Presented By:

Scientific Exploration and Expeditions

From the
Age of Discovery
to the
Twenty-First Century

Volume Two

Neil A. Hamilton

SHARPE REFERENCE
an imprint of M.E. Sharpe, Inc.

SHARPE REFERENCE

Sharpe Reference is an imprint of M.E. Sharpe, Inc.

M.E. Sharpe, Inc.

80 Business Park Drive

Armonk, NY 10504

© 2010 by M.E. Sharpe, Inc.

Library of Congress Cataloging-in-Publication Data

Hamilton, Neil A., 1949–

Scientific exploration and expeditions: from the age of discovery to the twenty-first century / Neil Hamilton.

    p. cm.

Includes bibliographical references and index.

ISBN 978-0-7656-8076-1 (hardcover: alk. paper)

1. Scientific expeditions—History. I. Title.

Q115.H167 2011

508—dc22
                                            010012118

Cover Images: Science & Society Picture Library/Getty Images (background map); left to right: David Boyer/National Geographic/Getty Images; NASA/Getty Images; Granger Collection, New York; Thomas J. Abercrombie/National Geographic/Getty Images; Robert Lackenbach/ Time & Life Pictures/Getty Images; Granger Collection, New York (astrolabe).

Printed and bound in the United States of America

The paper used in this publication meets the minimum requirements of American National Standard for Information Sciences Permanence of Paper for Printed Library Materials, ANSI Z 39.48.1984.

(c) 10 9 8 7 6 5 4 3 2 1

Publisher: Myron E. Sharpe

Vice President and Director of New Product Development: Donna Sanzone

Vice President and Production Director: Carmen Chetti

Executive Development Editor: Jeff Hacker

Project Manager: Laura Brengelman

Program Coordinator: Cathleen Prisco

Assistant Editor: Alison Morretta

Text Design: Patrice Sheridan

Cover Design: Jesse Sanchez

CONTENTS

VOLUME 2

M

Mackenzie, Alexander 193
Malinowski, Bronislaw 195
Maps and Mapmaking 199
Marsh, Othniel Charles 205
Mexia, Ynes 207
Mouhot, Henri 209

N

Nansen, Fridtjof 211
National Geographic Society 216
Nordenskjöld, Adolf Erik 219

O

Oceanography, History of........................ 222
Ostrom, John H. 229

P

Pacific Exploration................................. 231
Park, Mungo 238
Peary, Robert E. 242
Powell Expeditions 245

R

Royal Geographical Society.................... 250
Russian Exploration 252

S

Schliemann, Heinrich 259
Schultes, Richard 265
Schweinfurth, Georg August.................. 267
Scoresby, William 269
Scott, Robert Falcon............................. 272
Shackleton, Ernest................................ 278
Society of Woman Geographers 285
Space Exploration, Manned.................... 287
Space Exploration, Unmanned............... 301
Speke, John Hanning............................. 317
Stark, Freya... 321

T

Thomas, Elizabeth Marshall.................. 324

V

Van der Post, Laurens 326

W

Wallace, Alfred Russel............................ 331
Washburn, Bradford.............................. 336
Waterton, Charles................................. 340
Watkins, Gino...................................... 342
Wilkes Expedition 345

Glossary.. 351
Bibliography 356
Index.. I-1

Scientific Exploration and Expeditions

Volume Two

M

MACKENZIE, ALEXANDER (CA. 1764–1820)

ca. 1764: Born in Stornoway, Scotland
1779: Begins working for the Canadian trading firm Finlay, Gregory and Company
1789: Travels the Mackenzie River in Canada to the Arctic Ocean
1793: Reaches the Pacific Ocean by following the Bella Coola River from west of the Mackenzie Pass
1820: Dies on March 11 in Scotland

A Scottish-Canadian explorer and fur trader, Alexander Mackenzie journeyed west across the Continental Divide in the 1790s and reached the Pacific Coast.

Alexander Mackenzie was born sometime around 1764, probably in the fishing village of Stornoway on the Isle of Lewis in the Outer Hebrides of Scotland. When Alexander was about ten years old, his father took him to America—most likely to escape the poverty of the Scottish islands. After living briefly in New York, he was raised by two aunts in Montreal, Canada.

As a young man, Mackenzie entered the fur trade, which was then important to the British Canadian economy. At about age fifteen, he joined the firm of Finlay, Gregory and Company, which became Gregory, MacLeod and Company in 1783; he later worked for them as a trader in Detroit. The company came under increasing pressure from the two giants of the fur trade business, the Hudson's Bay Company and the North West Company, and it finally merged with the latter. Mackenzie became acquainted with one of the company's partners, Peter Pond, who believed that the Athabasca River could be followed west from the Cook Inlet to the Pacific Ocean. This northwest passage to the Pacific would provide a trade route to Asia.

Mackenzie resolved to test Pond's theory. He left Fort Chipewyan (which he had built on Lake Athabasca the previous year) on June 3, 1789. He was accompanied by a Chipewyan chief; five native women who served as guides, interpreters, and cooks; four Canadian voyageurs; and a general trader.

The expedition traveled in three canoes, battling strong northwest winds and treacherous rapids that often forced them to portage (cross overland with their canoes). The party reached Great Slave Lake on June 9 and found it still covered with ice. From there, beginning on June 29, they descended what Mackenzie called the River of Disappointment but was later renamed the Mackenzie River.

The trip took a total of 102 days. By the end of it, the expedition had reached not the Pacific Ocean but the Arctic Ocean. At Whale Island, where they stayed for four days, Mackenzie observed white whales and measured the tides.

Mackenzie began to think that the Peace River (in what is now western Alberta, Canada) was the most likely water route to the Pacific. Preparing for a journey to test that theory, he went to London in the winter of 1791 for training in navigation. He brought back a compass, a sextant, a chronometer, and a telescope, and set out in May 1793 with Alexander Mackay and eight other explorers in a 25-foot (7.6-meter) canoe.

As in the first expedition, the party encountered strong river rapids and engaged in arduous overland treks. Mackenzie had a difficult time convincing the men to forge ahead; however, they persevered, traveling along the Peace and Parsnip rivers and crossing the Continental Divide farther north than any other white men had to that time. On the western slopes of the Rocky Mountains, they discovered the Fraser River, traversed it for a short distance, and then, advised by the local Native Americans, crossed the West Road Valley and reached the Mackenzie Pass at an altitude of 6,000 feet (1,800 meters) in the Cascade Mountains.

Next, the expedition headed down the Bella Coola River and finally reached the Pacific Ocean, at the mouth of the river, on July 20, 1793. There, Mackenzie mixed a mineral with melted grease and used the concoction to make the following inscription on a rock:

> Alexander Mackenzie, from Canada, by land, the twenty-second of July, one thousand seven hundred and ninety-three.

It had taken the expedition seventy-four days to travel more than 1,200 miles (1,900 kilometers) to the coast. By the time Mackenzie returned home, the challenges of the journey had caused him to suffer from nervous exhaustion.

Although he failed to find the Northwest Passage, Mackenzie advanced British claims in the Pacific Northwest and added significantly to the geographical knowledge of the region. Albeit inadvertently, his explorations also influenced U.S. President Thomas Jefferson, who read Mackenzie's book, *Voyages from Montreal on the River St. Lawrence Through the Continent of North America to the Frozen and Pacific Oceans in the Years 1789 and 1793*, which was published in 1801. Already concerned about the growing British influence in the Pacific Northwest, President Jefferson became all the more determined to send an American expedition there, which he did under the leadership of Meriwether Lewis and William Clark.

From London, where he was hailed as a hero, Mackenzie founded and operated a trading firm called Alexander Mackenzie and Company, which merged with the North West Company in 1804. He returned to Montreal and was elected to the legislature of Lower Canada in 1805.

Three years later, he retired to Scotland, where he married, raised three children, and lived the rest of his life on a large estate near Moray Firth. He died on March 11, 1820, near Pitlochry.

Further Reading

Daniells, Roy. *Alexander Mackenzie and the North West.* Toronto, Canada: Oxford University Press, 1971.

Gough, Barry. *First Across the Continent: Sir Alexander Mackenzie.* Norman: University of Oklahoma Press, 1997.

Hayes, Derek. *First Crossing: Alexander Mackenzie, His Expedition Across North America, and the Opening of the Continent.* Seattle: Sasquatch, 2001.

See also: Lewis and Clark Expedition.

MALINOWSKI, BRONISLAW (1884–1942)

1884: Born on April 7 in Kraków, Poland
1908: Obtains doctorate from Jagiellonian University in Kraków
1915: Studies the Mailu people of New Guinea and begins studying the Trobriand Islanders
1916: Obtains doctor of science degree from the London School of Economics
1922: Publishes *Argonauts of the Western Pacific*
1927: Becomes chair of anthropology at the University of London
1939: Becomes visiting professor at Yale University
1942: Dies on May 16 at New Haven, Connecticut

Best known for his research on the Trobriand Islanders of the southwest Pacific, Polish-born cultural anthropologist Bronislaw Malinowski founded the functionalist approach to the study of culture, pioneered modern fieldwork techniques, and became known as one of the most influential anthropologists of the twentieth century.

Early Life and Studies

Bronislaw Malinowski was born on April 7, 1884, in Kraków, Austrian Poland, to Lucyan Malinowski, a professor of Slavic languages, and Jozefa Lacka. As a child he suffered from poor health, but he was an excellent student. In 1908, he obtained his first doctorate, in philosophy, physics, and mathematics, from Jagiellonian University in Kraków. After three semesters as a postgraduate student at the University of Leipzig, he received a scholarship to the London School of Economics.

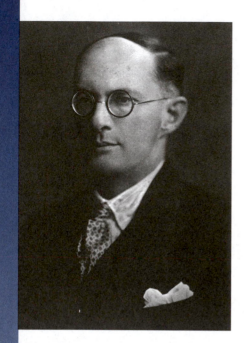

Polish-born cultural anthropologist Bronislaw Malinowski broke new ground in both methodology and theory with his years of fieldwork among the Trobriand Islanders of the southwest Pacific. (Hulton Archive/Stringer/ Getty Images)

During the course of his graduate studies, Malinowski became interested in anthropology when he read James Frazer's *The Golden Bough: A Study in Magic and Religion* (1890). Frazer, a Scottish anthropologist, discussed religion in a cultural context rather than a theological one.

In 1914, Malinowski obtained a fellowship to conduct anthropological fieldwork in New Guinea. He arrived there the following year and began his investigation among the Mailu people, who lived on the southern part of the island.

Although his work in New Guinea led to his earning a doctor of science degree from the London School of Economics in 1916, Malinowski discovered what he regarded as a weakness in his methodology. During his six months with the Mailu, he neither learned the native language nor spent much time living among the people. He determined to correct these faults in his future work.

In the Trobriand Islands

Malinowski decided to study the Trobriand Islanders, who lived on a coral archipelago (a group of islands) about 170 miles (275 kilometers) east of New Guinea in Melanesia, a subregion of the South Pacific. This time, adopting a new approach to his research, he immersed himself in Trobriand life and society. Rather than rely on occasional interviews with the natives—standard practice among anthropologists—he pitched a tent among them, learned their language, and took part in many of their cultural practices.

As he later advocated, "Each phenomenon ought to be studied through the broadest range possible of its concrete manifestations; each studied by an exhaustive survey of detailed examples." Malinowski advised other anthropologists,

> It is good for the Ethnographer to sometimes put aside camera, notebook and pencil and to join himself in what is going on. He can take part in the natives' games, he can follow them on their visits and walks, sit down and listen and share in their conversations. . . . Out of such plunges into the life of the natives . . . I have carried away the distinct feeling that their behaviour, their manner of being, in all sorts of tribal transactions, became more transparent and easily understandable than it had [been] before.

Malinowski developed what he believed were three important techniques in ethnographic fieldwork. First, he said, "[t]he organization of the tribe, and the anatomy of its culture must be recorded in firm, clear outline.

The method of concrete, statistical documentation is the mean through which such an outline has to be given." Second, he maintained, "[w]ithin this frame the imponderabilia of actual life, and the type of behaviour have to be filled in. They have to be collected through minute, detailed observations in the form of some sort of ethnographic diary, made possible by close contact with native life." And third, "[a] collection of ethnographic statements, collective narratives, typical utterances, items of folk-lore and magical formulae has to be given . . . as documents of native mentality."

On two expeditions—the first from June 1915 to May 1916, the second from October 1917 to October 1918—Malinowski studied the social practices of the Trobriand Islanders. Based on his experiences and findings, he wrote several books that reshaped the field of cultural anthropology, among them *Argonauts of the Western Pacific* (1922), perhaps the most influential; *Crime and Custom in Savage Society* (1926); *Myth in Primitive Psychology* (1927); and *The Sexual Life of Savages in North-Western Melanesia* (1929). In addition, he wrote numerous works about fishing, war and weapons, and language in Trobriand society.

In his writings, Malinowski advanced a theory of culture and an approach to its study known as functionalism. According to this view, "[t]he laws of behavior, in its technical, economic, legal, moral, and even magical aspects, form an integral whole which determines the actions of every individual in the group." Taken together, he believed, the social customs and

THE PARTICIPANT OBSERVER

In his groundbreaking research among the Trobriand Islanders, Bronislaw Malinowski acted as a particular type of anthropologist—namely, an ethnographer, someone who studies a human culture firsthand and reports on a people's way of life based on direct observation. In studying Trobriand society, Malinowski took the process a step further, to what anthropologists call "participant observation." In this case, the ethnologist goes beyond mere observation and engages in personal, hands-on experience of local customs.

Participant observation has the advantage of allowing the anthropologist to gain a deeper insight into social conditions and why people act as they do. But there are disadvantages to the method as well. Sometimes, the anthropologist is unwelcome from the start; in other cases, the people being studied begin to resist outside interference in their lives. In virtually any situation, it is difficult—some say impossible—for the anthropologist to climb out of his or her own "cultural skin" and fully and objectively experience the culture being investigated.

Thus, participant observation should be used judiciously and practiced carefully. Anthropologists and ethnographers need to be aware of the biases involved, even when, like Malinowski, they believe that they have left their own culture behind and become immersed in a new one. Above all, the norms and boundaries of the native culture must be respected.

practices create and maintain social order. Thus, Malinowksi maintained, it is important to study the parts of society as they interrelate; that is, to study society holistically.

The social order in Trobriand society, he found, had no need of European-style courts or of police. And yet, he also observed, the islanders pushed boundaries of order and tested its limits. So what, then, kept the order from breaking?

According to Malinowksi, it was a factor that can be observed in almost any society: the "reciprocity" needed in carrying on social or economic functions in the pursuit of self-interest. For example, among the Trobrianders (as in other societies), marriage establishes a bond not only between husband and wife but also between the families of each. Similarly, burial ceremonies serve not only to take care of the dead but also to comfort the survivors.

Academic Life and Later Fieldwork

Shortly after his return from the Trobriand Islands in 1922, Malinowski was made full-time lecturer at the London School of Economics. In 1926, he visited several universities in the United States, and he also studied the Pueblo Indians of the American Southwest. The following year, he began teaching at the University of London and was appointed its first chair of anthropology. His seminars there shaped the interests, work, and careers of the next generation of British anthropologists.

Journeying to Africa in 1934, Malinowski conducted fieldwork among the Bantu tribes. In 1941–1942, he conducted an extensive study of native peoples in the Oaxaca Valley of Mexico, focusing on the effects of outside influences on indigenous culture—a factor he had been criticized for undervaluing in anthropological research. In the meantime, Malinowski had become a visiting professor at Yale University in 1939. He held that post for the next three years.

An exiled member of the Polish Academy of Arts and Sciences during Germany's occupation of his home country, he was an outspoken critic of Adolf Hitler's Nazi regime. After attending the formal opening in New York City of the Polish Institute of Arts and Sciences at the Morgan Library on May 16, 1942, Malinowski returned to New Haven, Connecticut, where he died of a heart attack.

Although many of his ideas have been challenged or revised since his death, Malinowski continues to be regarded as a giant in the fields of social and cultural anthropology.

Further Reading

Thornton, Robert J., and Peter Skalnik, eds. *The Early Writings of Bronislaw Malinowski.* New York: Cambridge University Press, 1993.

Young, Michael W., ed. *The Ethnography of Malinowski: The Trobriand Islanders, 1915–18*. London: Routledge and Kegan Paul, 1998.

———. *Malinowski: Odyssey of an Anthropologist, 1884–1920*. New Haven, CT: Yale University Press, 2004.

MAPS AND MAPMAKING

1154: Arabian geographer Mohammed al-Idrisi draws a map of the known world

1311: Genoan cartographer Petrus Vesconte makes a navigation chart of the Mediterranean Sea

1507: German cartographer Martin Waldseemüller produces a map that includes the label "America"

1569: Flemish cartographer Gerardus Mercator produces his first world map, a large cylindrical projection that becomes the standard for ocean navigation

1879: The United States begins a geological survey for the purpose of making large-scale topographic maps

1966: The Pageos satellite is launched by the United States to conduct a geodetic survey of the Earth

1999: The seventh Landsat satellite is launched as part of the American geodetic survey program

The art and science of mapmaking, or cartography, has undergone tremendous change over the centuries, partly as a function of physical exploration and partly as a result of technological innovations and evolving scientific methods.

Mapmaking long predated the dawn of modern science in the fifteenth century. The first known maps date from ancient Babylonia (in the region of the Tigris and Euphrates rivers in present-day Iraq) in around 2300 B.C.E. Carved into clay tablets, these early diagrams showed the locations of towns, communities, and even property lines. One such map, from Nippur (near the Euphrates River in present-day Iraq) created circa 1300 B.C.E., depicts individual landholdings, along with irrigation canals and streams. In East Asia, maps drawn on silk dating to the second century B.C.E. have been found in China. In the Mediterranean, the Greek philosopher Anaximander drew a map showing all known lands around the Aegean Sea in the sixth century B.C.E.

A breakthrough came in about 240 B.C.E., when Eratosthenes of Cyrene made an important calculation. While serving as chief of the Alexandrian Museum in Egypt, he used a well and a vertical column to measure the angle of the sun and thereby determine the circumference of the Earth. Although his result was 16 percent too high, the calculation represented an important advance in human knowledge of the Earth. For that effort and others, including the invention of a system of latitude and longitude, Eratosthenes has been called the "father of geodesy," the science of Earth measurement.

In about 150 B.C.E., the Alexandrian scholar Ptolemy defined cartography as "a representation in pictures of the whole known world together with the phenomena which are contained therein." Most mapmakers today still hold with that basic definition.

Wanting cartographers "to survey the whole in its just proportions," Ptolemy recommended that whenever a large-area map distorted the representation of large or small areas, more localized maps should be used to provide a more accurate view. In 1154, the Arabian geographer Mohammed al-Idrisi drew a map of the world excluding unknown regions, such as the Americas. As early as the twelfth century, the Mayas and the Incas were making maps of lands in Central America.

By the thirteenth century, navigators in the Mediterranean Sea were making charts with lines connecting various points, although these charts did not include meridians or parallels. The earliest dated navigation chart was made by a Genoan, Petrus Vesconte, in 1311. Some historians consider this the first work of professional cartography.

Cartography in the Era of Modern Science

The rise of modern science, coinciding as it did with the Age of Discovery, brought major advances in cartographic accuracy and the charting of previously unknown lands. In 1507, the German cartographer Martin Waldseemüller produced a map that included the label "America" (after Amerigo Vespucci, an Italian navigator and explorer off the Atlantic coast) for the newly discovered lands across the Atlantic Ocean. For the first time, North and South America were shown as separate from Asia. In 1570, Abraham Ortelius, a Flemish mapmaker who lived in Antwerp, published the first modern atlas, *Orbis Terrarum*, which contained seventy maps drawn by different cartographers.

More precise methods of measuring latitude improved the accuracy of maps. Notably, in 1525, French physician Jean Fernel calculated the length of a degree of latitude with such accuracy that he was able to determine the circumference of the Earth within one-tenth of 1 percent. Fenel's was the first accurate measurement of a degree by a European; he performed this calculation in Paris using a quadrant and horse-drawn carriage.

Fenel used a quadrant to measure the angle of the noontime sun and the horizon; then he compared it to a published table in order to calculate his latitude. Based on the circumference of his carriage wheels and the number of their revolutions, he measured the distance from Paris to Amiens (near his birthplace). Upon arriving, he again measured the angle of the sun, to determine his new latitude. Paris and Amiens, it turned out, were almost exactly 1 degree arc apart; the distance between them, therefore, was equal to the distance of latitude. It would be another hundred years before better instruments allowed for more accurate measurements.

Perhaps the most famous name in cartography is that of Gerardus Mercator (1512–1594), a Flemish instrument maker whose charts helped generations of sailors make safer journeys across the oceans. Mercator's great innovation was a way to represent the spherical shape of the Earth on flat parchment. It is not clear how he came up with the idea, but, in 1569, he presented a world map based on a "new proportion and a new arrangement of the meridians with reference to the parallels."

To do this, Mercator took the rhumb lines from the globe—the straight lines between two points used by navigators—made them perpendicular to the equator, and drew them so they would not converge at the poles. Consequently, the meridians of longitude and the parallels of latitude intersected at right angles. To accomplish this, he had to increase the spacing of the parallels of latitude as they moved away from the equator toward the poles so that they would match the spreading of the meridians of longitude. One effect of this projection technique was to distort the shape of landmasses near the poles. Thus, for example, Greenland appeared to be the same size as South America.

Mercator's 1569 map reflected the growing knowledge of world geography during the Age of Discovery—at least to that time. It showed the west coasts of South and Central America, depicted Baja California as part of North America, and provided a more accurate outline of Asia. But the map showed nothing of the North American interior, as Europeans had yet to explore it; it also showed a landmass called *Terra Australis* where Antarctica is located, which was believed to be connected to the southern tips of Australia and South America.

Mercator's projection is referred to today as a "conformal map," meaning that the depiction of smaller surface areas are relatively accurate, but larger areas, such as continents, tend to be distorted. In a subsequent innovation, called "equal-area maps," 1 square inch (or square centimeter, depending on the scale used) on the surface of a map represents the same number of square miles (or square kilometers) of physical terrain as any other square inch (or square kilometer).

The great breakthrough in global cartography—which became a mainstay of ocean navigation—was a projection of the spherical world using straight lines to indicate latitude and longitude. The system took the name of its creator, Gerardus Mercator. *(Stringer/Hulton Archive/Getty Images)*

While it does provide greater accuracy in one respect, an equal-area map still distorts shapes and distances in areas near the poles. Indeed, any flat map of a spherical planet necessarily distorts the representation of shapes and distances. The question for any cartographer or map reader is which projection to use. (There are many variations within both the conformal and equal-area categories.)

The science of surveying—measuring distances and angles across three-dimensional space—matured significantly in the seventeenth and eighteenth centuries with advances in instrumentation. No longer was surveying confined to the measurement of small areas such as property lines. With improved instruments and more advanced mathematical techniques, surveyors could measure larger areas with greater accuracy.

Further improvements in cartography came as a result of a new scientific theory developed at about the same time. In the 1680s, Isaac Newton advanced the theory of centrifugal force, which had major implications for cartography because it held that the Earth was not perfectly round, but bulged at the equator. To test Newton's theory, the French Royal Academy of Sciences sponsored two expeditions, one bound for Peru in 1735 and one for the Arctic in 1736.

The Arctic explorers trekked into the wilderness of Lapland, where they battled giant, biting mosquitoes and foul weather. After calculating an arc of meridian from Tornio to Kittis (two Finnish towns), they measured a base line from the Torne River to Avasaksa by walking across the frozen river and placing 33-foot (10-meter) rods in their path. The leader of the expedition, Pierre Louis Moreau de Maupertuis, wrote,

> Judge what it must be to walk in the Snow two feet deep, with heavy Poles in our hands, which we must be continually laying upon the Snow and lifting again: In a Cold so extreme, that whenever we would taste a little Brandy, the only thing that could be kept liquid, our Tongues and lips froze to the Cup, and came away bloody; In a Cold that congealed the Fingers of some of us, and threatened us with yet more dismal Accidents.

The results of that Arctic expedition, along with the one to Peru, confirmed Newton's theory about the bulge in the Earth and marked a landmark event in the science of mapmaking. Cartographers were moving out of their workshops and libraries, and going out as explorers to survey land and sea.

New Horizons

If the more precise methods of measuring latitude that emerged in the eighteenth and nineteenth centuries improved the accuracy of maps, so, too,

Satellite imagery has revolutionized the field of cartography, providing real-time views of the Earth's surface in unprecedented resolution and detail. This view of the Chesapeake Bay was captured by one of the U.S. Landsat observation satellites in the 1990s. (*Science & Society Picture Library/ Getty Images*)

did the measuring of longitude. This awaited the development of an accurate mechanical clock—or marine chronometer—that could be carried on board a ship and continue to function. The device would keep the time of the prime meridian (Greenwich Mean Time). By comparing this time with the local time at sea, it was possible to determine a ship's longitudinal position relative to the prime meridian.

The problem was making a clock capable of withstanding the humidity, temperature, and barometric pressure of a long sea voyage. The solution came from John Harrison, an English clockmaker, who developed and built increasingly durable and accurate marine chronometers. Finally, in 1761, his H-4 timepiece, which was about the size of a soup plate, made it possible to gauge one's longitude at sea reliably and accurately. James Cook used a copy of the H-4, called the K-1, on his voyages to the Pacific Ocean and praised its accuracy. It proved invaluable in compiling the maps of his expeditions.

In another key development, topographic surveys intended to show the surface features of a place or region on a map (hills, valleys, rivers, and the like) were undertaken by European countries by the late eighteenth century, adding a new dimension to cartographic science. In 1793, the French completed a topographic survey of their entire nation; this was followed by similar national surveys in Austria, Great Britain, Spain, and Switzerland.

In the United States, the Geological Survey was begun in 1879 to survey and make large-scale topographic maps. In 1891, the International Geographical Congress proposed mapping the entire world, a project still under way today. Meanwhile, at sea, in the mid-nineteenth century, Matthew Maury of the U.S. Hydrographic Office began collecting data on winds, currents, ocean floors, and related phenomena—an effort regarded by some as the beginning of modern oceanography.

Mapmaking has undergone rapid change in the twentieth and twenty-first centuries as a result of modern technology. Aerial photography, which began during World War I, was used extensively in World War II. In the decades since, satellites have brought major advances in the collection and digital dissemination of detailed, real-time geographic information.

The United States began a geodetic survey of the Earth in 1966 with cameras mounted inside a balloon-launched satellite called Pageos (which circled the Earth in a polar orbit) and in three Landsat satellites launched in the 1970s. Landsat 1 was rocketed into space on July 23, 1972, to an altitude of 560 miles (900 kilometers); its nearly circular orbit provided a clear perspective of the Earth's surface with little distortion. A single image from Landsat was equivalent to 1,000 pictures taken from an airplane. In 1999, the seventh in the series of Landsat satellites was launched; it continues to transmit images of the Earth from space.

With all the improvement of modern technology, however, cartography still requires expeditions on the ground. As one cartographer recently put it,

> You have to steep yourself in the place, its trails and rocks and vegetation if you are to produce a map with more authenticity, one that has the right *feel* as well as the right mathematics.

Further Reading

Schwartz, Seymour I. *Putting "America" on the Map: The Story of the Most Important Graphic Document in the History of the United States.* Amherst, NY: Prometheus, 2007.

U.S. National Aeronautics and Space Administration Landsat Program: http://landsat.gsfc.nasa.gov.

Whitfield, Peter. *The Charting of the Oceans: Ten Centuries of Maritime Maps.* Rohnert Park, CA: Pomegranate Artbooks, 1996.

Wilford, John Noble. *The Mapmakers.* New York: Alfred A. Knopf, 1981.

See also: Space Exploration, Unmanned.

MARSH, OTHNIEL CHARLES (1831–1899)

1831: Born on October 29 in Lockport, New York
1867: Becomes curator at the Peabody Museum of Natural History at Yale University
1870: Begins exploring the American West in search of fossils when he leads a party of explorers from Fort McPherson, Nebraska
1899: Dies on March 18 in New Haven, Connecticut

American paleontologist, curator, and professor Othniel Charles Marsh led hundreds of fossil-finding expeditions to the western United States, discovered and named hundreds of fossil species, and provided strong corroborating evidence for Darwin's theory of evolution in its infancy. An early specialist in the field of vertebrate paleontology, Marsh also was known for his rivalry regarding fossil discoveries with Edward Drinker Cope.

Othniel Charles Marsh was born on October 29, 1831, in Lockport, New York. His father, Caleb Marsh, was a struggling farmer; his mother, Mary, died when Othniel was just three years old. Caleb Marsh expected his son to work on the farm, but as a boy Othniel liked to roam the fields and hunt in the woods. He became friends with geologist Ezekiel Jewett and through him became interested in natural history.

Financially strapped, Marsh was unable to enter Phillips Academy at Andover, Massachusetts, until he was twenty-one years old. He continued his studies at Yale University in New Haven, Connecticut, in 1856, supported largely by money from his uncle, George Peabody, who had become a successful banker. After earning his bachelor's degree in 1860, Marsh began graduate studies at Yale's Sheffield Scientific School, where he took courses in chemistry, physics, geology, botany, modern languages, and the history of science.

In 1861, he published his first paper, on the Nova Scotia goldfields. By this time, his collection of rocks and minerals had grown so large that it almost broke through the floor of the room where he was living. Fellow students considered him hard to get to know and called him "Daddy" because of his age.

With his interests shifting from geology to paleontology, Marsh studied at several German universities in the mid-1860s. Upon returning to America, he was named professor of vertebrate paleontology at Yale in 1866. Later that year, he persuaded his uncle to found the Peabody Museum of Natural History at Yale, of which Marsh was named curator in 1867. With money inherited from his uncle, Marsh built a large house in New Haven, where he entertained guests and stored his collec-

A pioneer of vertebrate paleontology, Othniel Charles Marsh discovered hundreds of fossils on expeditions to the American West in the late 1800s. His findings lent strong support for Darwin's controversial new theory of evolution. (*Granger Collection, New York*)

tion of fossils. (In 1898, he donated his collection to the Peabody, where it is still housed today.)

In 1870, Marsh departed with a small group of assistants from Fort McPherson, Nebraska, on the first of several expeditions he would lead to the West in search of fossils. One observer described him as "preeminently an outdoor man . . . a crack shot, a fisherman of repute, a seasoned camper." Marsh believed that the Nebraska plains had once been a lake bed and the Rocky Mountains a shallow sea, a theory confirmed by his discovery of a number of fish fossils as well as several remains of small mammals.

One fossil in particular, which Marsh discovered while he was riding along a buffalo trail, was the first of its kind to be found in North America—a bone from a flying reptile called the pterodactyl. From this evidence, along with a number of smaller bones collected by others, Marsh could estimate the size of the creature, the first vertebrate species known to have been capable of flying:

I . . . made a careful calculation of how large a Pterodactyl must be to have a wing finger corresponding to the fragment I had found, and ascertained that its spread of wings would be about twenty feet.

Marsh found proof for his theory on a second Western expedition in 1871, when he uncovered additional bones. Based on that evidence, he wrote,

I was soon able to determine that my calculations based on the original fragments were essentially correct, and that my first found American dragon was as large as my fancy had painted him.

Other Western expeditions followed in 1872, 1873, and 1874. During the last of these, Marsh collected more than 2 tons of fossils.

Collectors working for Marsh unearthed yet more fossil remains, from which he acquired specimens of other dinosaur species. Among these was the toothed Cretaceous bird *Hesperornis*, which he had identified previously. Based on the new evidence, about fifty fragments in all, Marsh was the first to show that birds had evolved from reptiles.

According to one contemporary, Marsh's discovery "removed Mr. Darwin's proposition . . . from the region of hypothesis to that of demonstrable fact." Indeed, Marsh fully supported Darwin's theory of evolution through natural selection.

As early as the 1860s, meanwhile, an intense rivalry—referred to as the Great Bone Wars—had developed between Marsh and the Philadelphia-based paleontologist Edward Drinker Cope. Each tried to outdo the other in collecting fossils, publishing papers, and advancing scientific theories. The competition resulted, in part, from Marsh's revelation, in 1869, that Cope had incorrectly reconstructed the skeleton of the *Elasmosaurus*, a long-neck reptile. (Cope had placed the skull on the skeleton's tail rather than its neck.)

The rivalry exploded into public view in 1890 when the *New York Herald* published a claim by Cope that Marsh was trying to take over the U.S. Geological Survey. The controversy drew widespread interest at a time when new findings and theories in natural science had captured the imagination of ordinary Americans.

Marsh died of pneumonia on March 18, 1899, in New Haven, where he had been teaching at Yale. In his lifetime, he had published some 300 scientific papers and books, named several hundred new species of fossil vertebrates, and, from 1883 to 1895, had served as president of the National Academy of Sciences.

Further Reading

Cohen, I. Bernard, ed. *The Life and Scientific Work of Othniel Charles Marsh: An Original Anthology.* New York: Arno, 1980.

Ostrom, John H., and John S. McIntosh. *Marsh's Dinosaurs: The Collection from Como Bluff.* New Haven, CT: Yale University Press, 2000.

Wallace, David Rains. *The Bonehunters' Revenge: Dinosaurs, Greed, and the Greatest Scientific Feud of the Gilded Age.* Boston: Houghton Mifflin, 1999.

See also: Cope, Edward Drinker.

MEXIA, YNES (1870–1938)

1870: Born on May 24 in Washington, D.C.
1925: Collects plant specimens at Mazatlán in Mexico
1928: Studies plants at Mt. McKinley National Park in Alaska
1929: Explores Brazil, Peru, and the Amazon River and collects 65,000 plant specimens
1935: Collects 15,000 specimens of plants and animals in South America
1938: Dies in Berkeley, California on July 12

A Mexican American botanist and explorer, Ynes Mexia collected an estimated 150,000 plant specimens—hundreds of them previously unknown species—on expeditions to Mexico, South America, and Alaska. A former social worker, she did not begin studying botany until she was in her fifties.

She was born Ynes Enriquetta Julietta Mexia on May 24, 1870, in Washington, D.C., to Enrique Antonio Mexia, who was serving as a diplomatic envoy at the Mexican consulate, and Sarah Wilmer Mexia. From infancy to the age of nine, she lived in Mexia, Texas, a town in Limestone County named for her grandfather. Thereafter, upon her parents' separation, she moved to Philadelphia to live with her mother and then to Mexico City to live with her father.

After the death of her first husband in 1904, Mexia remarried. She later suffered a nervous breakdown and not long after that divorced her second husband. She moved back to the United States, became an American citizen, and pursued a career as a social worker in San Francisco.

In 1921, at the age of fifty-one, Mexia began studying natural history at the University of California at Berkeley. Four years later, she took a summer course on flowering plants at Hopkins Marines Station in Pacific Grove, California, before joining a botanical expedition to Mexico.

At Mazatlán, Mexico, Mexia became a tireless collector and cataloger of plant specimens, continuing her activities despite a fall from a cliff in which she fractured her ribs. She took detailed field notes and photographed everything of potential importance. During the course of the expedition, Mexia displayed a preference for camping out in the field on her own. Although she established contacts with several leading scientists, she did not form any close relationships and sometimes complained of depression.

In the next twelve years, Mexia made a total of seven more collecting trips. In 1926 and 1927, she collected botanical specimens in western Mexico for the Department of Botany at the University of California at Berkeley. Near the end of that trip, she traveled over the Sierra Madre Mountains to collect local oak and plant samples. In all, she brought back hundreds of specimens to California, among them lichens, mosses, ferns, grasses, herbs, shrubs, and trees. The collection included fifty new species.

In 1928, on an expedition to Alaska, Mexia collected more than 6,000 species and studied plant life at Mount McKinley National Park (today Denali National Park), while living in complete solitude. The following year, she explored Brazil and Peru and traveled the Amazon River. She spent two months in the jungle and returned to the United States with 65,000 specimens. On an expedition to Peru, Argentina, Bolivia, and Chile in 1935, she collected another 15,000 specimens of plants and animals.

Mexia undertook her last expedition in 1937, to Guerrero and Oaxaca in Mexico. After falling ill the following year, she returned to California, where doctors told her she had lung cancer. She died at Berkeley on July 12, 1938.

A fellow botanist said of Mexia, "She was the true explorer type and happiest when independent and far from civilization."

Further Reading

Bonta, Marcia M. *Women in the Field: America's Pioneering Woman Naturalists.* College Station: Texas A&M University Press, 1991.

Goodspeed, Thomas Harper. *Plant Hunters in the Andes.* New York: Farrar and Rinehart, 1941.

MOUHOT, HENRI (1826–1861)

1826: Born on May 15 in Montbéliard, France
1858: Begins exploring Indochina on a journey up the Chao Phraya River from Bangkok to Ayuthaya
1860: Explores Angkor, including the Angkor Wat temple complex, in Cambodia
1861: Dies on November 10 in Luang Prabang, Laos

The French naturalist and explorer Henri Mouhot explored Southeast Asia in the mid-nineteenth century. Through his writings, he encouraged the archaeological exploration of the ancient Khmer capital of Angkor and called Western attention to the marvels of the temple complex located there.

Henri Mouhot was born on May 15, 1826, in Montbéliard, France, near the Swiss border. As a young professor of philology in the 1840s and 1850s, he traveled to Russia to teach and then toured Europe while studying photography. In 1856, he arrived in England and began studying zoology.

It was during this time that he read John Bowring's *The Kingdom and the People of Siam* (1857), whose vivid descriptions of Siam (present-day Thailand) made Mouhot want to visit. Bowring wrote,

> The appearance of the river is beautiful. Now and then a bamboo hut is seen amidst the foliage, whose varieties of bright and beautiful green no art could copy. Fruits and flowers hang by thousands on the branches.

With support from the Royal Geographical Society and the Zoological Society of London, Mouhot set out for Indochina in 1858. In the course of the next three years, he made four trips into the interior of Southeast Asia.

On his first expedition from Bangkok, he sailed up the Chao Phraya River to Ayuthaya, the former capital of Siam, and reported a discovery. He noted,

> I found animal footprints, mainly of tiger and elephant, everywhere up to the top of the mountain, in the valleys, caves, fissures. I have reached the conclusion that some of these footprints had been made by unknown antediluvian animals.

An English engraving of 1868 depicts Angkor Wat, the great temple of the ancient Khmer Empire in Cambodia. The historic site became an object of fascination among Europeans after firsthand descriptions by Frenchman Henri Mouhot. *(Granger Collection, New York)*

Other archaeologists have since determined that it is more likely that the marks were made by erosion in the limestone.

In December 1858, Mouhot began his second expedition, which lasted until April 1860. Surviving largely on rice and dried fish, and fighting mosquitoes every step of the way, he reached the ancient city of Angkor and explored its impressive Hindu temples. He took detailed measurements of Angkor Wat, the largest temple complex in the world, and marveled at its bas-relief artistry depicting warriors riding tigers, people entering paradise, and scenes of daily Khmer life. Mouhot wrote,

> At [Angkor], there are . . . ruins of such grandeur . . . that, at the first view, one is filled with profound admiration, and cannot but ask what has become of this powerful race, so civilized, so enlightened, the authors of these gigantic works?

Made of sandstone and laterite (a red, porous, clay-like soil), the Angkor Wat temple complex comprises five lotus-shaped towers, a large central tower, and other smaller towers. A series of terraces surrounds the central tower, and the entire structure is, in turn, surrounded by a moat.

The capital of the Khmer Empire, Angkor had been inhabited from the early ninth to the early fifteenth centuries, though Mouhot thought that it dated from a much earlier period. In addition to exploring the temples, he collected hundreds of insect specimens and shipped them back to Europe. All were lost when the steamer carrying them sank in Singapore harbor. Other items from his natural history collections later were received by the British Museum.

Contrary to popular accounts, Mouhot did not "discover" Angkor Wat. Western explorers and missionaries had visited the temple, and other nearby temples, as early as the 1500s. Yet Mouhot's descriptions and detailed sketches attracted considerable interest in Europe and encouraged archaeologists to explore the buildings.

Mouhot undertook a third expedition, to Petchaburi, in 1860, and a fourth one, to Laos, later that year. He died on November 10, 1861, in Luang Prabang, Laos, likely from a jungle fever.

Mouhot's travel notes appeared in a French magazine in 1863. And book editions of his writings were published in French and English in succeeding years.

Further Reading

Mouhot, Henri. *Travels in Siam, Cambodia, Laos, and Annam.* Bangkok, Thailand: White Lotus, 2000.

See also: Royal Geographical Society.

N

NANSEN, FRIDTJOF (1861–1930)

1861: Born on October 10 in Store Froen, Norway
1888: Walks across Greenland from east to west, arriving at the Inuit village of Godthaab in early October
1893: Begins his attempt to reach the North Pole aboard the *Fram*, a ship specially built to withstand ice floes
1906: Begins two-year term as Norway's ambassador to Great Britain
1921: Leads an international effort to save lives during a famine in Russia
1922: Awarded the Nobel Peace Prize
1930: Dies on May 13 in Oslo, Norway

A Norwegian explorer, oceanographer, diplomat, and humanitarian, Fridtjof Nansen fell short of his goal to reach the North Pole in the late 1800s but collected extensive scientific information about the Arctic. He was awarded the Nobel Peace Prize in 1922 for his work as high commissioner of refugees for the League of Nations.

Fridtjof Nansen was born on October 10, 1861, in Store Froen, Norway, near Oslo (then named Christiania). His father, Baldur Nansen, was a prosperous attorney, and his mother, Adelaide Nansen, came from a well-to-do family. Fridtjof lived in a large farmhouse with a younger brother and five older half-brothers and half-sisters.

As a young man, Nansen spent much time in the Norwegian forests skiing, hiking, and camping. In 1880, at age eighteen, he enrolled at the University of Oslo (then called the University of Christiania) and studied zoology. Two years later, he sailed to the Arctic as a crew member on the seal-hunting ship *Viking*, bringing with him equipment for collecting and investigating specimens. The *Viking* sailed to the coast of Greenland, where the beauty of the frozen land, which Nansen viewed from the crow's nest, inspired him with the idea of crossing the Arctic island on foot.

Back from his trip later that year, he was appointed curator of the Bergen Museum in Norway under zoologist Daniel Cornelius Danielssen. In 1888, Nansen received his doctorate from the University of Oslo upon completion of his dissertation, which was titled "The Structure and Combination of the Histological Elements of the Central Nervous System."

Norwegian explorer Fridtjof Nansen poses for a photo in his cabin on the *Fram*, while the ship was lodged in the Arctic ice cap in early 1895. Though the expedition failed to reach the North Pole, Nansen traveled farther north than any person to that time. *(Imagno/ Hulton Archive/ Getty Images)*

To the Arctic

Having received his degree, Nansen set about planning to trek across Greenland with five companions. The group decided to begin the journey from an ice floe along the east coast of the island, a dangerous plan, because the eastern region was devoid of villages from which help could be obtained if needed.

Nansen and his fellow explorers arrived on the east coast of Greenland in July 1888 and promptly encountered a setback. As they prepared to depart, the ice floe they were on broke apart, and on one of the pieces the explorers sailed south for ten days, which forced them to return north a considerable distance before beginning the trek across Greenland. All together, the incident cost them three weeks.

The purpose of the expedition was not purely adventure, and the explorers carried with them various scientific instruments, such as a sextant, barometers, theodolites, and three compasses—the last "for the testing of magnetic deviation," said Nansen, "as well as for trigonometrical observations." The party covered about 250 miles (400 kilometers), traversing hills and mountains and forging through blizzards, which put them ever farther behind schedule.

They finally reached Greenland's west coast and the Inuit village of Godthaab in early October, just as the harsh winter weather began setting in. Spending the winter there, Nansen used the time to learn more about Arctic travel from the villagers. He also learned their language and shared their meals of seal and whale blubber.

During this expedition, Nansen made extensive scientific observations, including descriptions of Inuit life, the geography, and weather conditions. He found that the inland ice and deep snows never melted. And, from his detailed meteorological observations, he concluded,

> The great difference between sun and shade temperature is plainly due to the excessive radiation in the dry, thin air of this high plateau. . . . The scale of our sling thermometers only read as low as -220 Fahr. (-300 Cent.), as no one had expected such cold at this time of the year in the interior of Greenland.

Upon his return to Norway in 1889, Nansen was hailed by his countrymen for his feat and was named curator of the zoological collection at the University of Oslo. Shortly thereafter, he published two books about his adventure, *The First Crossing of Greenland* (1890) and *Eskimo Life* (1891).

Nansen next determined to become the first person to reach the North Pole. With backing from the Norwegian government, he directed construction of the *Fram*, a ship with a rounded hull and pointed bow and stern that enabled ice floes to slip underneath it rather than crush it.

For the expedition itself, Nansen developed a bold plan: to freeze the *Fram* in the ice along the east coast of Siberia and then allow the ocean current to push it north. He derived this idea from having seen debris from Siberia wash up along the shores of Greenland. For his crew, Nansen recruited twelve Norwegians, later explaining: "Two Norwegians, alone of all other nationals, could sit face to face on a cake of ice for three years without hating each other."

After settling into the Siberian ice pack in September 1893, the *Fram* drifted across the polar ice cap, as planned. After two winters, however, it became clear to Nansen that the ship would pass hundreds of miles south of the North Pole. In March 1895, therefore, he decided to set out overland to complete the expedition.

Packing dogsleds with 100 days of rations, Nansen departed the vessel with fellow explorer Hjalmar Johanssen, and they began a grueling journey. Time and again, their sleds capsized on the treacherous terrain. The travail of having to carry their sleds "over hummocks and inequalities of the ground," as Nansen described it, exhausted them:

Sometimes we were so sleepy in the evenings that our eyes shut and we fell asleep as we went along. My head would drop, and I would be awakened by suddenly falling forward on my snowshoes.

Although Nansen and Johanssen ultimately failed to reach the North Pole, on April 8, 1895, they reached 86° 14' north latitude (at what is now called the Nansen Cordillera)—the farthest north anyone had ever traveled on the face of the Earth. In his diary, Nansen wrote about the decision to turn back:

The ice grew worse and worse, and we got no way. Ridge after ridge, and nothing but rubble to travel over. . . . I went on a good way ahead on snowshoes, but saw no reasonable prospect of advance, and from the highest hummocks only the same kind of ice was to be seen. It was a veritable chaos of ice-blocks, stretching as far as the horizon. There is not much sense in keeping on longer.

To make matters worse, Nansen and Johanssen lost track of the *Fram*. On their return trip, therefore, they headed south for Franz Josef Land, located some 400 miles (640 kilometers) away. In late July 1895, however, bad

NANSEN'S INSTRUMENTS

In *Farthest North* (1897), his memoir of his expedition to reach the North Pole, Fridtjof Nansen described the scientific instruments he brought along:

For meteorological observations, in addition to the ordinary thermometers, barometers, aneroids, psychrometers, hygrometers, anemometers, etc., etc., self-registering instruments were also taken. Of special importance were . . . [an] aneroid barometer (a barograph) and a pair of . . . thermometers (thermographs).

He also listed "a complete set of instruments" for taking magnetic observations; water samplers, deepwater thermometers, and the like to make hydrographic observations; and an "electric apparatus" to "ascertain the saltness of the water."

Nansen conducted his astronomical observations with a sextant and three theodolites. Theodolites, which began to appear in their modern form in the 1780s, consist of two graduated circles placed at right angles to each other and a telescope that turns on an axis and is situated at the center of the circles, all mounted on a pedestal.

With a theodolite, Nansen could measure horizontal and vertical angles and thus accurately survey the land. Before Nansen's expedition, British surveyors had used theodolites to map the Indian subcontinent.

weather prevented them from proceeding. The two explorers prepared for winter by hunting and storing polar bear, walrus, and seal meat; for shelter, they dug a pit in the ground and covered it with walrus skins.

The following May, they resumed their journey, now all but lost. Then came a stroke of good fortune. In June 1896, on an island just south of Franz Josef Land, they happened upon another explorer, Frederick Jackson of Great Britain. In August, they returned to Norway on board Jackson's ship a few days ahead of the *Fram*, which had just reached open water at Spitsbergen.

During the course of the expedition, the Norwegians aboard the *Fram* set up special weather stations and made numerous observations. They measured wind speeds, temperatures, and other meteorological events; recorded water temperatures; and found that the Arctic Ocean was a deep basin rather than a shallow sea. Around 1900, Nansen published six volumes of scientific information obtained on his Arctic expedition.

Scientist, Diplomat, Humanitarian

Back in Norway, Nansen was named professor of oceanography and zoology at the University of Oslo, where he did notable work in the fields of fluid dynamics and neurology. He also helped found the International Council for the Exploration of the Sea in 1902, advised scientists who wanted to explore the Arctic, and went on several oceanographic expeditions (1910–1914).

Increasingly, however, Nansen focused his attention on politics. A strong supporter of Norway's independence from Sweden, he served from 1906 to 1908 as his country's first ambassador to Great Britain. During World War I, he negotiated an agreement with the United States to receive supplies, and in 1920 he headed the Norwegian delegation to the League of Nations.

As high commissioner of refugees for the league, Nansen was instrumental in arranging the repatriation of 500,000 German and Austro-Hungarian prisoners of war from Russia. When famine swept that country in 1921, he led an international appeal for help that saved hundreds of thousands of lives. For his humanitarian efforts, Nansen was awarded the Nobel Peace Prize in 1922.

Nansen's other diplomatic accomplishments include a measure he proposed to alleviate tension between Greece and Turkey. It called for the "exchange of Turkish nationals of the Greek Orthodox religion [in Turkey] and of Greek nationals of the Moslem religion [in Greece]"; this measure was enacted at the Convention of Lausanne in 1923.

Nansen died in Oslo on May 13, 1930, likely as the result of overexertion on a skiing trip. He once said, "Our object is to investigate the great unknown regions that surround the pole, and these investigations will be equally important from a scientific view."

Further Reading

Greve, Tim. *Fridtjof Nansen*. 2 vols. Oslo, Norway: Gyldendal, 1973.

Huntford, Roland. *Nansen: The Explorer as Hero*. New York: Barnes and Noble, 1998.

Nansen, Fridtjof. *Farthest North*. New York: Modern Library, 1999.

See also: Arctic.

NATIONAL GEOGRAPHIC SOCIETY

1888: Founded in January in Washington, D.C., as a nonprofit scientific and educational organization; the first edition of *National Geographic Magazine* appears in October

1890: The society sponsors its first scientific expedition, which maps large areas of the Alaskan wilderness

1905: Eleven pages of photographs appear in the society's magazine

1965: The first National Geographic television special is aired

2002: The society's motion picture *March of the Penguins* wins an Academy Award

From its headquarters in Washington, D.C., the National Geographic Society has promoted geographical knowledge for more than 120 years through thousands of scientific expeditions and research projects, a popular consumer magazine, books, television shows, movies, traveling exhibitions, multimedia presentations, games, and toys.

The society was organized on January 13, 1888, when thirty-three men gathered at the Cosmos Club in Washington with the idea of forming an association dedicated to exploring the world and publicizing findings gathered from global expeditions. Among those in attendance were a teacher, a geologist, a lawyer, a topographer, a banker, a military officer, and a naturalist.

At the time, large areas of the world remained unmapped, despite numerous expeditions that had plied the seas and explored the continents since the beginning of the Age of Discovery in the fifteenth century. Those gathered in Washington resolved to establish a society dedicated to "the increase and diffusion of geographic knowledge."

The National Geographic Society was formally incorporated two weeks later, on January 27, 1888. Gardiner Greene Hubbard, a lawyer and financier who had organized the Bell Telephone Company, was elected as the group's first president. Upon his death in 1898, Hubbard was succeeded by his son-in-law, inventor Alexander Graham Bell, who declared, "The world and all that is in it is our theme."

The inaugural edition of the society's official journal, *National Geographic Magazine* (later shortened to *National Geographic*), appeared in October 1888. Under its first full-time editor, Gilbert H. Grosvenor, who served in the post beginning in 1903, the magazine pioneered the use of numerous photographs to enhance its stories, earning Grosvenor the title "father of photojournalism." In 1905, he filled eleven pages of the magazine with photographs. In another innovative move the following year, he published photographs of animals taken at night with the use of flash lighting. Despite the positive response of readers, the increasing number of photographs caused two of the society's board members to resign because, they claimed, he was turning the publication into a "picture book."

In 1910, the magazine opened one of the nation's leading color photo laboratories under Charles Martin and Edwin "Buddy" Wisherd. In the 1930s, it pioneered the use of Kodachrome, a color film known for its clarity. And in 1962, the magazine published its first all-color issue. Meanwhile, the maps that appeared in *National Geographic* elevated the standards of popular cartography.

Today, the total monthly circulation of *National Geographic* is nearly 9 million, and it is issued in thirty-two language editions. Subscribers are regarded as members of the society.

In 1975, the society also began publishing a magazine for children, *National Geographic World*, whose name was changed in 2001 to *National Geographic Kids*. Other magazines followed, including *National Geographic Traveler* in 1984 and *National Geographic Adventure* in 1999.

Over the years, the National Geographic Society has produced numerous television documentaries. Its first special, *Americans on Everest*, appeared on the CBS network in 1965. The society launched its own TV network, the National Geographic Channel, in several European countries and Australia in 1997, and in the United States in 2001.

The society produces motion pictures through its National Geographic Films subsidiary, which released its first feature film, *K-19: The Widowmaker*, in 2002. In 2006, its *March of the Penguins* (produced in partnership with Warner Independent Pictures) received an Academy Award for best documentary.

In addition to the acclaimed Web site nationalgeographic.com, which includes a wealth of multimedia content, the society has developed a number of other projects specifically in support of its mission to educate and inform. The Geography Education Program, begun in 1985, seeks to improve geography instruction in schools. And the society has funded and sponsored traveling exhibits, such as the treasures of the tomb of the ancient Egyptian King Tutankhamen in the 1980s, and one in 2008 titled "The Cultural Treasures of Afghanistan."

Gilbert Hovey Grosvenor served as the longtime editor-in-chief of *National Geographic* magazine (1899–1954) and president of the National Geographic Society (1920–1954), establishing both as respected scientific and cultural institutions. (*James Whitmore/Time & Life Pictures/Getty Images*)

At the same time, the organization has supported some 7,000 scientific activities and expeditions in the decades since its founding. It sponsored its first expedition in 1890, a mission led by Israel C. Russell and including explorers from the U.S. Geological Survey that mapped 600 square miles (1,550 square kilometers) of wilderness in Alaska and discovered the second-highest mountain in North America, Mount Logan. In 1902, after the volcanic eruption of Mount Pelée on the Caribbean island of Martinique, the society sent an expedition to collect data—thus beginning another regular endeavor: the study of major natural disasters.

On more than one occasion, society explorers have met with tragedy, ranging from serious injury to death. In 1980, when Mount St. Helens erupted in Washington State, Reid Blackburn, a twenty-seven-year-old photographer working for *National Geographic*, died under 4 feet (1.22 meters) of ash.

Expeditions sponsored or supported by the society have included some of the most notable in the modern history of exploration. In the early 1900s, it sponsored the expeditions of Robert E. Peary to the North Pole and Richard E. Byrd to Antarctica. In 1912, it supported expeditions led by Hiram Bingham to excavate Machu Picchu, the ancient Inca city in the Peruvian Andes. And, in the 1920s, it supported Howard Carter's quest for the tomb of Tutankhamen.

Beginning in the 1960s, the society supported such projects as the work of anthropologists Louis Leakey and Mary Leakey at the Olduvai Gorge in East Africa; the undersea explorations conducted by Jacques Cousteau; the research of chimpanzees by Jane Goodall and of gorillas by zoologist Dian Fossey; and the efforts by Robert Ballard to find the remains of the *Titanic*.

Former society president (until 1996) and chairman of the board of trustees since 1987, Gilbert Melville Grosvenor (grandson of Gilbert Hovey Grosvenor) received the Presidential Medal of Freedom in 2004 for the society's work in advancing geography education.

As stated by Peter H. Raven, chairman of the society's Committee for Research and Exploration, in *National Geographic Expeditions Atlas* (2000),

From the depths of the seas to the tops of the highest mountains; from tropical rain forests . . . to the most severe deserts; from the history of ancient civilizations to the wonderful ways humans have adapted to diverse habitats; the National Geographic has sponsored many key scientists and explorers who have helped build our basic knowledge of the world today.

Further Reading

National Geographic Society. http://www.nationalgeographic.com.
———. *National Geographic Expeditions Atlas.* Washington, DC: National Geographic Society, 2000.
Poole, Robert M. *Explorers House: National Geographic and the World It Made.* New York: Penguin, 2004.

See also: Byrd, Richard E.; Carter, Howard; Leakey Family; Peary, Robert E.

NORDENSKJÖLD, ADOLF ERIK (1832–1901)

1832: Born on November 18 in Helsinki, Finland
1855: Obtains doctorate from the University of Helsinki
1857: Banished from Finland for criticizing Russian control of his homeland
1858: Undertakes first expedition to Spitsbergen
1878: Begins navigation of the Northeast Passage
1881: Publishes *The Voyage of the Vega*
1901: Dies on August 12 in Stockholm, Sweden

A Finnish-Swedish geologist, mineralogist, and explorer, Baron Adolf Erik Nordenskjöld explored Spitsbergen (the largest island of the Svalbard archipelago in the Arctic Ocean) and Greenland before becoming the first person to make a continuous journey along the northern coast of Eurasia, through the Northeast Passage.

Nils Adolf Erik Nordenskjöld was born on November 18, 1832, in Helsinki, Finland (then called Helsingfors) to Nils Nordenskjöld, a superintendent of mining and a naturalist, and Sofia Margareta von Haartman, the daughter of a doctor. He was educated by a private tutor before enrolling in a grammar school at Porvoo, the town his family had moved to on the southern coast of Finland.

As a young man, Adolf liked to collect rocks and insects, and he explored part of the Ural Mountains with his father. As he later wrote, "I had been allowed to accompany my father in mineralogical excursions and had acquired from him a skill in recognizing and collecting minerals."

Nordenskjöld entered the University of Helsinki in 1849, earning a master's degree there in 1853 and a doctorate in 1855. He studied chemistry and geology and wrote a description of minerals found in Finland, along with several short papers on mineralogy. After receiving his doctorate,

Finnish-born Swedish explorer Adolf Erik Nordenskjöld, the first to navigate the Northeast Passage (1878–1879), was hailed as a national hero upon his return home. He spent his latter years writing about geography, cartography, and history. *(Hulton Archive/Stringer/ Getty Images)*

he became a mining engineer and was appointed to the university's faculty. In 1857, however, he lost his university position and was banished from Finland for his liberal politics and public criticism of czarist rule.

Emigrating to Stockholm, Sweden, in 1857, he became superintendent of the mineralogical department of the Swedish Museum of Natural History. He held that position for the rest of his working life, greatly expanding the museum's mineralogical and geological collection and adding a collection of meteorites.

Nordenskjöld undertook his first scientific expedition to Spitsbergen in 1858 under Otto Torell, a leading geologist of the time; he returned with Torell in 1861. Three years later, Nordenskjöld led his own expedition under the sponsorship of the Royal Swedish Academy of Sciences. In 1868, he traveled farther north in Spitsbergen than anyone to that time, exploring the island's northern coast as well as nearby North East Land.

He explored the inland ice sheet of Greenland in 1870 and led an expedition to try to reach the North Pole two years later. But severe weather forced him to spend the winter of 1872–1873 in Spitsbergen, where he collected geological specimens with other scientists before crossing North East Land. Among the results of this expedition, he later wrote, were,

> [T]he discovery on the Polar ice itself of a dust of cosmic origin, containing metallic nickel-iron; . . . researches on the aurora and its spectrum; . . . a complete series of meteorological and magnetic observations in the most northerly latitude where such observations had up to this time been carried on; . . . the discovery of numerous new contributions to a knowledge of the flora of the Polar countries during former geological epochs; a sledge excursion . . . whereby the north part of the North East Land was surveyed; and a journey, very instructive on a scientific point of view, made over the inland ice of North East Land.

After leading expeditions to the Kara Sea in 1875 and the Yenisei River in 1876, Nordenskjöld decided to traverse the entire Northeast Passage from Scandinavia along the length of the Russian Arctic coast to the Bering Sea. He began his journey on June 22, 1878, at Karlskrona, in southern Sweden on the Baltic Sea, aboard a steam-powered whaling ship called the *Vega*. In addition to the ship's captain, Louis Palander, and the crew, several other scientists accompanied Nordenskjöld. He was confident that the *Vega* could make the voyage that so many others had failed to complete.

On August 1, the expedition reached the Yugor Strait (the entry to the Kara Sea), where the scientists collected zoological and botanical specimens. Nordenskjöld worried that they would encounter the severe ice and fog in the Kara Sea that had forced other expeditions to turn back, but the weather proved favorable. At Preobraschenie Island (near the Taymyr Peninsula in Siberia, the northernmost area on the Asian continent), the scientists collected and labeled numerous mineral and botanical specimens. Nordenskjöld reported that the island was "free of snow and covered with a carpet of mosses mixed with grass."

Then came worsening winter and dangerous ice, forcing the expedition to a halt in the Bering Strait in late September. The ice threatened to crash against the ship and tear it apart. To guard against catastrophe, the explorers built a depot on shore and stocked it with supplies. As they waited out the winter, the scientists in the party built a magnetic observatory.

When the weather broke, Nordenskjöld and his men resumed the journey. They finally reached their goal, the Bering Sea, in the summer of 1879. From there, they sailed south along the Asian coast, west through the Indian Ocean to the Suez Canal, and then on to Europe, thereby completing a circumnavigation of all of Eurasia.

Back in Sweden in 1880, Nordenskjöld was hailed as a national hero; he was named a baron. His book on the expedition, *The Voyage of the Vega*, appeared the following year.

In 1883, Nordenskjöld again journeyed to Greenland. On this voyage, he succeeded in taking his ship through the island's great ice barrier, a feat no one else had accomplished to date.

Appointed to the Swedish Academy in 1893, Nordenskjöld spent his later years writing books on geography, cartography, and history. His expeditions and writings served as an inspiration to other Arctic explorers, including Norwegian Fridtjof Nansen and American Robert E. Peary.

Adolf Erik Nordenskjöld died on August 12, 1901, at Stockholm, Sweden. One observer wrote of him in 1882,

> The most striking characteristics of his various expeditions have been the small expense at which they were conducted, their modest but carefully-considered equipment, the clear and scientific methods on which they were planned, and the wealth and high value of the results obtained.

Further Reading

Häkli, Esko. *A.E. Nordenskiold: A Scientist and His Library*. Helsinki, Finland: Helsinki University Library, 1980.

Kish, George. *North-East Passage: Adolf Erik Nordenskiold, His Life and Times*. Amsterdam, The Netherlands: Nico Israel, 1973.

See also: Arctic; Nansen, Fridtjof; Peary, Robert E.

OCEANOGRAPHY, HISTORY OF

1841: Edward Forbes publishes *History of British Starfishes*

1855: Matthew Maury publishes *The Physical Geography of the Sea*

1872: The British ship *Challenger* begins a worldwide oceanographic expedition

1910: Prince Albert I founds the Oceanographic Museum in Monaco

1925: The German *Meteor* expedition begins in the South Atlantic

1960: An American bathyscaphe, the *Trieste*, explores the Mariana Trench

1968: The JOIDES program is begun to engage in deep-sea drilling

2004: The ship *Resolution* begins its journey of 28,000 miles to collect sample cores

Since the dawn of the Age of Discovery in the fifteenth century, oceanography—the exploration and study of the ocean and its phenomena—has emerged as a full-fledged scientific discipline. The means of oceanographic exploration and information gathering have evolved from sailing ships trolling the ocean surface for aquatic life to deep-sea diving vessels and drills that penetrate far beneath the ocean floor.

Oceanographers study the entire system of the world's oceans and seas. The discipline entails a number of scientific fields—especially geology, chemistry, geophysics, botany, zoology, meteorology, astronomy, and mathematics—which together form a detailed picture of the world's oceans, how they behave, and what lives in them.

The science of oceanography includes a number of subdivisions. Physical oceanography studies and describes the causes of the winds, currents, tides, and other water movements, along with temperature, salinity, and pressure. Chemical oceanography maps the chemical content of the seas. This involves organic chemistry, primarily the study of plants and animals, and inorganic chemistry, the study of compounds other than the carbon-based ones found in plants and animals. Biological oceanography explores the ways in which organisms interact with their environment and with each other. Geological oceanography examines the makeup of rocks, minerals, and fossils and the forces that bring about changes in the Earth's structure.

In addition, ocean engineers devise methods of controlling beach erosion, develop oceanographic instruments, and invent ways to retrieve natural resources without destroying animal and plant habitats. Meteorologists study weather conditions as related to the world's oceans, as well as how the oceans affect climate and vice-versa.

Nineteenth Century

In the fifteenth century, as Europeans explorers set out in search of new lands, their interest in the ocean expanded beyond the purview of the classical world, which had been largely confined to the Mediterranean Sea. The new interest was sparked by a variety of interwoven motivations, with intellectual curiosity generally taking a back seat to political and economic gain.

There was no single founder of modern oceanographic science. But Scottish naturalist Edward Forbes (1815–1854) and American naval officer Matthew Fontaine Maury (1806–1873) often are cited as pioneers.

After several scientific expeditions and years of academic research, Forbes published *History of British Starfishes and other Animals of the Class Echinodermata* in 1841; the work included 120 of his own illustrations. Forbes also is associated with the since-discredited azoic theory, according to which the deep sea is completely devoid of life. As severely misguided as that notion now seems, it at least was based on firsthand observation: the deeper Forbes cast his net, the fewer aquatic creatures he caught.

Meanwhile, in the United States, Maury—sometimes referred to as the father of oceanography—had been analyzing ocean currents and winds while serving in the armed forces as a midshipman in the U.S. Navy. He published his findings in *A New Theoretical and Practical Treatise on Navigation* (1836), which became a standard navy manual. Three years later, Maury was forced to retire from active service due to an injury suffered in a stagecoach accident.

In 1842, Maury was named superintendent of the Depot of Charts and Instruments at the U.S. Navy Department in Washington, D.C., where he began collecting oceanographic and meteorological data from old and current ship logs. Maury was the first person to conduct a systematic study of the world's oceans. By the early 1850s, he had become internationally recognized for his work.

His comprehensive, systematic mapping of the winds, currents, and physical geography of the world's seas in the mid-nineteenth century earned Matthew Fontaine Maury a reputation as the father of modern oceanography. *(Granger Collection, New York)*

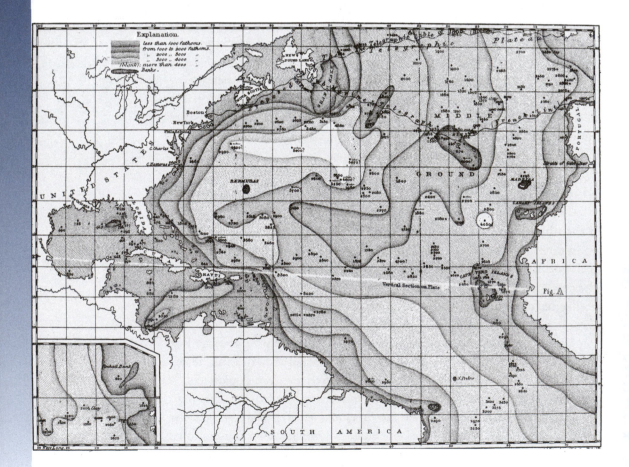

In 1855, Maury published what is widely regarded as the first textbook in the field of oceanography, *The Physical Geography of the Sea*. Reprinted five times in its first year and eventually published in several foreign languages, the work provided detailed information about winds and currents to guide sailing ships, extensive charts that reduced the sailing times for numerous voyages, and a kind of primer on methodology. In addition, Maury showed himself to be an adept writer who offered vivid descriptions of conditions at sea. For example, he wrote:

> There is a river in the ocean. In the severest droughts it never fails, and in the mightiest floods it never overflows. Its banks and its bottom are of cold water, while its current is of warm. The Gulf of Mexico is its fountain, and its mouth is in the Arctic Seas. It is the Gulf Stream. There is in the world no other such majestic flow of waters.

Even as seminal works in the field were being published, oceanography was being advanced by several nineteenth-century expeditions. In the 1830s, the British naturalist Charles Darwin (1809–1882) added to the knowledge of the seas and the islands in them on his famous journey aboard the *Beagle*. From 1839 to 1842, Lieutenant Charles Wilkes (1798–1877) of the U.S. Navy led an exploratory fleet of six ships in charting 1,500 miles (2,400 kilometers) of the Antarctic coast and taking deep soundings in its waters.

The first scientific oceanographic expedition is said to have been that of the British ship *Challenger*, whose team was headed by the Scottish naturalist Charles Wyville Thomson (1830–1882). Sailing from Portsmouth, England, in December 1872, the *Challenger* was equipped with more than 770,000 feet (235,000 meters) of line for measuring depth and 65,600 feet (20,000 meters) of cable for collecting sediment samples and marine organisms. Over the next three-and-a-half years, it sailed around the globe and made 362 oceanographic soundings. Thomson and his crew measured ocean depths of up to 26,000 feet (940 meters) and discovered 4,017 new marine species.

From the sediment samples gathered on the *Challenger*, the Scottish-Canadian marine biologist John Murray (1841–1914), who assisted Thomson on the expedition, began the study of underwater geology. He also edited and published some fifty volumes of *Challenger* reports.

Louis Agassiz (1807–1873), the great Swiss-American naturalist, laid the foundation for the study of marine biology in America. Since the 1840s and 1850s, professional naturalists had been dredging shallow seawater on the eastern coast of the United States to obtain marine specimens for teaching and research. In 1873, Agassiz established a summer marine station for teachers on Penikese Island, Massachusetts. A number of his former students established other marine laboratories in nearby locations. These led to the creation in 1888 of the Marine Biological Laboratory at Woods Hole on Cape Cod, Massachusetts.

Agassiz's son, Alexander Agassiz (1835–1910), made further breakthroughs, developing various devices to sample the ocean waters and floors. In 1877 and 1895, he made voyages to study seafloor sediments in the Pacific Ocean and marine biology in the Caribbean Sea.

Twentieth Century to the Present

Prince Albert I of Monaco (1848–1922), the ruler of that principality beginning in 1889, made notable contributions to the field, working with some of the world's leading oceanographers and marine scientists. His research on ocean currents showed that the Gulf Stream split in the northeastern Atlantic, with one branch flowing toward Ireland and Britain and another toward Spain and Africa before turning back west. In 1910, Prince Albert founded the Oceanographic Museum in Monaco, which houses equipment

The topography of the ocean floor in the southwest Pacific is rendered in unprecedented detail using altimeter data from the SEASAT oceanographic satellite. SEASAT was launched in 1978 to study the features and dynamics of the Earth's oceans. (*Science & Society Picture Library/ Getty Images*)

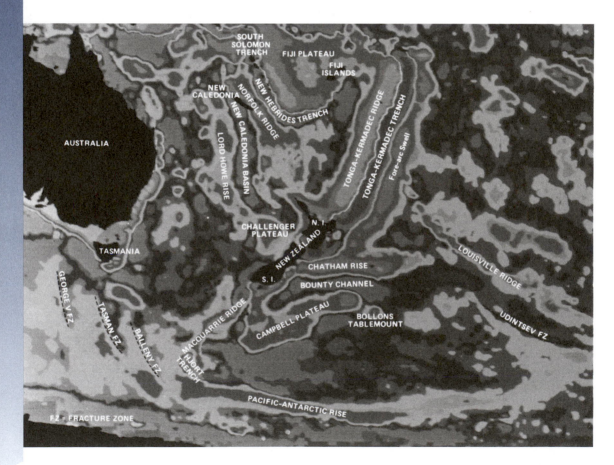

THE HARDY CONTINUOUS PLANKTON RECORDER

The British scientist Alister Hardy (1896–1985) developed a device called the continuous plankton recorder in the 1920s as a way to more efficiently collect plankton (tiny organisms in the water that form the basic food source for many larger marine animals).

Traditionally, plankton had been collected by towing a net made of fine silk gauze behind a slow-moving ship. The continuous plankton recorder also employed a fine silk gauze net that was pulled behind a ship; however, the silk was placed on a roll, and the forward motion of the ship supplied energy to unroll the silk in stages. This allowed for plankton to be collected at a rate that corresponded more closely with its concentration in the ocean.

Today, the Hardy continuous plankton recorder is housed in a metal case with a towline in the front and a propeller in the back to stabilize it. The recorder is towed at a depth of about 33 feet (10 meters). The plankton enter the front, are caught on the gauze, and then pass into a tank of preservative.

As the gauze is unwound, a record is made of the plankton through which the ship has passed. These records help scientists understand seasonal cycles and other changes in plankton density. In recent years, remote satellite sensing has added to the collection of plankton data.

he used in his research, specimens he collected, a scientific library, and an aquarium with species from the Mediterranean.

From 1925 to 1927, the German *Meteor* expedition, organized by the Institute of Marine Research in Berlin, traversed the South Atlantic to measure ocean depths, analyze temperatures and salinity, and study current patterns. Scientists on board showed for the first time that the ocean bottom consists of mountains, valleys, plateaus, and plains. Using sonar, the expedition discovered the Mid-Atlantic Ridge, a mountain range running down the middle of that ocean.

In the Pacific, an American bathyscaphe called the *Trieste*, carrying Swiss engineer Jacques Piccard and Lieutenant Don Walsh of the U.S. Navy, reached the ocean floor on January 23, 1960, at a site called Challenger Deep, the deepest known point in the Mariana Trench. Challenger Deep later was measured at 35,800 feet (10,900 meters).

In 1968, a program called Joint Oceanographic Institutions for Deep Earth Sampling, or JOIDES, was begun under an agreement by the Scripps Institution of Oceanography in La Jolla, California, the Lamont-Doherty Earth Observatory at Columbia University, the Woods Hole Oceanographic Institute, and the Rosenstiel School of Marine and Atmospheric Science at the University of Miami. As part of JOIDES, the specially equipped research vessel *Glomar Challenger* began drilling and coring the floors of the world's oceans in March 1968. Along an oceanic ridge between South America and Africa, the *Glomar Challenger* drilled seventeen holes at ten different sites; core samples provided solid evidence to support the theory of continental drift.

From August 1968 to November 1983, the *Glomar Challenger* took part in a total of ninety-six expeditions, covered 375,632 nautical miles (696,000 kilometers), recovered 19,119 cores, and drilled as deep as 5,712 feet (1,740 meters) beneath the ocean floor. The successor to the *Glomar Challenger*, the *JOIDES Resolution*, drilled cores in the Atlantic Ocean, Pacific Ocean, Mediterranean Sea, Black Sea, and Ross Sea. In 2004–2005 alone, it traveled nearly 28,000 nautical miles (52,000 kilometers), drilled 104 holes in the ocean floor, and recovered 1,826 cores.

Scientists also have found new ways to study seafloor topography. Advances came with the use of echo sounding to measure depths and objects. In the early 1950s, Maurice Ewing of the Lamont Geological Observatory, assisted by Bruce Heezen and Marie Tharp, used sounding profiles of the Atlantic to put together the first detailed maps of the ocean floor. These maps were updated in 1996 by Walter Smith and David Sandwell of the Scripps Institution of Oceanography.

The scientific investigation of the world's oceans is today assisted by new technology, including satellites designed to provide data on surface water temperatures, along with the movements of waves and currents. Ellen J. Prager and Sylvia A. Earle write in their book *The Oceans* (2000),

DIGGING INTO THE OCEAN FLOOR

Scientists use a variety of devices, called samplers and corers, to gather evidence from the ocean floors.

One sampler, called the Van Veen, uses a scoop that resembles a clamshell to examine the top 8 inches (20 centimeters) of the ocean floor. Before the Van Veen sampler is lowered into the ocean, its "jaws" are opened. When the device touches the ocean floor, stabilizing plates prevent it from digging too deeply or unevenly into the targeted area. Up top in the research ship, a cable is pulled that causes the jaws to close and capture sediment from a level depth with minimum of disturbance to the ocean floor.

The gravity corer consists of a weighted tube mounted within a frame. When lowered to the ocean floor, it digs within the targeted area to a given depth and the tube fills with sediment. The corer penetrates the ocean floor slowly to minimize disturbance, and it is raised back to the research vessel with a winch. The sediment core either can be stored for later analysis or be sampled directly on board the ship. Video cameras are sometimes attached to the corer to provide a view of the sediments before the collection process begins.

The gravity device has the advantage of allowing the sediment to be collected just as it is stratified on the ocean floor. Thus, when the sediment is retrieved, it can be analyzed with respect to size, texture, and composition, as well as dated in a way similar to the dating of geological strata on land.

Our understanding of the oceans has progressed immensely over the last century. Yet we have explored only a fraction of the ocean's depths. We are just beginning to understand the interactions between the ocean, the underlying Earth, and the climate and we still know precious little about the creatures that live in the sea's salty waters.

Further Reading

Bascom, Willard. *The Crest of the Wave: Adventures in Oceanography*. New York: Harper and Row, 1988.

Mills, Eric L. *Biological Oceanography: An Early History*. Ithaca, NY: Cornell University Press, 1989.

Prager, Ellen J., and Sylvia A. Earle. *The Oceans*. New York: McGraw-Hill, 2000.

See also:
Darwin, Charles;
Wilkes Expedition.

OSTROM, JOHN H. (1928–2005)

1928: Born on February 18 in New York City
1951: Begins job as research assistant at the American Museum of Natural History in New York City
1960: Receives doctorate in vertebrate paleontology from Columbia University
1964: Discovers *Deinonychus* while excavating fossils in Montana; shortly thereafter, he argues that some dinosaurs were warm-blooded
1970: Uncovers new specimen of the primitive bird species *Archaeopteryx*
2005: Dies on July 16 in Litchfield, Connecticut

American paleontologist John Ostrom revived lagging scientific interest in dinosaurs when he made a famous fossil discovery in 1964, on the basis of which he maintained that many dinosaurs were warm-blooded. He also is known for establishing the evolutionary link between dinosaurs and birds.

John H. Ostrom was born in New York City on February 18, 1928. Upon entering Union College in Schenectady, New York, in the late 1940s, he intended to become a doctor. While in college, however, he read *The Meaning of Evolution* (1949) by George Gaylord Simpson, a professor at Columbia University in New York City, and was drawn to the field of paleontology. Upon receiving his B.S. degree in 1951, Ostrom worked with Simpson as a field assistant on a fossil expedition in the San Juan Basin of New Mexico.

From 1951 to 1956, Ostrom served as a research assistant to Edwin H. Colbert at the American Museum of Natural History. He then enrolled at Columbia for graduate studies; in 1960, he received his doctorate in vertebrate paleontology. In 1961, Yale University in New Haven, Connecticut, hired him as an assistant professor in the Department of Geology and

Geophysics and as assistant curator of vertebrate paleontology at the university's Peabody Museum of Natural History.

Three years later, Ostrom made a discovery that proved critical to the modern study of paleontology. At an excavation site in Montana's Cloverly Formation, he and an assistant, Grant Meyer, were walking along a slope when they saw an animal's claws and hand bones protruding from the ground. "At that moment of discovery," Ostrom later wrote, "it was evident from the few fragments exposed on the surface that we had stumbled across something very unusual and quite unlike any previously reported dinosaur." He dubbed the site "The Shrine." Over the next two years, he and his field-workers excavated more than 1,000 bones from the site, dating from about 125 million years ago.

The fossil remains included those of what Ostrom concluded was a carnivorous dinosaur that walked on two legs and had claws, talons, and a long tail. He called it *Deinonychus*, meaning "terrible claw." Measuring about 3.5 feet tall (1.07 meters) and 9 feet long (2.75 meters), *Deinonychus* slashed with its claws and likely hunted in packs.

According to Ostrom, *Deinonychus* was fleet-footed and very active, characteristics associated with a high metabolic rate and, therefore, warm-bloodedness. Moreover, the foot bones of *Deinonychus* resembled those of modern-day emus and ostriches, meaning that it had more in common with mammals and birds than with reptiles. Ostrom further insisted that many dinosaur species had narrow foot placement and kept their legs under their bodies, giving them an erect posture. All of these characteristics suggested a warm-blooded animal.

Ostrom's interest in the connection between dinosaurs and birds was triggered by a 1970 visit to a museum in Haarlem, the Netherlands, where he found that a fossil that had been discovered in 1855 was mislabeled as a pterosaur, or flying reptile. Ostrom recognized that the fossil actually was a new specimen of *Archaeopteryx*, the earliest and most primitive known bird, dating from about 150 million years ago. He also recognized that it bore similarities to *Deinonychus*.

As a result of his discoveries, Ostrom wrote a succession of scientific papers from 1970 to 1976 arguing that birds were descended from dinosaurs. It was a revolutionary theory that shook up the world of paleontology. In fact, some scientists resisted it for decades.

In 1971, Ostrom had been made full professor at Yale and curator of vertebrate fossils at the Peabody Museum, where he oversaw one of the most important collections in the world. In the decades that followed, John Horner and others made fossil discoveries—such as dinosaur nests and eggs—that helped confirm Ostrom's theory of an evolutionary link between dinosaurs and birds. In 1997, Ostrom was part of an expedition to China that provided further evidence yet: the discovery of new feathered dinosaurs.

Ostrom died on July 16, 2005, in Litchfield, Connecticut. "John is basically responsible for the way we view dinosaurs," said Horner. "He is probably the most influential person in dinosaur paleontology in the last century."

Further Reading

Ostrom, John H. *The Strange World of Dinosaurs*. New York: G.P. Putnam's Sons, 1964.

P

PACIFIC EXPLORATION

1567: Álvaro de Mendaña de Neira discovers the Solomon Islands

1642: Abel Janszoon Tasman discovers Tasmania off the southern coast of Australia

1767: Samuel Wallis discovers Tahiti; Louis Antoine de Bougainville journeys to Samoa and the New Hebrides

1769: Captain James Cook explores New Zealand

1773: Cook crosses the Antarctic Circle

1872: The *Challenger* expedition begins the first oceanographic study of the Pacific

1960: The *Trieste* dives to the deepest point in the Mariana Trench

2006: The Integrated Ocean Drilling Program begins exploring beneath the Pacific floor

The vast Pacific Ocean has been the scene of explorations both above the sea and beneath it as nations have pursued territory, riches, and scientific knowledge. The largest body of water in the world, the Pacific covers approximately 64 million square miles (165 million square kilometers), double the area of the Atlantic Ocean and larger than that of the planet's entire landmass. In stretching from the Bering Strait in the north to the Antarctic in the south, it encompasses climate zones ranging from frigid to temperate to tropical.

Deep trenches cut through the ocean's floor, resulting from the collision of tectonic plates that cause one to be pushed under the other. In the East Pacific Rise, a submerged volcanic range parallels the South American coast. This range runs continuously through all of the Earth's ocean basins, for roughly 40,000 miles (64,000 kilometers); in the Pacific, it juts above the water to form Easter Island and the Galápagos.

Geologic formation is ongoing in the Pacific Ocean. In the northeastern ocean, the American Plate and the Pacific Plate continue to slip

The four-year voyage of the British corvette *Challenger* in the 1870s marked the beginning of modern oceanographic survey. The *Challenger* was the namesake of the second U.S. space shuttle, launched in 1983. (*Time & Life Pictures/Getty Images*)

past each other and produce new fracture zones. Meanwhile, the seafloor continues to spread (the extension occurs as sea plates move apart) at a rate of about 1.2 to 4 inches (3 to 10 centimeters) per year.

Early Exploration

The Age of Discovery resulted in the crisscrossing of the Pacific Ocean by sailing ships from Portugal, Spain, the Netherlands, England, and France from the sixteenth through the nineteenth centuries. Most of these expeditions were propelled by the desire for wealth and conquest; however, over time, more were inspired by the spirit of scientific discovery.

Spain sponsored several notable expeditions. In 1519, Ferdinand Magellan (ca. 1480–1521), a Portuguese navigator in the service of Spain, set sail in pursuit of a westward route to the Spice Islands of Asia. Magellan sailed around South America and into the Pacific. He was killed in a skirmish with an indigenous tribe in the Philippines in 1521. Nevertheless, the following September, one of the five original ships that had set out on the expedition reached Spain with a crew of just eighteen men, completing the first successful circumnavigation of the Earth.

In 1567 and again in 1595, the Spanish maritime explorer Álvaro de Mendaña de Neira led two expeditions into the Pacific in search of an undiscovered continent, gold, and natives who could be converted to Catholicism. On his first voyage, he discovered the Solomon Islands in Melanesia; on his second, he discovered the Marquesas Islands in Polynesia. Mendaña de Neira's missions were beset with illness and clashes with the islanders, and he found no gold.

Another Spanish navigator, Luis Váez de Torres (birth and death dates unknown), also set sail in search of the elusive southern continent. In 1606, Váez de Torres approached the southern coast of New Guinea, thus showing that the island was not attached to some great landmass to the south. The strait located between New Guinea and the Australian continent to the south later took his name—the Torres Strait.

In November 1642, Abel Janszoon Tasman (1603–1659), considered the greatest of the early Dutch navigators, discovered an island off the southeast coast of Australia that he named Van Diemen's Land, after the governor-general of the Dutch East Indies, Anthony van Diemen. The island was later renamed Tasmania in his honor. From there, he sailed east, sighting the northwest coast of New Zealand's South Island in December and reaching the northeastern Fiji Islands in January 1643.

On Tasman's second voyage, in 1644, he mapped the northern coast of Australia and was able to observe the people who lived there. After that, however, there was no further exploration of the continent to any significant degree until the voyages of Captain James Cook in the 1770s.

Among the notable early British explorers, Vice-Admiral John Byron (1723–1786) circumnavigated the globe from 1764 to 1766, discovering several islands in the Pacific along the way. Among these were the Tuamotu Archipelago in central Polynesia, Tokelau near the Samoan Islands, and Tinian in the northern Mariana Islands.

Samuel Wallis (1728–1795), captain of the HMS *Dolphin*, set sail in 1766 with secret instructions from the British Admiralty "to discover and obtain a complete knowledge of the Land or Islands supposed to be situated in the Southern Hemisphere." In June 1767, Wallis thought he had found the tip of a mysterious continent, but it turned out that he had discovered the island of Tahiti. He wrote in his log,

> At two in the morning, it being very clear, we made sail again; at day-break we saw the land, at about five leagues distant, and steered directly for it; but at eight o'clock, when we were close under it, the fog obliged us again to lie to, and when it cleared away, we were much surprised to find ourselves surrounded by hundreds of canoes. . . . When they came within pistol shot of the ship, they lay by, gazing at us with great astonishment.

Of the island they had discovered, George Robinson, the master of the *Dolphin*, wrote,

> The country hade the most Beautiful appearance its posabel to Imagin, from the shore side one two and three miles Back there is a fine Leavel country that appears to be all laid out in plantations.

Philip Carteret (1733–1796) sailed with Wallis's expedition as commander of the *Swallow*, but he became separated from the *Dolphin* in the Strait of Magellan and continued on his own. In July 1767, Carteret and his crew discovered Pitcairn Island, a volcanic island in the south-central Pacific. The island promptly was named for the fifteen-year-old midshipman who first spotted it, Robert Pitcairn. Carteret explained,

> It is so high, that we saw it at a distance of more than fifteen leagues, and it having been discovered by a young gentleman, son to Major Pitcairn of the marines, we called it Pitcairn's Island.

Captain James Cook (1728–1779) made his first voyage to the Pacific as captain of the *Endeavor* in 1768. With him was botanist Joseph Banks. At Tahiti the following year, Cook observed the transit of Venus across the sun. In October 1769, he arrived at New Zealand and spent the next six months exploring its coasts; he discovered that New Zealand consisted of two islands and was not a part of Antarctica. On April 19, 1770, Cook sighted the east coast of Australia; he named and explored Botany Bay. Banks, meanwhile, collected about 800 specimens of Australian flora.

In 1772, Cook began a second expedition to the South Pacific, this time with two ships, the *Resolution* and the *Adventure*. In December 1773, he crossed the Antarctic Circle, the southernmost point ever reached by a European explorer until then. By the time he returned home to England in July 1775—with only one sailor lost on the entire expedition—Cook had explored vast expanses of the previously unknown Pacific, had proved that there was no large continent in the temperate regions of the ocean, and had produced accurate maps of far-flung lands.

For the French, Louis Antoine de Bougainville (1729–1811) undertook a voyage of discovery around the globe in 1766. In the Pacific, he sailed to the Samoan and New Hebrides islands in 1767, continuing on to the Solomon Islands. He named Bougainville Island, to the northeast of Australia, for himself, before continuing on to the Moluccan Islands (in Indonesia).

In the nineteenth century, English naturalist Charles Darwin (1809–1882) added to the knowledge of the Pacific with his voyage to the west coast of South America and the Galápagos Islands aboard the *Beagle* in the 1830s. In addition to his groundbreaking insights into animal and plant life, he also gathered important information on the natural history of the sea and the geology of the islands.

The modern era of oceanographic expeditions is said to have begun with the voyage of the British *Challenger* from 1872 to 1876. Under the direction of Scottish naturalist Charles Wyville Thomson (1830–1882) and Canadian scientist John Murray (1841–1914), it was the first major sea expedition organized to gather extensive data on ocean features, including temperature, seawater chemistry, currents, marine life, and the geology of the seafloor.

Murray wrote,

> Our knowledge of the ocean was, literally speaking, superficial. No systematic attempts had been made to ascertain the physical and biological conditions of that vast region of the earth's surface occupied by the deeper waters of the ocean.

To fill that void, the *Challenger* sailed almost 69,000 nautical miles (130,000 kilometers) in the Atlantic, Pacific, and Antarctic oceans with a full staff of scientists on board. One of the outcomes of the expedition was the publication of the *Report of the Scientific Results of the Exploring Voyage of H.M.S. Challenger During the Years 1873–1876*, which Murray called "the greatest advance in the knowledge of our planet since the celebrated discoveries of the fifteenth and sixteenth centuries."

THE PACIFIC FLOOR

If all the water were drained from the Pacific Ocean, a seabed of extremely rugged terrain would be revealed. Prominent among this terrain's features are four massive fissures that cut through the northern Pacific from east to west: the Mendocino Escarpment, which runs roughly midway between Hawaii and Alaska, and the Murray, Clarion, and Clipperton Fracture Zones. Each of these fissures measures up to 30 miles (48 kilometers) wide, 3,300 miles (5,300 kilometers) long, and 10,500 feet (3,200 meters) deep. In the South Pacific, the Marquesas Fracture Zone runs approximately 1,500 miles (2,400 kilometers) east to west, reaching a width of 30 miles (48 kilometers) and a depth of 4,000 feet (1,200 meters).

The peaks of mountains that tower up from the ocean floor form the Hawaiian Islands, the Marshall Islands, and the Fiji Islands, among others. Abutting many of the islands in the Pacific Ocean are deep trenches, the deepest of which is the Mariana Trench in the western North Pacific. The Tonga-Kermadec Trench extends from New Zealand northeast to the Samoa Islands, a distance of 1,600 miles (2,600 kilometers), and reaches a depth of nearly 34,900 feet (10,600 meters).

Earthquakes frequently shake the region between New Zealand, Tonga, and New Guinea, as they do the continental mountains around the eastern South Pacific. A northward shift of the ocean floor and a southward slide of the South American plate have produced massive earthquakes in Chile. Shifts in the Pacific and North American plates have produced earthquakes along and near the San Andreas Fault in California.

In all of these ways, the floor of the Pacific Ocean is a dynamic environment that invites scientific discovery.

THE *TRIESTE*

The research bathyscaphe *Trieste* was the brainchild of Swiss physicist and balloonist Auguste Piccard (1884–1962), who began pursuing his idea for a deep-sea diving vessel in the 1930s.

The project was interrupted by World War II; full-scale development began in 1952. Construction took place in the Italian city of Trieste and at other locations.

With scientific and navigation equipment provided by Germany, Italy, and Switzerland, the *Trieste* made its first dive on August 11, 1953. On board were Auguste Piccard and his son, Jacques, who took the vessel to a depth of 5 fathoms (30 feet, or 9 meters).

The *Trieste* consisted of a float chamber, to provide buoyancy and allow the vessel to return to the surface, and a separate pressure sphere, creating an arrangement Piccard called a "bathyscaphe" (a Greek term meaning "deep ships"). Unlike similar sea-diving vessels, also known as deep submergence vessels, the *Trieste* could be used without attachment to a ship's cable, giving it more freedom of movement.

The crew occupied the pressure sphere, which was attached to the underside of the floats and connected to the deck by a vertical shaft that ran through the float chamber and down to the sphere hatch. The pressure sphere held two people; cylinders provided oxygen in the sphere.

The *Trieste* later was modified to withstand higher pressure in deeper water. For the historic 1960 dive into the Mariana Trench, the vessel departed San Diego, California, in October 1959 aboard the freighter *Santa Maria* and was taken to to the island of Guam. The descent, with Jacques Piccard and Don Walsh aboard, took 4 hours and 48 minutes—of which only 20 minutes were spent on the ocean floor. The dive went smoothly except for the cracking of the outer Plexiglas windows, which caused the entire vessel to shake, at a depth of about 30,000 feet (9,000 meters).

The *Trieste* was replaced by the *Trieste II* in the early 1960s. According to the Historic Naval Ship Association, *Trieste II* since has been improved and changed so many times that few of its original parts remain.

The deep-sea bathyscaphe *Trieste* is retrieved from the western Pacific Ocean after its record dive to the floor of the Mariana Trench—the deepest point on the Earth's surface—in 1960. (*Thomas J. Abercrombie/National Geographic/Getty Images*)

Indeed, the *Challenger* expedition engaged in nearly 500 deep-sea soundings, more than 100 bottom dredges, 151 open-water trawls, and 263 water temperature observations. Among its discoveries were 4,715 new species of marine life and the Mariana Trench—later shown to contain the deepest point on the Earth's surface—in the western Pacific.

Modern Exploration

In the latter part of the twentieth century, with space satellites photographing and collecting data on geographic features across the Earth, scientists turned their attention to the depths of the world's oceans—especially the Pacific—and the seabed beneath.

In 1958, the U.S. Navy bought a Swiss-designed deep-sea submersible called the *Trieste*, which on January 23, 1960, reached the ocean floor at a site in the Mariana Trench called Challenger Deep. At a depth of about 35,800 feet (nearly 7 miles), or 10,900 meters (nearly 11 kilometers), Challenger Deep was—and remains—the deepest known point on the Earth's surface. On board the *Trieste* were the Swiss engineer Jacques Piccard and Lieutenant Don Walsh of the U.S. Navy, who reported seeing a kind of flatfish on the ocean floor. Sediment samples identified various simple organisms, confirming that life could be sustained under the enormous pressure found at such depths.

In 1964, the United States began exploring *beneath* the Pacific Ocean, as part of its Deep Sea Drilling Project, with the goal of penetrating the sediment and crust to learn more about how the ocean evolved. In 1984, that project was succeeded by the Ocean Drilling Program, and, in 2006, by the Integrated Ocean Drilling Program (IODP), an American-led consortium of twenty-three nations cooperating to explore the Pacific and other seas. Within the structure of the IODP, the United States operates the drilling vessel *JOIDES Resolution*, Japan operates the drilling vessel *Chikyu*, and the European Union operates stationary platforms capable of drilling in environments unsuitable for ships.

In 2008–2009, drilling expeditions in the Pacific were conducted near the equator at Australia's Great Barrier Reef, in New Zealand's Canterbury Basin, near Antarctica's Wilkes Land, and off the southeast coast of Japan. According to a report by the IODP,

> Core sediments from the Pacific show evidence of 90 billion tons of microbial organisms living in the deep biosphere. For a long time, scientists believed that extreme conditions such as high pressure, lack of oxygen, and low supply of nutrients and energy would make deep, sub-seafloor environments uninhabitable for any life form. Nonetheless, sea-going investigations have proven the existence of the deep biosphere.

Thus, findings from the IODP added to a long line of discoveries both above and beneath the Pacific Ocean that enhance our understanding of the Earth and the processes shaping it.

See also:
Bougainville, Louis-Antoine de; Cook, James; Darwin, Charles.

Further Reading

Doubilet, David. *Pacific: An Undersea Journey*. Boston: Little, Brown, 1992.

Lambert, David. *The Pacific Ocean*. Austin, TX: Raintree Steck-Vaughn, 1997.

PARK, MUNGO (1771–1806)

1771: Born on September 11 in Selkirkshire, Scotland

1793: Journeys to Sumatra in Southeast Asia

1795: Leads an expedition into the African interior via the Niger River for the purposes of geographical exploration and trade

1805: Leads a second expedition to explore the Niger River

1806: Drowns in the Niger River during an attack by natives

A Scottish explorer trained in medicine, Mungo Park led two expeditions to West Africa, where he explored the Niger River and collected numerous plant specimens, along with valuable ethnographic and geographic information. On his second expedition, he died while trying to escape an attacking tribe.

Born on September 11, 1771, in Selkirkshire, Scotland, Mungo Park was raised in a large family of twelve or thirteen children (accounts vary). His father, also named Mungo Park, was a tenant farmer of modest means who worked on an estate called Foulshiels; his mother, Elspeth Hislop, was the daughter of another tenant farmer. The younger Mungo was first educated by a private tutor and then attended the local grammar school.

In 1788, Park entered the University of Edinburgh, where he studied medicine and botany as he trained to become a surgeon. In 1792, however, he left the university before completing his final oral examinations. Later that year, he toured the Scottish Highlands with his brother-in-law, James Dickson, a prominent botanist.

Through Dickson, Park met the great botanist Joseph Banks, then president of the Royal Society. In 1793, after Park passed his exam at the Company of Surgeons in London, Banks appointed him assistant surgeon aboard the *Worcester*, which set sail in February 1793 for Sumatra in Southeast Asia. After returning to London the following spring, Park presented Banks with several exotic Sumatran plants and watercolors he had painted of twenty species of fish.

Excited by his experiences on the journey to Sumatra, Park began contemplating a scientific expedition to Africa. His desire dovetailed with the plans of the African Association, which, in 1790, had sponsored an expedition up the Niger River by Major Daniel Houghton to learn about this unknown (at least to Europeans) territory and to open a new trade route for Britain into the African interior. Houghton died before he could complete the mission.

Park now offered to lead a new expedition, for reasons that he later explained in his book, *Travels in the Interior of Africa* (1799):

> I had a passionate desire to examine into the productions of a country so
> little known; and to become experimentally acquainted with the modes of
> life, and character of the natives. . . . If I should succeed in rendering the
> geography of Africa more familiar to my countrymen, and in opening to their
> ambition and industry new sources of wealth, and new channels of com-
> merce, I knew that I was in the hands of men of honour.

The African Association instructed Park to follow the Niger River, to find out where the river began and ended, and to visit such settlements as Timbuktu and Houssa.

Park sailed from Portsmouth on May 22, 1795, and reached the north bank of the Gambia River in June. He then journeyed from Pisania, a British trading station 200 miles (320 kilometers) inland, and headed for the Niger

Scottish explorer Mungo Park recounted his West African adventures in a popular 1799 work titled *Travels in the Interior of Africa*. Engravings in the book included the Mandinka village of Kamalia, where Park recovered from a life-threatening fever. (*Granger Collection, New York*)

River. As he traveled, he kept detailed records of the geography and tribal cultures he encountered, noting how the people looked and describing their foods, languages, and societies.

Park encountered many troubles. In the spring of 1796, a band of Moors captured him and held him prisoner at Benowm, in the Ludamar region. He escaped in July and reached the Niger a few days later. By then, however, he was overwhelmed with hunger and fatigue and had been robbed of all his gold, so he made the decision to forgo trying to reach Timbuktu and instead turned back to Pisania. On the return trip, he followed the Niger for 300 miles (480 kilometers) to Bamako. At the settlement of Kamalia, he had to stop in order to recover from a serious fever.

On June 10, 1797, Park finally reached Pisania, where he obtained passage on an American slave ship headed for South Carolina. At the West Indies, he transferred to a British ship and arrived back in England that December. He brought with him a wealth of information and eighty plant specimens.

MUNGO PARK'S ESCAPE AND HIS DISCOVERY OF THE NIGER

In his book *Travels in the Interior Districts of Africa*, Mungo Park describes what happened immediately after he escaped from the Moors, who had taken him captive in spring 1796 (he escaped that July):

It is impossible to describe the joy that arose in my mind, when I looked around and concluded that I was out of danger. I felt like one recovered from sickness; I breathed freer; I found unusual lightness in my limbs; even the Desert looked pleasant. . . . I soon became sensible, however, that my situation was deplorable; for I had no means of procuring food, nor prospect of finding water. . . . I became faint with thirst, and climbed a tree in hopes of seeing distant smoke, or some other appearance of human habitation; but in vain; nothing appeared all around but thick underwood, and hillocks of white sand.

He also describes his first encounter with the Niger River:

The circumstance of the Niger's flowing towards the east, and its collateral points, did not . . . excite my surprise; for although I had left Europe in great hesitation on this subject, and rather believed that it ran in the contrary direction, I had made such frequent enquiries during my progress concerning the river; and received from Negroes of different nations, such clear and decisive assurances that its general course was *towards the rising sun*, as scarce left any doubt on my mind.

Park was married to Allison Anderson in 1799, and he began practicing medicine two years later in the Scottish town of Peebles. Then, in the fall of 1803, the British government invited him to lead another expedition to trace the Niger River. Park, who at this time thought the Niger and Congo rivers were one, agreed to go.

He left Portsmouth on January 31, 1805, arrived at the Gambia River a few weeks later, and led his expedition inland in April. Battling 100-degree Fahrenheit (38-degree Celsius) heat and muddy terrain, he reached Pisania on May 4 and Badoo on May 28. As the party traveled farther inland, the rains grew heavier and the hordes of mosquitoes grew worse. Fevers and dysentery ravaged the Europeans.

Park reached the Niger River in August 1805, but, by then, his party of forty-four had been reduced to twelve, the rest having fallen victim to disease. The fatalities included Park's brother-in-law, Alexander Anderson, who was stricken by dysentery at Sansanding. Park wrote several letters in mid-November, including one to his wife, in which he said,

> I do not intend to stop or land anywhere, till we reach the coast; which I suppose will be sometime in the end of January.

Through it all, Park remained focused on a single objective, namely "the fixed resolution to discover the termination of the Niger or perish in the attempt." His resolve proved reckless, however, as it made him attempt to overcome obstacles that neither he nor his remaining party was in any condition to face. Indeed, he was never heard from again.

In 1812, searchers from England finally uncovered what had happened to the determined explorer. Apparently, by early 1806, Park's party had dwindled to just five Europeans, including himself and one man who had gone insane. After leaving Sansanding, the party encountered the Bussa Rapids on the Niger River below its confluence with the Sokoto River, in what is now western Nigeria. At that point, their boat became stuck, and native tribesmen attacked them with arrows and spears.

In an attempt to escape, Park and his men jumped into the river. They drowned in the swift current. One of the expedition's slaves survived the incident and later recounted what had happened.

Further Reading

Hudson, Peter. *Two Rivers: Travels in West Africa on the Trail of Mungo Park.* London: Chapmans, 1991.

Lupton, Kenneth. *Mungo Park: The African Traveler.* New York: Oxford University Press, 1979.

Park, Mungo, with Kate Ferguson Marsters, ed. *Travels Into the Interior of Africa.* Durham, NC: Duke University Press, 2000.

See also: African Association; Banks, Joseph.

PEARY, ROBERT E. (1856–1920)

1856: Born on May 6 in Cresson, Pennsylvania
1881: Joins the U.S. Navy as a civil engineer
1886: Makes his first journey to Greenland and resolves to reach the North Pole one day
1900: Reaches the northernmost point of the Greenland ice cap
1908: On April 6, leads the first team to reach the North Pole
1920: Dies on February 20 in Washington, D.C.

The American Arctic explorer and U.S. Navy engineer Robert Peary generally is credited as the first person to reach the North Pole, in April 1908—though some doubt and controversy continue to surround the accomplishment.

Robert Edwin Peary was born on May 6, 1856, in Cresson, Pennsylvania, to Charles Nutter Peary and Mary Webster Wiley. His father died when he was still a young child, and he moved with his mother to Portland, Maine. As a youngster, he preferred the outdoors and enjoyed hiking in the woods with friends.

After graduating from Bowdoin College in 1877, Peary worked as a draftsman in the Office of Coast Survey. In 1881, he joined the U.S. Navy as a civil engineer with the rank of lieutenant. In 1884–1885, he served in Nicaragua, helping survey the land for a possible canal through Central America, connecting the Atlantic and Pacific oceans.

Peary made his first two trips to Greenland in 1886 and 1891 and became determined to reach the North Pole. In 1892, he traveled across the extreme northern part of the Greenland ice cap from Bowdoin Bay, on the west coast, through what came to be called Peary Land, and then on to Independence Fjord, on the east coast. (His expeditions were well north of where the Swedish-Norwegian explorer Fridtjof Nansen had crossed Greenland in 1888.) Other Peary-led expeditions to the Arctic, from 1893 to 1895, proved notable for the collection of meteorites he brought back to the United States.

From 1898 to 1902, Peary mapped large parts of the Greenland coast, although he got no closer than 340 miles (550 kilometers) from the North Pole. During one of these expeditions, in 1900, he reached the northernmost point of Greenland and named it Cape Morris Jesup in honor of the president of the American Museum of Natural History at that time. He also discovered the northernmost point of land in the world, a small island called Oodaaq Qeqertaag, also in Greenland (situated 438 miles, or 705 kilometers, south of the North Pole). The trip proved that the Greenland ice cap ended at 82° north latitude, well short of the North Pole.

Aside from the lands explored and the knowledge obtained, Peary's journeys to the Arctic provided valuable information for his ultimate goal of reaching the North Pole. To endure the harsh conditions, he relied heavily on the Inuits, the native peoples of the region. Peary and his companions studied their way of life and learned essential skills for surviving in the frigid north. The Inuits taught them how to build an igloo and how to dress warmly in animal fur. Some even traveled with Peary, helping him hunt for game, drive the dogsleds, and navigate the land. These natives proved indispensable to the success of his expeditions.

In his next push for the pole, Peary and his men reached 87° 6′ north latitude in April 1906, leaving him less than 175 miles (280 kilometers) from his goal. Although cold and hunger forced Peary to turn back, it was the farthest north anyone had ever traveled.

His next attempt began in July 1908. He left New York City with twenty-three men aboard the *Roosevelt*, bound for the Arctic. The party arrived at Ellesmere Island (in northern Canada) and spent the winter there preparing for the final assault. Peary and his men left the island on February 28, 1909, with nineteen sleds and 133 dogs. The men were organized into teams, each team moving north in stages and setting up supply depots. This technique was subsequently called the Peary System.

The expedition was fraught with danger. Blankets of snow fed by fierce winds pounded the explorers, glare made vision difficult, and the ice proved unpredictable. One night, while he was trying to sleep, Peary wrote, he heard "thundering noises" and "felt the ice floor on which I lay quivering." He went on:

> In an instant it was clear what had happened. A crevasse had suddenly opened through our igloo, directly under the spot whereupon I slept; and I . . . with tumbling snow blocks and ice and snow crashing about and crushing me, with the temperature 48° below zero, was floundering in the open sea!

Fortunately, two of Peary's Inuit companions saved him.

Peary, along with his African American colleague, Matthew Henson, and four Inuits, made the final push to the North Pole, reaching the site on April 6, 1909. From that point on, Peary said little to Henson and kept him at a distance, apparently because Henson had reached the pole several minutes ahead of him.

Commander Robert E. Peary returns home aboard the USS *Roosevelt* in September 1909, five months after reaching the North Pole. En route home, Peary learned of Frederick Cook's claim to have beaten him to the pole—an enduring source of controversy. (*Hulton Archive/Stringer/Getty Images*)

In any event, that September, Peary sent a telegram from Newfoundland to *The New York Times* to announce his triumph. He wired,

> I have the pole, April sixth. Expect arrive Chateau Bay, September seventh. Secure wire control for me there and arrange expedite transmission big story.

Peary's claim proved controversial from the outset, not least because the American explorer Frederick Cook had announced days earlier that he had reached the North Pole in April 1908, a full year earlier. Despite the dubious aspects of Cook's claim—and of his reputation—Peary's doubters maintained that he had not made it to the pole but had purposefully or unknowingly miscalculated his location. They said that he could not have returned to his base camp as soon as he did if he had traveled from the true location of the North Pole.

Photographic evidence, however, suggests that Peary indeed made it all the way to the pole, or at least within 5 miles (8 kilometers) of it. Moreover, it was argued, he could have made the return trip as rapidly as he claimed for several reasons: The trail back already was familiar; his sleds were carrying fewer supplies and weighed less; the dogs were excited to be returning

PEARY VERSUS COOK

Robert E. Peary did not stand alone in claiming to have reached the North Pole. In September 1909, just five days before Peary sent a telegram from Newfoundland announcing his feat, a similar claim was made by Frederick Cook (1865–1940), a physician from Hortonville, New York.

Cook had served as a surgeon on Peary's 1891 expedition to Greenland. He reported that he had reached the North Pole on April 21, 1908, nearly a full year before Peary. Bad weather, he said, had delayed his return and the announcement of his achievement.

In the months and years that followed, Peary and his supporters and Cook and his supporters battled over whose claim was legitimate. Peary submitted his evidence—including photographs, his log, and depth charge measurements—to the National Geographic Society. The society, a cosponsor of Peary's expedition, concluded that he had passed at least within a few miles of the pole. Cook's case was damaged by a dubious claim he had made, that he had reached the summit of Mount McKinley, and by his criminal conviction for mail fraud in 1924.

In yet another take on the controversy, historian Robert Bryce concludes in his exhaustive work, *Cook and Peary: The Polar Controversy Resolved* (1997), that both men lied. Neither one, he says, reached the North Pole, with Cook getting no closer than 400 miles (640 kilometers) and Peary getting no closer than 100 miles (160 kilometers).

Nevertheless, most scholars continue to support Peary's claim to have been the first person to reach the North Pole—or very close to it.

and moved faster; there was a tailwind; and they were able to save time by using the camps they already had set up. That argument gained support in 2005, when a team of British adventurers repeated Peary's return journey with replica equipment in less time than it had taken Peary. But none of this has definitively answered the objections of Cook's supporters or proven the case on behalf of either explorer.

Upon his return to the United States, Peary was showered with honors and awards, including a gold medal from the National Geographic Society, a formal citation of thanks from Congress, and a promotion by the U.S. Navy to rear admiral in 1911.

Peary died in Washington, D.C., on February 20, 1920. Surviving him was his wife, Josephine Diebitach Peary, who had accompanied him on several expeditions and given birth to a daughter in the Arctic. The couple also had a son, and Peary fathered several children with Inuit women outside of marriage.

According to *The New York Times* (an ardent Peary supporter), his feat of reaching the North Pole had "crowned a life devoted to the exploration of the icy north and the advancement of science."

Further Reading

Bryce, Robert. *Cook and Peary: The Polar Controversy Resolved*. Mechanicsville, PA: Stackpole, 1997.

Henderson, Bruce. *True North: Peary, Cook and the Race to the Pole*. New York: W.W. Norton, 2005.

Herbert, Wally. *The Noose of Laurels: The Discovery of the North Pole*. London: Hodder and Stoughton, 1989.

See also: Arctic; Henson, Matthew.

POWELL EXPEDITIONS

1834: John Wesley Powell is born on March 24 in Mount Morris, New York
1867: With his wife, Emma, Powell climbs Pike's Peak in Colorado
1869: Begins his exploration of the Colorado River system on May 24
1871: Leads a second expedition down the Colorado River
1879: With Powell's help, the Bureau of American Ethnology is founded
1881: Becomes director of the United States Geological Survey
1903: Dies on September 23 in Maine

In 1869 and 1871, Civil War veteran and geology professor John Wesley Powell led two daring expeditions down the Colorado River in pursuit of scientific information, to acquire plant and animal specimens, and to map the canyon country. Among his other accomplishments, he was the first to explore the Colorado and Green River canyons, the first to pass through the Grand Canyon, and, later, the first to classify Native American languages.

John Wesley Powell had science and adventure in his blood long before he conquered the Colorado. He was born in Mount Morris, New York, on March 24, 1834, to Joseph Powell and May Dean; his family eventually settled on a farm in Boone County, Illinois. A tailor and lay preacher, Joseph Powell wanted his son to become a minister, but the young man resisted him. Instead, John Wesley Powell studied natural science at Illinois College, Wheaton College, and Oberlin College without taking a degree.

In 1855, Powell walked across Wisconsin for four months, and in 1856 he rowed down a portion of the Mississippi River. Over the next two years, he journeyed down the Ohio River from Pittsburgh to St. Louis and rowed portions of the Illinois, Mississippi, and Des Moines rivers.

With the outbreak of the Civil War, Powell served in the Union army. He lost most of his right arm when he was struck by a musket ball at the Battle of Shiloh in 1862. He rose to the rank of major before receiving a disability discharge in January 1865.

Upon leaving the army in 1865, he became professor of geology at Illinois Wesleyan University and then, in 1867, at Illinois State Normal University. At that time, he also helped found the Illinois Museum of Natural History at Bloomington and became its director.

Powell journeyed west for the first time in 1867, when he led an expedition to the Rocky Mountains in Colorado and, with his wife, Emma, climbed Pikes Peak. (She was the first woman known to scale the peak.) The trip gave Powell the idea to explore the Colorado River, to add what he called a "mite to the great sum of human knowledge." Although there had been some previous exploration of the lower Colorado in the 1850s, the river was largely unknown.

Powell's expedition party of ten men included his brother, Walter; O.G. Howland, a printer and editor; and William Dunn, a hunter and trapper. Powell assembled four boats for the journey, three of which were made of oak and contained a watertight compartment. The fourth, called the *Emma Dean*, was a 16-foot (4.9-meter) pilot boat made of pine. Powell brought along sextants, barometers, chronometers, compasses, and thermometers for mapping and for recording geographic and weather conditions. From conception, the journey was to be part adventure and part scientific expedition, including a search for specimens, geologic studies, and detailed surveying and map work.

The canoes cast off on the Green River in the Wyoming Territory on May 24, 1869. By the end of the month, the expedition had entered the northeast corner of Utah, where they were dwarfed by red sandstone cliff walls that Powell named Red Canyon. As the party continued down the Green River, Powell studied geological formations and collected plants and

Major John Wesley Powell and his party gather on the Green River in Wyoming in 1871 for a second expedition (retracing the first, two years earlier) to explore the Colorado River and Grand Canyon. The second trip yielded a map and scientific records. (*Stringer/ Hulton Archive/ Getty Images*)

fossilized shells. He commanded the pilot boat, looking out for rapids and other dangers, often ordering it ashore so that the waters could be tested for depth and current before continuing on.

In early June, while still on the Green River, one of the oak boats got caught in a rapid and smashed into the rocks. The three men aboard were rescued, though some of the scientific instruments were lost; Powell later retrieved the barometers that had been swept downriver. Indeed, the Green River proved to be a considerable challenge. As one of the men wrote, "The river in this canyon is not a succession of rapids as we have found before, but a continuous rapid."

On July 21, the expedition finally reached the Colorado River, with its more than 150 rapids, and soon entered a magnificent, winding sandstone chasm that Powell named Glen Canyon. He wrote,

Past these towering monuments, past these mounded billows of orange sandstone, past the oak-set glens, past these fern-decked alcoves, past these mural curves, we glide hour after hour, stopping now and then, as our attention is arrested by some new wonder.

Then came the Grand Canyon, which the expedition reached on August 13. Powell described their arrival:

We are now ready to start our way down the Great Unknown. We have but a month's rations remaining. . . . We have an unknown distance yet to run, an unknown river to explore. What falls there are, we know not; what rocks beset the channel, we know not; what walls rise over the river, we know not.

On August 28, three of the men, exhausted by the journey and concerned about the dangers ahead, quit the expedition. They later were killed by Native Americans.

Also on August 28, Powell and his party encountered—and survived—the most dangerous rapids of the entire trip. They completed their journey the following day at Grand Wash. Powell later wrote, "The first hours of convalescent freedom seem rich recompense for all pain and gloom and terror."

Indeed, toward the end, the expedition had become a struggle for survival. Little "science" was conducted, and much of the scientific data and all of the specimens the men had collected were lost.

Powell, though, became a national hero. He was able to recount much about a river system Americans knew nothing of. Moreover, his second ex-

THE GRAND CANYON AS GEOLOGICAL PARK

With its sheer red cliffs towering thousands of feet above the Colorado River, the Grand Canyon is a kind of natural temple—American conservationist John Muir called it the "grandest of God's terrestrial cities"—as well as a geological park. "There is not a place on Earth," says William Breed of the Museum of Northern Arizona, "where geology is revealed on such a fantastic scale and in so much detail."

The canyon was created about 6 million years ago by a combination of the uplifting of the Earth's surface and the cutting action of the Colorado River. It winds 217 miles (349 kilometers) across northwestern Arizona, measuring up to 18 miles (29 kilometers) wide and 1 mile (1.6 kilometers) deep.

Within it, there are a number of layers of exposed rock. The top layer consists of Kaibab limestone, deposited as sediment about 250 million years ago and containing fossils of coral and early sharks. Below that is a layer of Toroweap limestone, which is some 255 million years old, which is followed by Coconino sandstone, dating to about 260 million years ago, and soft Hermit shale, from about 265 million years ago.

Lower yet is a layer of inter-bedded shales and sandstones called the Supai formation, dating from 140 million to 290 million years ago. Next comes a layer of Redwall limestone about 500 feet (150 meters) thick and dating from 330 million to 360 million years ago, followed by a thin layer of sandstone, the Temple Butte, deposited 360 million to 410 million years ago.

The next three layers date back 500 million to 570 million years and consist of brown Mauv limestone, green Bright Angel shale, and rust-red Tapeats sandstone. At the very bottom of the canyon are the oldest of rocks, Vishnu schists and gneisses, from half a billion to a billion or more years ago.

Whether one views the Grand Canyon from the rims or delves into its inner secrets, the experience is one of coming into contact with a scale of time almost incomprehensible next to the relatively brief period of human existence.

pedition down the Colorado, in 1871, proved much more successful from a scientific point of view. He returned home with extensive scientific records, including a map, photographs, and drawings, as well as biological and geological specimens.

Thereafter, Powell studied the rivers and rainfall of the West and the ways in which Native Americans, Spanish settlers, and Mormons used the land. Concluding that water was the region's critical resource, in 1878, he issued a far-reaching land use plan that called for the sharing of scarce water reserves and advised the federal government to build dams. Settlers, Powell insisted, would have to learn to work with nature rather than fight it.

Powell's experience with Native American tribes and culture made him an ideal director of the new Bureau of American Ethnology, which he helped found in 1879. As director, he led a group of linguists into the field to compile the first distributional map of Native American languages—a valuable resource in Native American studies for decades to come.

From 1881 to 1894, Powell served as only the second director of the United States Geological Survey. The government agency had been established in 1879 and charged with "classification of the public lands, and examination of the geological structure, mineral resources, and products of the national domain."

Powell died on September 23, 1902, in Maine. By then, he was a renowned geologist and ethnologist. Nevertheless, he is best remembered for his Colorado River expeditions of 1869 and 1871, and his explorations of the previously unknown river system and the natural world that surrounded it.

Further Reading

DeBuys, William, ed. *Seeing Things Whole: The Essential John Wesley Powell.* Washington, DC: Island, 2001.

Dolnick, Edward. *Down the Great Unknown: John Wesley Powell's 1869 Journey of Discovery and Tragedy Through the Grand Canyon.* New York: HarperCollins, 2002.

Worster, Donald. *A River Running West: The Life of John Wesley Powell.* New York: Oxford University Press, 2001.

R

ROYAL GEOGRAPHICAL SOCIETY

1830: The Royal Geographical Society is founded in London
1832: The society publishes its first journal
1892: The *Geographical Journal* begins publication
1933: The Institute of British Geographers is formed when a splinter group breaks away from the Royal Geographical Society
1995: The Royal Geographical Society and the Institute of British Geographers merge

A British learned society established in 1830 to "promote the advancement of geographical science," the Royal Geographical Society (RGS) has pursued its mission by sponsoring numerous scientific expeditions, publishing journals and magazines, staging exhibits and lectures, and recognizing notable achievements in the field.

The Royal Geographical Society evolved from a male-only dining club in London, an exclusive gathering whose members held informal dinner debates on current events and scientific issues. In 1830, a small group of members—including the Admiralty official and geographer John Barrow, naval officer and Arctic explorer John Franklin, and hydrographer Francis Beaufort—founded the society, which received its royal charter under Queen Victoria in 1859. Initially, members convened at the offices of the Horticultural Society on Regent Street.

By 1840, the RGS had about 700 members and was beginning to compile an impressive library, including some 380 books and 290 maps and charts. "No work relating to geography, no map or chart extant," said the annual report, "should be wanting to the library of the Royal Geographical Society in London."

From 1854, the RGS met at 15 Whitehall Place; it moved to Saville Row in 1870. The new venue provided a suitable place for explorers to discuss their findings and projects, study in the library and map room, and present speeches to audiences. In 1913, the society moved to its present site, Lowther Lodge in Kensington Gore. It also ended its ban on women members at that time.

During the nineteenth century, the RGS sponsored expeditions to advance scientific knowledge, especially of unknown or little-known regions. Integral to that mission, at least to some, was extending the reach of British power and influence. Many members supported the growth of the British

Empire with the imperialistic attitude that this would bring civilization to those who they viewed as the "uncivilized" people of the world.

In addition, expeditions sponsored by the society often entailed the inventorying of resources to be exploited. For example, in an 1876 speech to the Royal Geographical Society, Lieutenant Verney Lovett Cameron observed of East Africa,

> Most of the country from the Tanganyika to the West Coast is one of almost unspeakable richness. Of metals, there are iron, copper, silver and gold; coal also is to be found; the vegetable products are palm oil, cotton, nutmegs, besides several sorts of pepper and coffee, all growing wild.

Among the noteworthy expeditions sponsored by the RGS were those in Guyana by Robert Schomburgk; in Africa by David Livingstone, Richard Burton, John Hanning Speke, James Augustus Grant, and Joseph Thomson; and in the Arctic by John Franklin and George Strong Nares.

The society published its first journal in 1832, with news from its meetings recorded in the *Proceedings* beginning in 1855. This was succeeded in 1892 by the *Geographical Journal*, which the society has continued to publish on a quarterly basis to the present day. (Since 2000, the *Geographic Journal* has ceased reporting RGS news in order to focus exclusively on original research papers.) From its inception, the society also has promoted geography as a discipline in British universities, funding the first geography faculty positions at the universities of Oxford and Cambridge.

The growth of the RGS has not been without turbulence. By the late 1920s, younger members were chafing at their inability to get their papers read before the society or to get them published. As a result, several of them broke away in 1933 to form a splinter group called the Institute of British Geographers (IBG). The new society organized conferences and seminars separate from the RGS, though the two groups ultimately cooperated in several endeavors. The RGS and IBG began discussing a merger in 1992, came to an agreement two years later, and formally merged in 1995.

In May 1890, at a reception organized by the Royal Geographical Society at London's Albert Hall, Henry Morton Stanley describes his successful search in Central Africa for the lost Scottish explorer David Livingstone. *(Hulton Archive/Stringer/Getty Images)*

The official name of the society became the Royal Geographical Society (with the Institute of British Geographers). Today, the society is headed by a president and governed by a board of trustees called the Council. The latter consists of twenty-five members, twenty-two of whom are elected by the fellowship and serve three-year terms; the three other members are honorary. To become a fellow requires five years of membership in the society and nomination by an existing fellow.

In addition to honorary members and fellowships, the society presents about a dozen awards and medals for "excellence in geographical research and fieldwork, teaching and public engagement." The most prestigious are the Founder's Medal and the Patron's Medal. Recipients of these awards have included the Scottish missionary and African explorer David Livingstone in 1855 and naturalist Alfred Russel Wallace in 1892.

The Royal Geographical Society is Europe's largest learned society in the field and one of the largest in the world, with eight branches in the United Kingdom and one in Hong Kong. As of 2009, membership exceeded 15,000 from more than 100 countries—including academics, professional geographers, researchers, and adventurers—with an estimated 150,000 taking part in RGS events and activities.

See also: Arctic; Burton, Richard Francis; Livingstone, David, and Henry Morton Stanley; Speke, John Hanning.

Further Reading

Cameron, Ian. *To the Farthest Ends of the Earth: 150 Years of World Exploration by the Royal Geographical Society.* New York: E.P. Dutton, 1980.

Royal Geographical Society: http://www.rgs.org.

RUSSIAN EXPLORATION

1728: Vitus Bering, a Dane serving in the Russian navy, sails through the strait between eastern Siberia and Alaska

1733: Bering becomes the leader of the Great Northern Expedition

1735: Vasili Pronchishchev journeys down the Lena River through Siberia

1820: Ferdinand Petrovich Wrangel begins exploring northern Siberia, where he finds an open sea (the East Siberian Sea), rather than dry land, north of the Kolyma River and Cape Shelagski

1821: Count Fyodor Petrovich Litke begins his journey to map the west coast of Novaya Zemlya, an Arctic archipelago in northern Russia

1826: Litke collects specimens in the Bering Strait

1854: Nikolay Nikolayevich Muravyov-Amursky journeys down the Amu River between southeastern Siberia and northeastern China

1884: Aleksandr Mikhaylovich Sibiryakov travels across the Ural Mountains to Tobolsk in southwestern Russia

1902: Vladimir Klavdiyevich Arsenyev begins exploring the forests of the Ussuri River near Manchuria
1913: Boris Vilkitsky leads a hydrographic expedition to study the Northeast Passage

In addition to Western Europeans, a number of Russians—or explorers operating under the Russian flag—took part in scientific expeditions to investigate Arctic Russia, Siberia, and points farther south and east.

While Western European nations during the Age of Discovery were searching for a Northwest Passage connecting the Atlantic and Pacific Oceans, Russia was seeking a *Northeast* Passage connecting its western lands and Asian ports, including those in China, India, Japan, and, eventually, the Americas.

Vitus Bering and the Great Northern Expedition

At the turn of the eighteenth century, Czar Peter the Great was eager to find the Northeast Passage so as to establish a sea link with Asia. In addition, he wanted to spread Russian influence to North America and engage his nation in the kind of scientific research and exploration that had brought so much prestige to Western European nations.

To pursue those goals, Czar Peter turned to Vitus Bering (1681–1741), a Dane who had been serving in the Russian navy for years. In 1724, the czar appointed Bering leader of an expedition to determine whether Asia and America were connected by land.

The question had, in fact, been answered earlier. In 1648, Semyon Dezhnyov (ca. 1605–1672), a Cossack sailor, had guided seven ships through what later would be named the Bering Strait, which separated the two continents. Dezhnyov's report, however, was lost until 1736.

Czar Peter's instructions to Bering read:

I. At Kamchatka or somewhere else two decked boats are to be built. II. With these you are to sail northward along the coast, and as the end of the coast is not known this land is undoubtedly America. III. For this reason you are to inquire where the American coast begins, and go to some European colony; and when European ships are seen you are to ask what the coast is called, note it down, make a landing, obtain reliable information, and then, after having chartered the coast, return.

Bering sailed from the Siberian peninsula of Kamchatka in 1728 and, in the course of one month, entered the Bering Strait and journeyed north into the Arctic Ocean. Although fog kept him from seeing the North

American coast, his voyage, like Dezhnyov's eighty years earlier, proved that there was no land bridge between Asia and America.

From 1733 to 1743, Bering was in charge of Russia's Great Northern Expedition, which he conceived and proposed to Czarina Anna (Anna Ivanovna), who was then in power. Departing again from Kamchatka, the expedition would map the west coast of North America, sail west to Japan, and chart the Arctic coast of Siberia.

Czarina Anna accepted the proposal and, in the spirit of Czar Peter's fondness for science and exploration, expanded it. The expedition would include nearly 1,000 seamen, divided into four squads. One squad was to travel from Archangel to the mouth of the Ob River, a second from the Ob to the mouth of the Yenisei River, a third from the mouth of the Lena River to the mouth of the Yenisei, and a fourth from the mouth of the Lena to the Chukchi Peninsula and Kamchatka.

Bering himself sailed from Kamchatka aboard the *St. Peter* in June 1741, accompanied by a second ship, the *St. Paul,* under the command of Aleksi Illich Chirikov (1703–1748). The two ships soon became separated in a thick fog.

In late July, Bering, aboard the *St. Peter,* landed in Alaska at Kayak Island. Accompanying him was German botanist Georg Wilhelm Steller (1709–1746), who studied the North American plant and animal species he found on the island.

In November, Bering sighted the Commander Islands east of Kamchatka. By then, however, disease had felled many of his crewmen.

The death of Danish navigator Vitus Bering, on an island near Siberia's Kamchatka Peninsula in 1741, is dramatized in this painting. The island, like the sea in which it is located, now bears his name. (*Granger Collection, New York*)

RUSSIAN EXPLORERS IN ALASKA

Vitus Bering's expedition of 1741 is said to mark the "discovery" of Alaska. In mid-July of that year, while Bering was anchored farther north near Cape St. Elias, Aleksi Chirikov—the commander of the *St. Paul*, the second ship in Bering's expedition—sighted land in southeast Alaska.

Chirikov headed west and anchored in the Shumagin Islands (in the Aleutian chain). There, the *St. Paul* was approached by two kayaks bearing Aleuts (native Alaskans), and the two groups exchanged goods. The Aleuts invited the Russians ashore, where they exchanged goods again the next day. Then, the Russians departed. It was the first direct encounter between Europeans and the native people of Alaska ever recorded.

Russian explorers conducted more than sixty exploratory and colonization voyages to Alaska between that first encounter and 1861, when the territory was sold by Russia to the United States. In their voyages, the Russians mapped the coast of the Bering Sea and portions of the Arctic, studied the native people, and recorded extensive information on animal and plant life, rocks and minerals, geological features, the ice pack, and the region's climate.

Shortly thereafter, the *St. Peter* was shipwrecked on the island that would bear Bering's name. He died there in December 1741, a victim of scurvy, along with twenty-eight of his men.

The Great Northern Expedition continued, however, and forty-five of the seventy-seven officers and men on the *St. Peter* survived, arriving back in Siberia on a small ship they had built. Based on this expedition, Steller wrote *De Bestiis Marinis* (*The Beasts of the Sea*), published in 1751, in which he described the fauna of Bering Island, including the northern fur seal, the sea otter, and the northern sea lion.

Meanwhile, Chirikov and his crew continued to the east. In July 1741, they reached Prince of Wales Island in extreme southern Alaska. Chirikov anchored near Cape Addington and sent two parties inland to explore; neither party was ever heard from again.

In October, Chirikov weighed anchor and sailed to Kamchatka. In spring 1742, he led an expedition to search for Bering but failed to find him. He later received the news of Bering's death from the survivors of the *St. Peter*.

Vasili Pronchishchev (1702–1736), a lieutenant in the Russian imperial navy, headed one of the squads in the Great Northern Expedition, with the assignment to map the shores of the Arctic Ocean from the mouth of the Lena River to the mouth of the Yenisei River. In 1735, he journeyed down the Lena on the sloop *Yakutska*.

Although many of Pronchishchev's crew became sick from scurvy, in 1736, he reached the eastern shore of the Taymyr Peninsula, where he discovered several islands. The expedition was notable for several firsts. Pronchishchev was the first person to map large parts of the Lena River,

THE SEA BEAR CONFRONTED

Georg Wilhelm Steller's classic 1751 account of his expedition with Vitus Bering to the Bering Sea, *De Bestiis Marinis (The Beasts of the Sea)*, includes descriptions of animal life observed on various islands. Among them were the manatee, sea otter, sea lion, and sea bear (fur seal), one of which he found to weigh about 800 pounds (360 kilograms). Steller describes an encounter with a group of sea bears:

All the males have a strong odor. . . . These old animals are very cross and very savage. They live a whole month in one place without food or drink; they sleep all the time, but rage with exceeding fierceness at all who pass by. Indeed they are so very fierce and jealous that they would a hundred times rather die than give up their place. And so if they see a man they go out to get in his way and prevent his passing; one of the others meanwhile gets his place and is ready to fight with him. When we were obliged to come into conflict with them because of the necessity of continuing our journey, we threw great stones at them. They in turn would rage at the stone thrown at them just as a dog would, and start up in defiance and fill the air with their terrible roaring. . . .

and his wife, Maria, who sailed with him, is believed to have been the first European woman to explore the Arctic. Both Vasili and Maria died from scurvy during the journey.

The Great Northern Expedition's detachments mapped much of Russia's Arctic coast. On May 20, 1742, Semyon Chelyuskin (1700–1764) reached the northernmost point of Eurasia.

Other Eighteenth- and Nineteenth-Century Expeditions

From 1817 to 1819, Count Fyodor Petrovich Litke (1797–1882), who had joined the imperial navy in 1812, took part in a voyage around the world aboard the *Kamchatka*. From 1821 to 1824, he mapped the west coast of Novaya Zemlya—an archipelago in the Russian Arctic—and studied the southwestern Barents Sea.

Litke took part in another around-the-world voyage from 1826 to 1829. This was a scientific expedition during which he collected specimens in the Bering Strait as well as on Bonin and Caroline islands in the western Pacific. Litke also journeyed to Alaska, arriving at Sitka in 1827, and surveyed the Pribilof Islands, St. Matthew Island, and the Commander Islands. From Petropavlovsk, he sailed the Siberian coast all the way to St. Lawrence Bay at Nova Scotia in northeastern Canada.

In addition to being known for his explorations, Litke is known as one of the founders of the Russian Geographical Society (in 1845); he served as its first vice president. Also an inventor, he developed a device to record and measure ocean tides that was installed along the Arctic and Pacific coasts in 1841.

Ferdinand Petrovich Wrangel (1797–1870), who was born into a German noble family and graduated from a Russian naval cadet college in 1815, led an expedition from 1820 to 1824 to explore Siberia. He sailed into the Arctic Ocean and mapped the still largely obscure Siberian coast, where he found an open sea (the East Siberian Sea) north of the Kolyma River and Cape Shelagski, near latitude 70° north. "We beheld," he wrote, "the wide, immeasurable ocean spread before our gaze, a fearful and magnificent, but to us a melancholy spectacle."

In the course of this expedition, Wrangel collected information about glaciers, magnetic fields, and climatic conditions; he also tried but failed to find a large island he thought was in the Arctic Ocean. That island finally was discovered in 1867 by an American, Thomas Long, who named it Wrangel Island.

Nikolay Nikolayevich Muravyov-Amursky (1809–1881) was a major general in the Russian army until he retired due to illness in 1841. Six years later, he was appointed governor-general of Irkutsk and Yeniseysk in eastern Siberia. From 1854 to 1858, he led expeditions down the Amur River; the first one included the steamship *Argun* and seventy-seven barges and rafts. Muravyov-Amursky's journeys expanded Russian knowledge of the region and led to a treaty with China that relocated the border between the two countries and added significant new territory to Russian Siberia.

In the late nineteenth century, Aleksandr Mikhaylovich Sibiryakov (1849–1893), a wealthy mine owner, financed several expeditions to

Russian hydrologists drill for samples in the frozen Amur River after explosions at a Chinese chemical plant in 2005. The river is named after Nikolay Nikolayevich Muravyov-Amursky, who explored the frontier between eastern Russia and China in the 1850s. (*Viktor Drachev/ AFP/Getty Images*)

Siberia, including those of the Finn Adolf Erik Nordenskjöld (1832–1901) and the Russian Alexander Mikhaylovich Grigoryev (1849–1933). In addition, Sibiryakov led expeditions of his own. In 1880, he journeyed to the Kara Sea on the north-central coast of Russia. And in 1884, he traveled by steamer to the mouth of the Pechora River on the Barents Sea, then overland east across the Ural Mountains and south along the Tobol River to Tobolsk, in Kazahkstan.

Twentieth-Century Expeditions

In the early 1900s, the Russian explorer Vladimir Klavdiyevich Arsenyev (1872–1930) described and documented the Ussuri River basin and the Sikhote-Alin mountain range in the Far East. From 1902 to 1907, he explored the forests, or taiga, of the Ussuri along the Sea of Japan to Vladivostok, collecting flora and fauna along the way. His account of three expeditions, *Dersu Uzala (Dersu the Hunter)*, published in 1923, describes his relationship with his guide and teacher, Dersu Uzala of the Nanai tribe, and extols the practical knowledge and wisdom of the Ussurian native. Arsenyev also wrote several stories dedicated to the native people.

From 1913 to 1915, the hydrographer and surveyor Boris Vilkitsky (1885–1961) led an Arctic expedition to explore the Northeast Passage. On this trip, he discovered the Severnaya Zemlya archipelago, along with Vilkitsky Island, Maly Taymyr Island, and Starokadomsky Island. The later phase of the expedition included the first through voyage from Vladivostok to Archangel. Vilkitsky's two ships were forced to winter on the west coast of Taymyr in 1914–1915 and completed their journey to Archangel the following summer.

All told, Russian explorations of the eighteenth to twentieth centuries added immeasurably to the knowledge of Siberia, other areas of the Arctic region, and the northern Far East. They also served to expand Russian territory to the North American continent in Alaska and southeast to Chinese Manchuria.

Further Reading

Alekseev, A.I. *Fedor Petrovich Litke*. Fairbanks: University of Alaska Press, 1996.

Collins, David N., ed. *Siberian Discovery*. 12 vols. Surrey, UK: Curzon, 2000.

Fisher, Raymond Henry. *Bering's Voyages: Whither and Why?* Seattle: University of Washington Press, 1994.

Frost, Orcutt. *Bering: The Russian Discovery of America*. New Haven, CT: Yale University Press, 2003.

See also: Arctic.

S

SCHLIEMANN, HEINRICH (1822–1890)

1822: Born in Neubuckow, Germany, on January 6

1844: Begins working for an import-export company, traveling throughout Europe

1863: Retires from business a millionaire; devotes himself to archaeology

1871: Begins excavation in search of ancient city of Troy at Hissarlik, Turkey; uncovers several layers of ruins

1873: Discovers a cache of gold and other artifacts, which he calls "Priam's Treasure"

1874: Begins excavation at Mycenae, Greece

1876: Inside the Lion Gate at Mycenae, discovers ancient royal grave shafts and gold death masks

1890: Dies on December 26 in Naples, Italy

A German-born businessman and archaeologist whose work was surrounded by controversy, Heinrich Schliemann unearthed the site of the ancient city of Troy in Turkey and discovered rich artifacts at the ruins of Mycenae in Greece.

Heinrich Schliemann was born on January 6, 1822, in Neubuckow, Mecklenburg, Germany, to Ernst and Luise Schliemann. His father was a Protestant minister who enjoyed studying the classics. Heinrich later said that he first was attracted to studying ancient Troy when, at age eight, his father gave him a book containing Greek and Roman myths and legends. Many historians doubt this story, however, and trace his first interest in Troy to a much later time.

In any event, young Schliemann developed an intense interest in the *Iliad* and the *Odyssey*, the two epic poems by the ancient Greek poet Homer. These classics pertain to the Trojan War and its aftermath. This war is said by historians to have been fought in the twelfth century B.C.E. between the Greeks of Mycenae and the inhabitants of Troy, in Anatolia, part of present-day Turkey.

Schliemann received an erratic education. His schooling began at a private academy, but he was forced to leave it when his father was accused of embezzling church funds. The boy left public school at age fourteen and went to work for a grocer in Furstenburg, dedicating himself to making money and learning languages. He proved extraordinarily adept at both. He saved much of what he earned and taught himself six foreign languages within a two-year period: Dutch, English, French, Spanish, Italian, and Portuguese.

Schliemann's proficiency in languages helped him secure a position in 1844 with a large import-export firm, B.H. Schroder, which sent him to St. Petersburg, Russia, two years later to act as an agent. Schliemann made considerable money for the company as an indigo trader, traveled throughout Europe, and eventually came to represent the interests of a number of trading firms. In 1848, he founded his own merchant house and continued to prosper.

In 1850, Schliemann set out for California to make his fortune in the gold rush. Once there, he started a bank in Sacramento that bought gold dust from prospectors and sold it on the open market, and soon he amassed a fortune. While Schliemann became a naturalized U.S. citizen when California became a U.S. state in 1850, two years later, he decided to sell his business and return to Russia. Later that year, he married Ekaterina Petrovna Lyshina. They had three children, but the marriage proved difficult. The couple grew apart, lived separately, and eventually divorced.

In the meantime, Schliemann continued to pursue his interests in languages and archaeology. He retired from business in 1863 as one of the wealthiest men of the time and traveled extensively—to India, Singapore, China, Japan, Cuba, Mexico, France, Italy, and Greece—before settling in Paris. Schliemann then devoted his energies to archaeological research and further language study. He undertook graduate studies in Paris and would become fluent in as many as sixteen languages during his lifetime.

In June 1868, Schliemann spent three days at Pompeii in southern Italy, where excavations led by Giuseppe Fiorelli were under way. In July, he visited Mount Aetos, on the island of Ithaca in the Ionian Sea. This was believed to be the location of the palace of Odysseus, king of Ithaca. At Mount Aetos, Schliemann participated in his first archaeological dig.

In 1869, Schliemann wrote a book in which he maintained that a mound at Hissarlik in Anatolia was the site of ancient Troy. That year, he also submitted a dissertation on this subject (in ancient Greek) to the University of Rostock in Germany and received a Ph.D.

His theory conflicted with those of archaeologists who believed ancient Troy was situated at Bunarbasi (also called Pinarbasi), or at Alexandria Troas, located on the northwest coast of Asia Minor, or what is today Turkey. Schliemann had done some excavating at Alexandria Troas in 1868; however, he turned his attention to Hissarlik when he met British archaeologist Frank Calvert, who had dug trenches at Hissarlik and thought the site held valuable artifacts.

Also in 1869, Schliemann married Sophie Engastromenos. Her interest in the works of Homer and related history reinforced his.

Finding Troy

Schliemann began his excavation at Hissarlik in 1871. He soon uncovered several layers of ruins—a total of eleven cities of Troy from over the centuries. (Archaeologists have since found thirty levels of habitation dating back to 3000 B.C.E.) He called the bottom layer Troy I and the next layer Troy II. Since the latter showed evidence of having been burned, as had the city in the *Iliad*, Schliemann concluded that this was Homer's Troy. He and his team then dug for the treasure said to belong to Priam, the ruler of Troy at the time of the war. During the course of the search, much of the second layer was inadvertently destroyed.

In June 1873, Schliemann noticed a copper jug protruding from an excavation shaft. He later recounted the discovery:

> In excavating this wall further and directly by the side of the palace of King Priam, I came upon a large copper article of the most remarkable form, which attracted my attention all the more as I thought I saw gold behind it. On top of this article lay a stratum of red and calcined ruins ... as hard as stone, and above this ... lay [a] ... wall of ... fortification ... which was built of large stones and earth, and must have belonged to an early date after the destruction of Troy. In order to withdraw the Treasure from the greed of my workmen, and to save it for archaeology, I had to be most expeditious. ... While the men were eating or resting, I cut out the Treasure with a large knife, which it was impossible to do without the very greatest exertion and the most fearful risk of my life, for the great fortification-wall beneath which I had to dig, threatened every moment to fall down upon me.

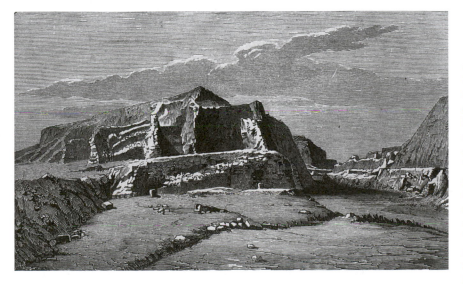

An engraving of 1873 depicts Heinrich Schliemann's excavations at Hissarlik, Turkey, the archaeological site of ancient Troy. That same year, Schliemann unearthed a cache of gold and other artifacts he dubbed "Priam's Treasure." (*Rue des Archives/ Granger Collection, New York*)

To this, he added,

> It would have been impossible for me to have removed the Treasure without the help of my dear wife, who stood by me ready to pack the things which I cut out in her shawl and to carry them away.

Among the items Schliemann found were golden earrings and necklaces; a copper shield and copper lances and daggers; and a silver dish and goblet and silver vases. Breaking a promise he had made to the Turkish government to turn over half of his findings, Schliemann smuggled the artifacts out of the country.

He eventually donated the treasure to a museum in Berlin. He published his findings in *Trojan Antiquities* (1874), *Troy and Its Remains* (1875), and *Ilios: The City and Country of the Trojans* (1880).

Mycenaean Tombs

With his mission accomplished at Hissarlik, Schliemann turned his attention to the site of Mycenae in Greece. Mycenae was the home of Agamemnon, the Greek king at the time of the Trojan War. In 1876, having received permission to dig inside the Lion Gate, the entrance to the royal citadel, Schliemann and his team discovered a grave circle measuring about 90 feet (27 meters) in diameter that contained five tombs. (In 1951, archaeologists found a second grave circle.)

Called the Dome Tombs, this was the burial sites of Mycenaean royalty, whose skeletons were adorned with gold death masks. Upon making his discovery, Schliemann sent a telegram to the king of Greece stating,

> With great joy I announce to Your Majesty that I have discovered the tombs which the tradition proclaimed by Pausanias indicated to be the graves of Agamemnon, Cassandra, Eurymedon and their companions, all slain at a banquet by Clytemnestra and her lover Aegisthos.

Upon uncovering a gold death mask in grave V, Schliemann is said to have declared, "I have gazed upon the face of Agamemnon." He wrote this description of the mask:

> Its features are altogether Hellenic, and I call attention to the long thin nose, running in a direct line with the forehead, which is but small. The eyes, which are shut, are large and well represented by the eyelids; very characteristic is also the large mouth with its well-proportioned lips. The beard is also well represented, and particularly the moustaches, whose extremities are turned upwards to a point, in the form of crescents.

IS AGAMEMNON'S MASK A HOAX?

Archaeologists today continue to debate the truth of a number of Heinrich Schliemann's claims. Foremost among these debates is the one about whether a golden mask Schliemann discovered in 1876 in grave V at Mycenae was the death mask of Agamemnon or, in fact, a forgery.

William Calder III, an American professor of classics and an expert on the work of Schliemann, argued in the 1960s that the forgery theory is supported by the following evidence:

1. The Agamemnon mask is different in style from all other Mycenaean masks yet uncovered.

2. Schliemann's contemporaries accused him of planting finds and then claiming to have discovered them.

3. Schliemann may have obtained the mask from a relative of his wife who was a goldsmith.

4. Schliemann later claimed to have excavated objects that he was known to have purchased.

5. The mask includes a moustache, the upturned position of which was maintained, Schliemann says, by a pomade; the ancient Greeks had no known pomades.

Katie Demakopoulou, director of the prehistoric collection of the National Archaeological Museum in Athens (where the mask now resides), points out that most experts accept the authenticity of the artifact, which bears similarities to other Mycenaean artwork found in the same grave circle.

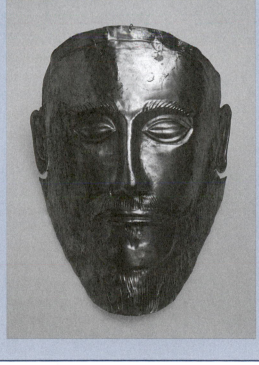

Moreover, it has been pointed out, Schliemann's excavation was closely supervised by the Greek Archaeological Society and the director of Greek antiquities. Kenneth D.S. Lapatin, an art historian at Boston University, has called for microscopic examination and materials analysis that might help reveal the true source and age of the artifact.

A gold mask discovered by Heinrich Schliemann at Mycenae in 1876 continues to be debated among archaeologists today. Is it the death mask of King Agamemnon, the legendary Greek leader in the Trojan War, or a forgery? (*Science & Society Picture Library/ Getty Images*)

The artifact became the most famous of those uncovered at Mycenae. It has been referred to as "Agamemnon's Mask," despite questions regarding its authenticity and age.

Later Work and Legacy

In 1878, Schliemann discovered more treasures at Troy. The following year, he hired an assistant, Wilhelm Dörpfeld, to oversee further archaeological work at the location. (Dörpfeld concluded that Troy VI, not Troy II, was the Troy of Homer, but changed his view in 1932 when American archaeologist Carl William Blegen found substantial evidence suggesting that Troy VII was the Homeric city.)

Schliemann went on to excavate other sites in Greece, including Ithaca, Orchomenus, and Tiryns. In the latter location, a dig in 1884 and 1885 uncovered the ruins of a great palace also referred to by Homer.

In 1886, Schliemann sailed down the Nile River with British Egyptologist E.A. Wallis Budge. Also that year, in the Mediterranean, he uncovered Aphrodite's Temple on the island of Kíthira and found Spartan remains on the island of Sphacteria, which is located at the entrance to the bay of Pylos in the Peloponnese.

Suffering from chronic ear infections, Schliemann underwent surgery in August 1890. Following the operation, he became ill and died on December 26, in Naples, Italy.

Schliemann's archaeological work remains controversial. Some experts have charged that he forged or altered some of his finds to make them seem to be more important. Others have suggested that he combined discoveries from different locations to make them appear as if they had come from a single archaeological site. Moreover, according to subsequent researchers, the treasure he found at Troy predated the Trojan War by more than 1,000 years, and the so-called Mask of Agamemnon has been the object of skepticism in some quarters. All things considered, however, businessman-turned-archaeologist Heinrich Schliemann contributed major discoveries about the classical age and the historical truth of ancient legend.

Further Reading

Moorehead, Caroline. *Lost and Found: The 9,000 Treasures of Troy*. New York: Viking, 1996.

Selden, George. *Heinrich Schliemann: Discoverer of Buried Treasure*. New York: Macmillan, 2000.

Traill, David A. *Schliemann of Troy: Treasure and Deceit*. New York: St. Martin's, 1995.

SCHULTES, RICHARD (1915–2001)

1915: Born on January 12 in Boston
1941: Earns doctorate in botany with dissertation on the use of psychedelic mushrooms by natives of Oaxaca, Mexico; makes his first trip to the Amazon River region in South America
1953: Becomes curator of the Oakes Ames Orchid Herbarium at Harvard University
1979: Publishes *Plants of the Gods: Origins of Hallucinogenic Use*, with Albert Hofmann
1980: Named director of the Botanical Museum and Edward C. Jeffrey Professor of Biology at Harvard
2001: Dies in Waltham, Massachusetts, on April 10

American plant researcher, educator, and curator Richard Evans Schultes has been called the "father of ethnobotany" and the "last Victorian explorer" for his seminal studies of the relationship between plants and native societies and for his prolonged field expeditions to remote regions of Mexico and the Amazon River basin. During the course of a career that spanned more than half a century, he documented hundreds of new plant species and cataloged the medicinal uses of thousands of plants.

Schultes was born on January 12, 1915, in Boston, where his father was a plumber and his mother a homemaker. He was inspired to become a scientist when, at age six, his parents read him *Notes of a Botanist* by English naturalist Richard Spruce. Published in 1908, Spruce's book recounted a vivid story of hunting for plant life along the Amazon River and in the Andes Mountains in South America. About the Andes, Spruce wrote,

> I have been much interested to meet here several tribes of plants which I had not seen since leaving England. I have got, for instance, a Poppy, Horsetail, a Bramble. . . . In a deep dell on the way to Moyobamba I was delighted to find a few specimens of that rare plant the Chickweed.

Schultes received his bachelor's degree from Harvard University in 1937. For his senior thesis, he lived among the Kiowa Indians in Oklahoma and studied their use of peyote in religious ceremonies.

Working under botanist Oakes Ames at Harvard, Schultes received his Ph.D. in 1941, with a dissertation again based on fieldwork among indigenous peoples. This time, he lived among the medicine men in the Mexican state of Oaxaca, detailing their use of psychedelic mushrooms in his dissertation, "Economic Aspects of the Flora of Northeastern Oaxaca."

Later in 1941, Schultes made his first trip to the Upper Amazon, as a Harvard research associate. In Colombia, he studied curare, a plant derivative used by shamans as a muscle relaxant. It also was used by other tribal people as a deadly substance on arrowheads.

Upon the outbreak of World War II in December of that year, Schultes's efforts in Amazonia were redirected by the U.S. government, which asked him to search for a species of rubber tree that would be resistant to disease. Ultimately, it was believed, this would reduce U.S. dependence on rubber from Asia, which had come under the domination of Japan. Although his wartime efforts failed, Schultes later discovered a new species of rubber tree in Sri Lanka and Malaysia.

In the early 1950s, Schultes lived among the native people of the Amazon basin for extended periods. His work there triggered a lifelong concern for the environmental integrity of the region and ongoing efforts to help save the rain forest and the culture of the people who inhabited it. As one of his students later observed,

> He believed ours would be the last generation fortunate enough to be able to live and work among these tribes as he had to experience their traditional way of life firsthand, and to record their vast ethnobotanical knowledge before the plant species—or the people who used them—succumbed to the march of progress.

Schultes made extended annual visits to the Amazon region; he even lived among native peoples who had never seen a white person before. He plied rivers in a simple aluminum canoe, carrying a single change of clothing, a machete, a hammock, a camera, and clippers for cutting and collecting plants. His diet consisted of instant coffee, baked beans, and food provided by the local tribes. To preserve the plant specimens he collected, he soaked them in formaldehyde diluted with water and then pressed them between newspaper sheets.

In all, Schultes collected an estimated 24,000 plant specimens, 120 of which came to bear his name. Also named for him is a 2.2 million-acre (890,000-hectare) tract of protected rain forest, established by the government of Colombia in 1986. Schultes documented the use of more than 2,000 medicinal plants by a dozen tribes. His studies of plants with hallucinogenic properties would make his books cult favorites among young people in the United States who experimented with drugs during the 1960s. His findings also influenced such writers as Aldous Huxley and Carlos Castaneda, who used and promoted the use of such hallucinogens as a way to gain better understandings of the inner self.

In 1953, Schultes became curator of the Oakes Ames Orchid Herbarium at Harvard, and in 1958 , he became curator of economic botany at the same institution. In 1970, he was named director of the Botanical Museum and Edward C. Jeffrey Professor of Biology.

Writing into his eighties, Schultes published a total of ten books and more than 450 scientific articles. He also took thousands of photographs, many of which appeared in his published works. Richard Evans Schultes died in 2001 at age eighty-six in Waltham, Massachusetts, outside Boston.

Further Reading

Davis, Wade. *One River: Explorations and Discoveries in the Amazon Rain Forest*. New York: Simon and Schuster, 1996.

Schultes, Richard. *Hallucinogenic Plants*. New York: Golden Press, 1976.

Schultes, Richard, and Albert Hofmann. *Plants of the Gods: Origins of Hallucinogenic Use*. New York: McGraw-Hill, 1979.

Schultes, Richard, and Siri von Reis. *Ethnobotany: Evolution of a Discipline*. Portland, OR: Dioscorides, 1995.

SCHWEINFURTH, GEORG AUGUST (1836–1925)

1836: Born on December 29 in Riga, Latvia

1856–1862: Educated at universities in Berlin, Heidelberg, and Munich, Germany

1863–1866: Explores the Red Sea region and travels into Africa to Khartoum, Sudan

1869–1871: Explores interior of eastern Africa, discovering the Uele (Welle) River and the Akka pygmies

1871: Writes *The Heart of Africa*, a book about his journey to Eastern Africa.

1873–1876: Conducts expeditions into the Libyan and Arabian deserts

1925: Dies on September 20 in Berlin

Latvian-German explorer, ethnographer, and botanist Georg August Schweinfurth journeyed into the interior of eastern Africa during the 1860s and 1870s, making important discoveries about the geography, native peoples, and plant life of the region, and contributing as well to knowledge of North Africa and the Arabian Peninsula.

Schweinfurth was born on December 29, 1836, in Riga, Latvia. He was educated at the universities of Berlin, Heidelberg, and Munich, in Germany. He pursued interests in botany and paleontology and completed his studies in 1862.

Commissioned to organize collections recently brought from the Sudan, Schweinfurth resolved to carry out his own explorations of Africa. In 1863, he journeyed to the Red Sea and spent the next three years exploring the region that bordered it, including Egypt, traveling inland to the Nile River and then to Khartoum, in the Sudan, and to the Abyssinian Highlands in present-day Ethiopia. Along the way, he collected numerous plant specimens.

In 1868, Schweinfurth received funding from the German scientific research foundation Humboldt-Stiftung to return to Africa and explore the region known as the Bahr-al-Ghazal, in what is now southwestern Sudan. Leaving Khartoum in January 1869, Schweinfurth headed south (upstream) on the White Nile River, studying the vegetation along the way. His journey took him into the midst of several indigenous tribes, namely the Bongo, Dinka, Diur, Niam-Niam, Mangbetu (Mombuttoo), and Shilluk. Only a few Europeans, mainly ivory traders, had encountered these peoples before.

While among the Mangbetu (in what is today the Democratic Republic of Congo), Schweinfurth discovered the Uele, or Welle, River. He concluded that it was connected to the Niger River rather than the Nile. In fact, it is a major tributary of the Ubangi River, which flows into the Congo River.

During the course of his travels in eastern Africa, as part of the expedition that began in 1869, Schweinfurth became the first European to encounter the Akka pygmies, confirming centuries-old speculation about a dwarf race in Africa. He attempted to bring one of the Akka back with him to Europe, but the captured man died along the way. Schweinfurth collected numerous plants and insects, but nearly all of his specimens collected to that date were destroyed in a fire at his campsite in December 1870.

Returning to Khartoum in July 1871, Schweinfurth wrote a book about his expedition titled *The Heart of Africa*, which was published two years later. In the account, he offered a number of original and insightful ethnographic descriptions. About the Mangbetu, for example, he wrote,

> My relationship with the natives became closer with each passing day. There was always a considerable crowd around my dwelling, avidly watching my slightest gesture. [The] . . . women, so cheeky when they are in a group, tend to be shy when they are on their own. I wanted to observe the details of their daily lives, but whenever they saw me coming they would scamper into their dwellings and shut the door in my face.

He also commented on the Niam-Niam, who filed their teeth to sharpen them and engaged in cannibalism. These were a people, reported Schweinfurth, "with whose name the Mohammedans of the Soudan were accustomed to associate all the savagery which could be conjured up by a fertile imagination."

From 1873 to 1874, Schweinfurth journeyed through the Libyan Desert with Gerhard Rohlfs, a fellow German explorer. In 1875, he founded a geographic society in Cairo, Egypt, where he was appointed curator of museums. He undertook the first of a series of expeditions into the Arabian Desert in 1876 and in the early 1890s made several trips to Eritrea, then an Italian colony in eastern Africa.

Schweinfurth devoted the rest of his life to African and Arabian studies and published several more books, including *Artes Africanae; Illustrations and Descriptions of Productions of the Industrial Arts of Central African Tribes* (1875). He died in Berlin on September 20, 1925.

Further Reading

Schweinfurth, Georg. *The Heart of Africa: Three Years' Travels and Adventures in the Unexplored Regions of Central Africa from 1868 to 1871.* Trans. Ellen E. Frewer. 2 vols. Chicago: Afro-Am Books, 1969.

SCORESBY, WILLIAM (1789–1857)

1789: Born on October 5 near Whitby, England
1799: Takes first whaling trip as a stowaway on his father's ship
1806: Begins studying chemistry and natural philosophy at the University of Edinburgh in Scotland
1811: Becomes the captain of a whaling ship; investigates atmospheric refraction at sea
1822: Surveys 400 miles (650 kilometers) of Greenland's east coast; quits whaling to become a clergyman
1823: Publishes *Journal of a Voyage to the Northern Whale-Fishery*
1831: Helps found the British Association for the Advancement of Science
1856: Sails to Australia; discovers that a ship's polarity reverses in the southern magnetic hemisphere, thus making an important discovery in the development of the mariners' compass
1857: Dies on March 21, 1857 in England

An English whaling ship captain, Arctic explorer, scientist, and clergyman, William Scoresby mapped the east coast of Greenland in the 1820s and researched magnetism to improve the performance of the mariner's compass.

Scoresby was born on October 5, 1789, near Whitby in Yorkshire, on England's northeast coast. His father, also named William Scoresby, was the captain of a whaling ship, on which the boy stowed away in 1799, at age ten, and took his first trip to sea. Three years later, William began an apprenticeship with his father, whaling near Greenland in the summer and attending school in the winter.

Arctic Scientist

In 1806, as first officer aboard the whaling ship *Resolution*, William Scoresby sailed to latitude 81° 30', the farthest north anyone had sailed in the eastern hemisphere to that time. Later that year, back on land, he began studying chemistry and natural philosophy at the University of Edinburgh in Scotland.

At Edinburgh, Scoresby became friends with Robert Jameson, a professor who encouraged him to undertake research in the northern seas. Scoresby later would provide Jameson with specimens from the Arctic, and the professor would present Scoresby's papers to natural history societies.

In 1811, Scoresby took over command of the *Resolution*. That same year, he was married for the first time. (He would be married a total of three times.)

On successive whaling voyages, he made scientific studies of the atmosphere, the sea, wildlife, and the workings of the mariner's compass. He compiled detailed weather reports made in the Greenland Sea, including comparisons of the temperature and humidity at the sea's surface, at deck level, and at the masthead. Using a diving thermometer of his own invention, he established that Arctic waters are warmer at lower depths than at the surface—the opposite of what is found in tropical waters. In another study, careful investigation of atmospheric refraction led him to conclude that mirages and fogs in the Arctic are caused by layers of air with contrasting temperatures.

With each whaling expedition, Scoresby undertook a new scientific investigation of Arctic conditions and natural phenomena. On one trip, he made a rigorous study of snowflakes, which he placed under a microscope. He drew pictures of the flakes and classified them according to the weather conditions in which he found them. He concluded that snowflakes were more varied in shape in the Arctic than those found in milder climates.

In 1819, Scoresby was elected to Britain's Royal Society to which he presented an original paper, "On the Anomaly in the Variation of the Magnetic Needle." The following year, he published *An Account of the Arctic Regions*, a two-volume work that brought together all of his own observations and those of other Arctic explorers. It was a landmark work in the field of Arctic science.

In 1822, Scoresby surveyed and charted some 400 miles (650 kilometers) of Greenland's east coast, designating place-names that, for the most part, still are used today. His exploration provided the first detailed information about the region.

Humphry Davy, a British scientist renowned for his work in chemistry, recognized the importance of Scoresby's expedition in a letter to him:

> I congratulate you on your safe return and on the success that has attended your researches. Your spirit of enterprise and your devotion to the cause of science amidst pursuits of so different a character entitle you to the warmest thanks of all those who are interested in the progress of natural knowledge and do honour to your country.

New Horizons

The journey to Greenland, as it turned out, would be Scoresby's last voyage to the Arctic. Upon returning to England, he learned of his first wife's death and quit whaling to study for the ministry in the Church of England. After two years of study at Cambridge University, he obtained his degree from Queen's College and was ordained in 1825.

Scoresby's decision to forsake the sea, however, did not deter him from his passion for science. In 1823, he had published *Journal of a Voyage to the Northern Whale-Fishery, Including Researches and Discoveries on the Eastern Coast of West Greenland*, which earned him yet more recognition within the scientific community and helped him gain election as a fellow of the Royal Society of London in 1824.

Becoming the first chaplain at the Mariners' Floating Church in Liverpool in 1827, Scoresby remarried the following year and moved on to the chaplaincy at Bedford Chapel in Exeter. As he carried out his clerical responsibilities, he remained heavily involved in the scientific community, helping to found the British Association for the Advancement of Science in 1831.

In 1837, Scoresby became vicar at Bradford, and, in 1839, he obtained his doctor of divinity degree. At Bradford, he dedicated himself to helping the poor and founded five schools for the children of mill workers.

Exhausted by church work, Scoresby took a trip to the United States in 1844 to restore his health but returned to England some six months later. With his strength continuing to decline, in 1847 he resigned from the ministry.

Upon the death of his second wife, in 1848, he returned to America and, during the trip, compiled important data on the height of waves in the Atlantic Ocean. Back in England, he married for a third time, in 1849, and moved to Torquay (now part of Torbay) in coastal Devonshire.

During his years away from the sea, Scoresby engaged in a number of scientific investigations. The most prominent was his study of magnetism and its effect on the mariner's compass. In general, he believed, the compasses of the time were poorly constructed and rendered inaccurate by the iron used in ship construction. To solve the problem, he would need to identify the grade of steel that would be most accurate for the instrument, determine the optimal shape for the needle, and measure the degree of deviation on ships with iron hulls or steam engines. After extensive research, he favored the use of compound magnets for additional strength and the best grade of steel to compensate for differences in bar quality.

In 1856, Scoresby sailed to Australia aboard the iron-hulled passenger ship *Royal Charter* with the goal of recording the ship's magnetic effects and determining if its polarity reversed in the southern magnetic hemisphere.

He confirmed the reversal for all the iron on the ship and concluded that compasses on board should be positioned aloft to avoid distortion. In addition, he advised, a ship's compass could not be set just once on a long voyage but had to be regularly checked for accuracy and adjusted when needed.

Scoresby died on March 21, 1857, at his villa in Torquay. His *Journal of a Voyage to Australia and Round the World, for Magnetical Research* was published two years later.

Further Reading

Scoresby, William, Jr. *An Account of the Arctic Regions.* 1820. New York: Augustus M. Kelley, 1969.

———. *Journal of a Voyage to the Northern Whale-Fishery.* 1823. Whitby, UK: Caedmon, 1980.

Stamp, Tom, and Cordelia Stamp. *William Scoresby, Arctic Scientist.* Whitby, UK: Caedmon, 1976.

See also: Arctic

SCOTT, ROBERT FALCON (1868–1912)

1868: Born on June 6 near Devonport, England

1883: Becomes a midshipman in the Royal Navy

1900: Appointed commander of the British National Antarctic Expedition

1901–1904: Explores Antarctica and becomes the first person to travel as far south as the 80th parallel

1910: Leaves England as commander of the *Terra Nova* in an attempt to become the first person to reach the South Pole

1911: Begins assault on the South Pole on October 24

1912: Learns that Norwegian explorer Roald Amundsen has reached the South Pole; reaches the Pole himself on January 17; dies in late March on the return trek to base camp

An English naval officer and explorer, Captain Robert Falcon Scott led what turned out to be the second expedition to reach the South Pole. He arrived there in January 1912, a month and three days after the Norwegian explorer Roald Amundsen. Scott and four other men died on the trip back to their base camp.

Robert Falcon Scott was born on June 6, 1868, near Devonport, England, to John Edward Scott, a brewer and the owner of a small country estate, and Hannah Cunning, who came from a well-to-do family. At age thirteen, Robert, nicknamed "Con" by his parents, entered the British Royal Navy as a cadet. He attended naval school at Dartmouth and was made a midshipman in 1883. From 1887 to 1888, he attended the Royal Naval College at Greenwich.

British National Antarctic Expedition

Scott had no burning ambition to become a polar explorer, but he saw it as a route to promotion through the ranks of the Royal Navy to commander and eventually captain. In 1899, therefore, when he was still a lieutenant, he accepted an offer to lead an expedition to Antarctica.

The Royal Society and the Royal Geographical Society were working together to raise money for such an effort, and Scott was selected by expedition organizer Clements Markham in May 1900. His official designation was commander of the British National Antarctic Expedition. Because the mission was principally scientific, other members of the expedition included naturalist Thomas Vere Hodgson, director of marine biological laboratories at the Marine Biological Station in Plymouth; geologist Hartley Ferrar, a recent graduate of Cambridge University; and physicist Louis Bernacchi, veteran of a recent Antarctic expedition.

Scott commanded the three-masted sailing ship *Discovery*, which was specially designed and built for Antarctic research. The expedition left England on August 6, 1901, and headed south from New Zealand in late December. Members of the *Discovery* Expedition, as it was referred to, began charting the Antarctic coastline and established a settlement on a cove in McMurdo Sound that they christened Winter Quarters Bay.

In November 1902, Scott and two other men—Ernest Shackleton and Edward Wilson—set out on foot, heading south. They became the first humans to reach as far south as latitude 82° 17', some 500 miles (800 kilo-

Robert Falcon Scott (rear, center) and members of his ill-fated Antarctic mission pose for a self-timed photograph at the South Pole in January 1912. The five men had trouble finding their route back and perished in the harsh conditions. (*Granger Collection, New York*)

meters) from the South Pole. "Certainly dog driving is the most terrible work one has to face in this sort of business," Scott wrote.

On December 5, he observed,

> The events of the day's march are now becoming so dreary and dispiriting that one longs to forget them when we camp; it is an effort to record them in a diary. Our utmost efforts could not produce more than three miles for the whole march.

During the course of the expedition, which continued until 1904, Scott and his fellow explorers also surveyed the coast of Victoria Land and made the first penetration of the rim of the Polar Plateau. In the latter instance, Albert Armitage, Scott's second-in-command, became the first person to cross the western mountains and reach the Antarctic ice cap. (Scott, at the time, was venturing south.) Bernacchi recorded the event:

> A typical [Antarctic] glacier followed to its source. . . . A distance of about 140 miles . . . sledged over in a mountainous, glacial region at 78 deg. South [reaching] an altitude of about 14,500 feet . . . accomplished by men [with] little or no previous experience of glacial traveling.

The *Discovery* Expedition garnered much public interest in Great Britain, and Scott returned home a hero. Nevertheless, the scientific record of the expedition met with considerable criticism from the scientific community. The president of the Physical Society of London, for example, called for a "scientific court martial" when it was shown that the expedition had confused true and magnetic compass bearings and that wind measurements had been botched as well.

Terra Nova Expedition

In 1908, Scott married Katherine Bruce, a sculptor, and they had a son, Peter Markham Scott, in 1909. In 1910, Scott took up command of a new scientific expedition to the Antarctic. Funded by private donors and the British government, the voyage would be undertaken on the ship *Terra Nova*, for an express purpose. Scott announced,

> The main object of the expedition, is to reach the South Pole and secure for the British Empire the honour of that achievement.

At the same time, however, science was to be an important part of the expedition. The party included three geologists, a physicist, a meteorologist, two biologists, a person to conduct magnetic measurements, and a specialist to oversee hydrographical surveys.

Also on board the *Terra Nova* were twenty Siberian-bred ponies and thirty-four sled dogs. According to Scott's plan, the ponies would haul supplies part of the way inland and then be killed for meat. The key means of transportation would be three motorized sleds, which had been little tested, "man-hauling," whereby sleds would be pulled by the explorers themselves, and sleds pulled by dogs and ponies.

The *Terra Nova* left England on June 1, 1910, with Scott staying behind to raise more money, which helped fund the expedition. He joined the ship in South Africa and sailed from there to New Zealand, departing for Antarctica on November 26, 1910. By then, Scott had learned that Amundsen also was on his way to Antarctica with the goal of becoming the first person to reach the South Pole.

THE *TERRA NOVA*

Robert Falcon Scott praised the *Terra Nova* as a "fine ice ship" that withstood repeated collisions with ice floes in the frigid waters of Antarctica. Yet at the time he acquired the vessel, in 1910, the *Terra Nova* had been in use for twenty-five years and was showing its age. Originally built as a whaling ship, it had sailed to McMurdo Sound to help free the *Discovery* on Scott's first Antarctic expedition, in 1903.

On the trip to the South Pole in 1910, the *Terra Nova* presented a number of challenges to its captain and crew. It took on large amounts of water and had to be pumped constantly to remain seaworthy. One particularly bad leak required the ship to be dry-docked in New Zealand before it could set off on the final leg of the voyage.

Moreover, the ship was dangerously overloaded. It was heavily laden with the dogs, ponies, coal, oil, motorized sleds, and other supplies and equipment Scott had resolved to take with him.

With giant waves sweeping across its deck and fire breaking out in the engine room, the *Terra Nova* was nearly lost in a storm at latitude 52° south. Its bilge pumps, essential for removing excess water, became clogged when coal dust and oil combined with water to form a thick sludge. Only the clearing of the valves by a mechanic restored the pumps and saved the ship.

After delivering Scott and his expedition party to McMurdo Sound, the *Terra Nova* departed for the winter. It returned in 1912 to resupply the expedition. It arrived for a third time in 1913, to bring home a triumphant Scott and his team—only for the ship's crew to learn of the explorers' tragic deaths.

With the expedition over, the *Terra Nova* resumed its role as a fishing vessel. In 1943, it sprang a leak and sank off the coast of Greenland.

Establishing a base camp at Cape Crozier, as Scott had intended, was made impossible by rough seas, and the expedition moved on to Cape Evans in McMurdo Sound. After setting up operations there, Scott and his men began erecting supply depots along the route to the pole. Meanwhile, others in the expedition, dubbed the Western Party, explored the Koettlitz Glacier; a Northern Party conducted research at Cape Adare; and a group in the main party began a study of emperor penguins at Cape Crozier.

Scott's trek to the South Pole began on October 24, 1911. Several men set out on motorized sleds; Scott joined them with dogsleds and ponies on November 1. A total of sixteen men, ten ponies, and twenty dogs began the journey.

Bad weather hampered the explorers from the start, and the motorized sleds broke down repeatedly; the team had failed to bring along the tools and parts needed to keep the sleds running. The ponies also proved to be a mistake, as they suffered from exhaustion from struggling through the deep snow. Despite his earlier expedition to Antarctica, Scott had failed to anticipate how extreme the conditions really would be.

As the party crossed the Polar Plateau, the men's energy began to wane. Then, on January 16, 1912, they came across the remains of a camp and tracks left by dogs and sleds. Amundsen had been there before them. In his diary, Scott noted,

> This told us the whole story. The Norwegians have forestalled us and are first at the Pole.

Scott chose four men to join him for the final assault on the South Pole: Henry Robertson Bowers, Edward Wilson, Lawrence Oates, and Edgar Evans. Despite insufficient food and clothing, the band of explorers soldiered on through blizzards and numbing cold. They began suffering from dehydration as well, a result of severe exertion in the frigid environment.

Finally, on January 17, Scott and his four partners reached the Pole. The temperature was -22 degrees Fahrenheit (-30 degrees Celsius), with a bitter wind whipping the air. Even more bitter was their sighting of the Norwegian flag. Amundsen had reached the pole thirty-four days earlier. Scott wrote in his diary,

> The Pole. Yes, but under different circumstances from those expected. We have had a horrible day . . . Good God! This is an awful place and terrible enough for us to have laboured to it without the reward of priority.

On the return trip to base camp, the five men had trouble finding the path they had taken. Scott had marked his supply depots poorly. On February 11, amid a raging blizzard, the members of the party became lost in a series of ice ridges while making their way down Beardmore Glacier. When the weather cleared briefly, Scott stopped to collect geological specimens, when he should have forged ahead.

Just before running out of food, the men finally found a supply depot. But on February 17, Evans died from complications resulting from a concussion. Then in mid-March, Oates wandered from his tent and never returned.

The expedition party now consisted of Scott, Wilson, and Bowers, who soon found themselves trapped in a blizzard with their food supply dwindling. The three men set up a tent on March 21 and lay down to await death. The last of them, perhaps Bowers or Scott, died some eight days later. Their bodies were found on the Ross Ice Shelf on November 12, 1912, a mere 11 miles (18 kilometers) from a supply depot but with at least 130 miles (210 kilometers) still between them and the base camp.

In his diary, which was discovered with his body, Scott left a departing statement:

> The causes of the disaster are not due to faulty organization but to misfortune in all risks which had to be undertaken. We took risks, we knew we took them; things have come out against us, and therefore we have no cause for complaint, but bow to the will of Providence, determined still to do our best to the last.

In truth, although the elements played an important role in what happened, Scott's preparation and planning paled in comparison to those of Amundsen. His supply depots were too few, too small, and too far apart. He relied too much on man-hauling, when dogsledding would have been more efficient and less exhausting. And he failed to leave clear instructions with the expedition members left behind at the base camp about what to do should he be delayed on the return trip. Irregardless of such mistakes in judgment and the expedition's failure to reach the Pole first, the real tragedy was the loss of life, despite their heroic efforts, of Scott and his four fellow explorers.

Further Reading

Baughman, T.H. *Pilgrims on the Ice: Robert Falcon Scott's First Antarctic Expedition.* Lincoln: University of Nebraska Press, 2008.

Crane, David. *Scott of the Antarctic: A Life of Courage and Tragedy.* New York: Vintage Books, 2007.

Huntford, Roland. *Scott and Amundsen: The Race to the South Pole.* New York: Atheneum, 1984.

Jones, Max. *The Last Great Quest: Captain Scott's Antarctic Sacrifice.* New York: Oxford University Press, 2003.

See also: Amundsen, Roald; Antarctica.

SHACKLETON, ERNEST (1874–1922)

1874: Born on February 15 in County Kildare, Ireland

1898: Is certified as a master mariner, which qualifies him to command a British ship

1901: Sails for Antarctica as part of Robert Falcon Scott's *Discovery* Expedition

1909: On the *Nimrod* expedition, comes within about 110 miles (175 kilometers) of the South Pole on January 9, the closest approach by any explorer to date; is knighted in November

1915: Reaches Antarctica aboard the *Endurance* in attempt to journey across the continent; the ship is trapped in ice and the men are forced to abandon it

1916: On May 10, reaches South Georgia Island with two other men on a mission to rescue the *Endurance* crew

1920: Plans the Shackleton-Rowett Expedition to circumnavigate Antarctica

1922: Dies of a heart attack on South Georgia Island on January 5

Anglo-Irish explorer Ernest Shackleton was one of the preeminent figures of the Heroic Age of Antarctic Exploration, known for his bravery in leading his stranded men to safety during a scientific expedition in 1914–1917 that failed to reach the South Pole.

Shackleton was born on February 15, 1874, in County Kildare, Ireland, to Henry Shackleton, a farmer, and Henrietta Letitia Sophia Gavan. When Ernest still was a child, his father quit farming to train for a career in medicine at Trinity College in Dublin. In 1884, Henry moved the family to Sydenham, now part of London, where he worked as a doctor.

Ernest loved to read and, after receiving schooling at home, at age thirteen he entered Dulwich College, a top public school for boys. He found school to be boring, however, and earned only mediocre grades. At age sixteen, he decided to apprentice on a sailing ship, the *Hoghton Tower*, operated by the North Western Shipping Company.

Discovery Expedition with Robert Falcon Scott

Enamored of seafaring and seeking the kind of adventure he had read about in books, Shackleton thrilled at the chance to sail around the world. After four years at sea, he passed the exam required to become a first mate. By 1898, he had been certified as a master mariner, which meant he could command a British ship anywhere in the world.

The following year, Shackleton was hired by the Union-Castle Line to operate a passenger ship between Southampton in England and Cape Town in South Africa. With the outbreak of the Boer War (1899–1902) in southern Africa that October, he commanded a troop ship for Britain.

It was at this time that Shackleton met Cedric Longstaff, an army lieutenant whose father was helping to finance the British National Antarctic Expedition, known as the *Discovery* Expedition after its ship. Through this connection and thanks to the impression he made on Clements Markham, an explorer who was overseeing the expedition as president of the Royal Geographic Society, Shackleton was appointed to the *Discovery* as third officer. The appointment brought him one step closer to realizing a dream he had once had, which he related to a reporter:

> [S]trangely enough, the circumstance which actually determined me to become an explorer was a dream I had when I was twenty-two. We were beating out from New York to Gibraltar, and I dreamt I was standing on the bridge in mid-Atlantic and looking northward. It was a simple dream. I seemed to vow to myself that some day I would go to the region of ice and snow and go on and on till I came to one of the poles of the earth, the end of the axis upon which this great round ball turns.

Under the leadership of Robert Falcon Scott, the *Discovery* Expedition left London on July 31, 1901. The explorers stopped at Cape Town before proceeding to New Zealand and reaching Antarctica in early January 1902.

With scientists Edward Wilson and Hartley Ferrar, Shackleton sledded from McMurdo Sound to the Great Ice Barrier. Scott then chose Shackleton and Wilson to join him on an exploratory probe toward the South Pole. The team departed on November 2, 1902, and eventually reached as far south as latitude 82° 17′, about 500 miles (800 kilometers) north of the pole. Fighting frostbite, snow blindness, and scurvy, the party trudged its way back to the *Discovery* by February 4.

The journey greatly weakened Shackleton, whose scurvy caused him to spit up blood, and Scott sent him back to England on a relief ship. Some historians have claimed, inconclusively, that Scott removed Shackleton from the expedition because he was popular with fellow crewmen and thereby posed a challenge to Scott's leadership.

Voyage of the *Nimrod*

Upon his return to England, Shackleton worked briefly as a reporter for *Royal Magazine*. In January 1904, he became a secretary of the Royal Scottish Geographical Society.

By that time, he had already begun his campaign to lead a return expedition to Antarctica, raising money and then presenting a proposal to London's Royal Geographical Society for reaching the South Pole. He laid out his plan in the March 1907 edition of the *Geographical Journal*. He would employ three separate parties. He wrote,

> One party will go east, and, if possible, across the Barrier to the new land known as King Edward VII Land, follow the coastline there south, if the coast trends south, or north if north, returning when it is considered necessary to do so. The second party will proceed south over the same route as that of the southern sledge-party of the *Discovery*; this party will keep from fifteen to twenty miles [24 to 32 kilometers] from the coast, so as to avoid rough ice. The third party will possibly proceed westward over the mountains and, instead of crossing in a line due west, will strike towards the magnetic Pole.

Shackleton made no bones about his priorities, adding,

> I do not intend to sacrifice the scientific utility of the expedition to a mere record-breaking journey, but say frankly, all the same, that one of my great efforts will be to reach the southern geographical Pole. I shall in no way neglect to continue the biological, meteorological, geological, and magnetic work of the *Discovery*.

The *Nimrod* left Lyttelton Harbor in New Zealand, bound for Antarctica, on January 1, 1908. Three weeks later, Shackleton and his crew reached Great Barrier Inlet near the Ross Ice Shelf. Seeing numerous whales at the location, he renamed it the Bay of Whales.

In early February, Shackleton established a settlement at Cape Royds, not far north of where the *Discovery* had been based at McMurdo Sound. At the lodging site built by the crew, meteorologist Jameson Adams set up equipment to measure air temperature, wind speed and direction, and water evaporation. On a nearby ridge, Adams measured wind speeds in excess of 100 miles (160 kilometers) per hour. Biologist James Murray built a sled to lower beneath the ice and drag along with a bucket attached to it to collect small fish and other marine animals. Other crew members studied the local geology and the aurora.

Shackleton, along with Adams, Eric Marshall, and Frank Wild, departed base camp on October 29, 1908, in an attempt to reach the South Pole. By January 2, 1909, however, they had neared exhaustion. Shackleton wrote in his journal,

> I cannot think of failure yet. I must look at the matter sensibly and consider the lives of those who are with me. . . . Man can only do his best.

Members of Ernest Shackleton's Antarctic odyssey of 1914–1916 pull an open whaleboat across the snow. Shackleton and five others sailed just such a vessel 1,200 miles (1,900 kilometers) across icy seas to save themselves and other members of the expedition. *(Hulton Archive/Stringer/Getty Images)*

Two days later, he wrote,

The end is in sight. We can only go for three more days at the most, for we are weakening rapidly.

Finally, on January 9, stopped by a raging blizzard, the expedition members marked their farthest assault by planting the Union Jack and a brass cylinder containing documents. They had reached 88° 23' south latitude, which was about 110 miles (175 kilometers) from the pole, by far the closest anyone had yet come. The men nearly starved to death on their return to base camp. Shortly after their arrival, the *Nimrod* sailed for England.

Despite their failure to reach the South Pole, the members of the expedition were hailed as heroes upon reaching home. Other achievements by members of the team included the first ascent of Mount Erebus and reaching the South Magnetic Pole.

Within months of his return in 1909, Shackleton published a book about the expedition, *The Heart of the Antarctic*. He received a gold medal from the Royal Geographic Society and was knighted by King Edward VII.

Voyage of the *Endurance*

In the months that followed, Shackleton undertook a succession of business ventures that proved largely unfruitful, earning his livelihood with a heavy schedule of lectures about the *Nimrod* Expedition. All the while, he harbored a desire to return south.

THE BUILDING OF THE *ENDURANCE*

The ill-fated vessel in which Ernest Shackleton and his crew left England for Antarctica in 1914 may well have been the strongest wooden ship ever built. The *Endurance* was designed by Ole Aanderud Larsen, a Norwegian businessman who founded a company to sell specialized paints and coatings to the shipping industry, and the ship was constructed at the Framnaes shipyard in Sandefjord, Norway.

The project was supervised by Christian Jacobsen, who hired only shipwrights who had been to sea on whaling or sailing ships. He believed that their direct experience with such ships in operation gave them more expertise and a greater concern for the quality of their work.

Jacobsen was a stickler for detail. The *Endurance*, originally christened the *Polaris*, had been built for other owners to carry tourists to the Arctic to hunt polar bear. To withstand the harsh Arctic conditions, Jacobsen installed double framing throughout the ship and made the bow more than 4 feet (1.2 meters) thick, using wood from a single oak tree, the shape of which provided a natural curved design.

When it was completed, the ship measured 144 feet (44 meters) long and 25 feet (8 meters) wide at the beam. It weighed 392 tons.

The *Polaris* was launched on December 17, 1912, but it was never used in the tourist trade. Instead, Shackleton bought it for $67,000 and renamed it the *Endurance* after his family's motto: *Fortitudine vincimus*, meaning "By endurance we conquer."

Ernest Shackleton's three-masted *Endurance*, said to be the strongest wooden ship built to date, heels to port, after becoming trapped in ice in the Weddell Sea of Antarctica. It sank there in November 1915. (*Rue des Archives/Granger Collection, New York*)

Two events in particular influenced Shackleton's plans for another journey to Antarctica. In December 1911, Norwegian explorer Roald Amundsen reached the South Pole, ending any hope Shackleton had of making it there first. Then, in early 1912, German explorer Wilhelm Filchner failed in his attempt to make a continental crossing of Antarctica, because an iceberg split apart and made it impossible for him to establish a base. Shackleton resolved to accomplish the continental crossing based on plans devised by Scottish explorer William Speirs Bruce.

Shackleton dubbed his journey the Imperial Trans-Antarctica Expedition. He employed two ships: the *Endurance*, from which he and five other men planned to cross Antarctica starting at Vahsel Bay, and the *Aurora*, which was to be stationed about 1,800 miles (2,900 kilometers) away, on the opposite end of the continent at McMurdo Sound. The expedition was financed mainly by private funds, with some monies contributed by the British government.

Shackleton's mission ran into trouble from the start. The *Endurance* reached Antarctica at the Weddell Sea in January 1915, but it promptly became entrapped in ice. Pressure from the frozen mass soon damaged the hull, which began taking on water in late October. The men were forced to abandon ship, and the *Endurance* sank about a month later.

For weeks, Shackleton and his colleagues camped on ice floes, hoping they would drift to safety at Paulet Island, where a supply cache was located. In early April 1916, however, the floe on which they had settled broke apart, and the men were forced to take to their lifeboats. Five days later, they reached Elephant Island, a deserted outcropping in the Southern Ocean. From there, it was decided that Shackleton and four other men would set sail for South Georgia Island and arrange for the rescue of those left behind.

The small party left Elephant Island in April 1916 aboard one of the expedition's open lifeboats, the *James Caird* (named for the mission's chief sponsor), which had been substantially refitted and strengthened by ship's carpenter Henry McNish. Shackleton and his team took with them four weeks' worth of food. "For if we did not make South Georgia in that time," he wrote, "we were sure to go under."

The men sailed for fifteen days, during which the *James Caird* nearly capsized and illness brought two of the men close to death. One of the party later wrote,

> It might be said that [Shackleton] kept a finger on each man's pulse. Whenever he noticed that a man seemed extra cold and shivered, he would immediately order another hot drink of milk be prepared and served to all. He never let the man know that it was on his account, lest he become nervous about himself.

Finally, on May 8—after 1,200 miles (1,900 kilometers) at sea—the five men came within sight of South Georgia Island. A ferocious gale nearly hammered the boat against the shore, and roiling water tore open parts of the hull. "I think most of us had a feeling that the end was very near," wrote Shackleton. Two day later, however, the *James Caird* reached shore safely. The men disembarked, staggered to a nearby stream, and fell to their knees to drink.

Yet another arduous journey awaited them, for they had landed far from any human settlement on the island. Rather than take to the sea again in search of the South Georgia whaling station, at Stromness, Shackleton sent two of the men, Frank Worsley and Tom Crean, across the island on foot. For thirty-six hours, Worsley and Crean labored across mountainous terrain and glacial mud, reaching the station on May 9.

A boat was dispatched to pick up the three other men, and Shackleton promptly began planning a mission to rescue the twenty-two men still on Elephant Island. After three unsuccessful attempts, foiled by sea ice, the mission was accomplished with the help of a small tug, the *Yelcho*, on loan from the Chilean navy. The crew of the *Endurance* was saved.

In May 1917, Shackleton returned to England, which was in the midst of World War I. Volunteering his services, he was sent to South America that October as a goodwill ambassador and diplomat. Not having been in foreign service, however, he proved unsuccessful at persuading the Argentine and Chilean governments to side with the Allies in the conflict. He returned home in May 1918.

By 1920, Shackleton was planning another expedition to Antarctica, this time with the goal of circumnavigating the continent. He obtained financing from John Quiller Rowett, a wealthy businessman and patron of science, for what was designated the Shackleton-Rowett Expedition. Shackleton, however, had been drinking heavily and was suffering from heart problems. In fact, he had suffered a heart attack in Rio de Janeiro, Brazil, but refused medical treatment.

A refitted Norwegian whaling ship, the *Quest*, was purchased for the Shackleton-Rowett Expedition. The *Quest* reached South Georgia Island on January 4, 1922. Shackleton summoned the ship's doctor early the next morning. He suffered another heart attack and died shortly thereafter.

At the request of his wife, Emily, Shackleton was buried on March 5, 1922, on South Georgia Island. He had once written: "Sometimes I think I am no good at anything but being away in the wilds just with men."

Further Reading

Alexander, Caroline. *The Endurance: Shackleton's Legendary Antarctic Expedition*. New York: Alfred A. Knopf, 1998.

Huntford, Roland. *Shackleton*. New York: Carroll and Graf, 1998.

Plimpton, George. *Ernest Shackleton*. New York: DK, 2003.

See also: Antarctica; Royal Geographical Society; Scott, Robert Falcon.

SOCIETY OF WOMAN GEOGRAPHERS

1925: The society is founded in New York City; Harriet Chalmers Adams becomes the organization's first president

1930: The society presents its first medal, to aviator Amelia Earhart

1984: Astronaut Kathryn D. Sullivan carries the society's flag as a member of the space shuttle *Challenger* crew

The Society of Woman Geographers (SWG) was founded in 1925 to bring together women who took part in world exploration; were interested in geography, anthropology, or related fields; and had "done distinctive work [that] added to the world's knowledge." Established in New York City, the society first organized chapters in New York and Washington, D.C., and then expanded to Chicago, San Francisco, and Los Angeles.

A nonprofit professional society and social organization, SWG was established at a time when women were excluded from the most prestigious exploration and research societies, and indeed from many scientific organizations and institutions. For decades, women had been barred from the most prominent geographical associations, such as the Royal Geographical Society in London (though it began admitting women in 1913) and the Explorers Club in New York (which maintained its ban until 1981). It was in response to such exclusion that four friends in New York, all of whom had traveled and written extensively—Marguerite Harrison, Blair Niles, Gertrude Emerson Sen, and Gertrude Mathews Shelby—decided to begin the society.

Harrison was a reporter and travel writer who became a spy for the United States in 1918. She expected to begin an assignment with U.S. military intelligence in Germany, but the war ended before she could do so. During the early 1920s, she served as a spy in Japan, China, and Russia, where she gathered information on the Bolshevik Revolution.

Blair Niles—the pen name of Mary Blair Rice—was a novelist and travel writer who had written about her life among native peoples in Mexico and South America. In 1926, she visited Devil's Island, the French penal colony off the coast of French Guiana, and recorded the life of one of its prisoners. The resulting book, *Condemned to Devil's Island* (1928), was an international best seller that prompted prison reform.

Gertrude Emerson Sen, an expert on Asia, eventually settled in India and reported on its culture. And Gertrude Mathews Shelby engaged in ethnographic research, including the study of African languages in America.

Harriet Chalmers Adams was named the SWG's first president in 1925, and she served in that position for eight years. Adams was an

American explorer, writer, and photographer who traveled extensively in South America, Asia, and the South Pacific and published accounts of her journeys in *National Geographic* magazine.

In 1930, the society presented its first gold medal (for a contribution of "major significance") to aviator Amelia Earhart, who had become the first woman to fly solo across the Atlantic Ocean two years before. Other early SWG members included first lady Eleanor Roosevelt, photographer Margaret Bourke-White, mountain climber Annie Peck, and anthropologist Margaret Mead.

Membership in the society is gained through nomination and election. Active members are individuals who have conducted research and fieldwork; are prominent in their disciplines; specialize in a particular geographic area; and have recorded their work in books, articles, films, photographs, or art. Associate members are frequent travelers who have made contributions to geographic education, research, and exploration but have not recorded their findings in permanent form.

Although members share a strong interest in geography and exploration, their pursuits are diverse. Those elected to the SWG have included anthropologists, ethnologists, explorers, mountain climbers, big-game hunters, environmentalists, aviators, artists, journalists, photographers, librarians, and archivists.

Today, the Society of Woman Geographers has approximately 500 members. Its headquarters in Washington, D.C., also is the site of a library, archive, and museum of works by members. As opposed to formal organization activities, the SWG emphasizes "personal association and interchange of ideas" among members.

In addition to its Gold Medal, awarded periodically to women of special accomplishment in their field, the society regularly bestows an Outstanding Achievement Award (for a contribution of "lasting benefit to Science, the Arts, or Humanity") and designates "Flag Carriers" to bring the SWG banner on expeditions of distinction. For example, astronaut Kathryn D. Sullivan was chosen to carry the society's flag as a member of the space shuttle *Challenger* crew in 1984.

Further Reading

Anema, Durlynn. *Harriet Chalmers Adams: Adventurer and Explorer*. Aurora, CO: National Writers Press, 2004.

Olds, Elizabeth. *Women of the Four Winds*. Boston: Houghton Mifflin, 1985.

Society of Woman Geographers. http://www.iswg.org.

See also:
Explorers Club.

SPACE EXPLORATION, MANNED

1961: Soviet Yuri Gagarin reaches outer space and orbits Earth aboard *Vostok 1*, April 12; Alan Shepard is first American in space, aboard the *Freedom 7*, May 5

1962: John Glenn makes the first manned orbital flight of Earth for the United States, on the *Friendship 7*

1963: Soviet Valentina Tereshkova, aboard *Vostok 6,* is the first woman in space

1965: Soviet Alexei Leonov walks in space, March 18; the United States launches its first manned Gemini space capsule

1968: The United States launches its first manned Apollo flight; *Apollo 8* orbits the Moon

1969: The Soviet Union docks space capsules *Soyuz 4* and *Soyuz 5*, and men transfer between them, January 14–15; American Neil Armstrong sets foot on the Moon, July 20

1971: The Soviet Union launches the Salyut 1 orbiting space laboratory

1975: Historic joint space mission begins when *Apollo 18* docks with *Soyuz 19*

1981: The United States launches its first space shuttle, *Columbia*

1998: The International Space Station, developed by the United States, Russia, Japan, Canada, and the European Space Agency, is assembled in orbit

2003: The People's Republic of China launches into space its first astronaut, aboard the *Shenzhou 5* capsule; the spacecraft makes fourteen orbits of Earth

2009: U.S. space shuttle *Endeavour* carries seven astronauts to the International Space Station, setting a record for the most people in the same space vehicle at the same time: thirteen

The first nations to launch humans into space, the Soviet Union and the United States, did so as much—or more—to gain political and military advantage in the cold war as for scientific reasons. The early missions, in the 1960s, consisted of suborbital and orbital flights around the Earth that led, on the part of the United States, to the landing of men on the Moon.

With the end of the cold war and the breakup of the Soviet Union in 1991, Russia continued to send people into space on a regular basis, as did the United States. China began human space flight in 2003.

From the outset, space flights have been more than propaganda stunts. They have contributed significantly to knowledge of the Moon and other celestial bodies; they have expanded greatly the information needed for humans to function more effectively in space; and they have contributed directly to scientific knowledge pertaining to the Earth's environment, human life, and supporting technologies.

First Humans in Space

After a decade or more of rocket testing, artificial satellite missions, and even the launching into space of a stray Russian dog (Laika, aboard *Sputnik 2* in 1957), the era of human space flight began on April 12, 1961, when Soviet air force Colonel Yuri Gagarin was hoisted out of the Earth's atmosphere from the Baikonur Cosmodrome in Kazakhstan. He was aboard the *Vostok 1* space capsule designed by rocket scientist Sergey Pavlovich Korolyov. Gagarin completed a single orbit of the Earth, reentered the atmosphere, ejected himself from the capsule, and parachuted to the ground in the Saratov Oblast in southeastern Russia. Gagarin was one of twenty original cosmonauts, six of whom were trained for early space flight at Zvezdny Gorodok, or Star Town, near Moscow. Gagarin's mission had been preceded by several flights that had carried a dummy, Laika, or nothing.

Gagarin was chosen for the historic flight just four days before its launch. *Vostok 1* circled the Earth at an altitude of 112 to 203 miles (180 to 326 kilometers) for one hour and forty-eight minutes. It traveled at a speed of 5 miles (8 kilometers) per second. Although a last-minute glitch in the firing of the reentry rockets nearly doomed the flight, the Soviet space program received worldwide acclaim for its accomplishment and enjoyed a major propaganda boost in its competition with the United States.

Barely four months later, on August 6, the Soviets followed up Gagarin's mission with a seventeen-orbit flight by cosmonaut Gherman Titov aboard *Vostok 2*. Once again, problems beset the spacecraft. The capsule's heating system ceased functioning, resulting in a frigid interior and a disoriented cosmonaut. Nevertheless, the mission reinforced Soviet prowess in human space exploration.

During this time, the United States had been pursuing Project Mercury (1959–1963) to send men into space. The project was under the direction of the National Aeronautics and Space Administration (NASA). As a result of the Soviet success with Gagarin, NASA decided to move up its first flight, a suborbital mission to be undertaken by Alan Shepard, one of the program's seven original astronauts, cho-

The age of manned space exploration began on April 12, 1961, with the 108-minute flight of *Vostok 1*, which carried Soviet cosmonaut Yuri Gagarin on a single Earth orbit. *(Rolls Press/ Popperfoto/Getty Images)*

sen for training in 1959. Shepard flew on May 5, 1961, aboard a Mercury capsule dubbed *Freedom 7*. He was lifted into space from Cape Canaveral, Florida, by a Redstone rocket.

The flight lasted a mere fifteen minutes, during which Shepard barely had time to experience weightlessness. Still, the mission achieved its goal of proving that NASA could launch a man into space and that the capsule would work. Three weeks later, in a historic address to Congress, President John F. Kennedy committed the United States to "landing a man on the Moon and returning him safely to the Earth" before the end of the decade.

The United States launched a second suborbital flight on July 21, 1961, carrying another member of the Mercury Seven, Virgil "Gus" Grissom. The mission was another success for NASA, even though the door to the capsule, *Liberty Bell 7*, opened prematurely upon landing in the Atlantic, nearly drowning Grissom. The *Liberty Bell 7* was lost at sea, but America celebrated another manned space flight.

The first manned orbital flight for the United States took place on February 20, 1962, with John Glenn aboard the *Friendship 7*, launched from Cape Canaveral by an Atlas rocket. Glenn circled the Earth three times on a flight that lasted some five hours. The mission included a few glitches, including a faulty automatic orientation system that forced Glenn to revert to manual control, and concern upon reentry that the capsule's heat shield was loose, a potentially fatal problem. But the capsule splashed down safely, and the mission demonstrated the capability and promise of the American space program at a time when the Soviets seemed to be dominating the headlines.

The six manned flights of Project Mercury produced little in the way of pure scientific knowledge, as they included few true experiments. They were intended mainly to test the effects of space travel on humans and to advance flight capabilities so that future astronauts could be sent to the Moon.

The Soviets, meanwhile, achieved another historic first in June 1963, when they sent the first woman into space. Cosmonaut Valentina Tereshkova flew aboard *Vostok 6*.

About two years later, on March 18, 1965, a pair of cosmonauts were sent aloft in the *Voskhod 2* capsule equipped with a collapsible airlock, which allowed pilot Alexei Leonov, attached to a 17-foot (5-meter) tether, to engage in the first-ever space walk. The extravehicular activity (EVA) lasted nearly twenty minutes.

Project Gemini

NASA made the transition to a two-person space capsule with Project Gemini (1965–1966). The broad goal of this program was to develop the capabilities and technologies necessary for advanced space flight.

The first manned mission in the program, *Gemini 3*, took place on March 23, 1965, with astronauts Grissom and John Young making three Earth orbits. *Gemini 4*, on June 3, featured a flight time of nearly eighteen hours (sixty-six orbits) and the first space walk by a U.S. astronaut, Edward White. For twenty-three minutes, White propelled himself in space while tethered to the capsule and using a hand-held maneuvering gun, which fired short bursts of gas.

The Gemini program included many more scientific experiments than had been undertaken in Project Mercury. In 1963, NASA began soliciting research proposals through its Office of Space Sciences and Office of Manned Space Flight. The Manned Space Flight Board, created in 1964, decided which experiments would be performed on which missions. (The procedure would be continued with Gemini's successor, Project Apollo.)

One approved experiment explored the possibility of radiation damage to human cells, certainly a concern for any space flight of long duration. Human blood samples, sealed in an aluminum box, were exposed to a precise amount of radiation in zero gravity and chromosomal aberrations then studied. Another experiment examined how cells might be affected by near weightlessness. The eggs of a sea urchin were fertilized, and changes brought about by low gravity were observed as the eggs developed.

Among other highlights of the Gemini program were the 220 orbits and 330 hours in space recorded by *Gemini 7* astronauts Frank Borman and James Lovell in December 1965; the first rendezvous in space, when *Gemini 6* (with Walter "Wally" Schirra and Thomas Stafford on board) and *Gemini 7* closed to within 1 foot (.3 meters) of each other on December 15; and the first retrieval of an object (a test package) in space by Michael Collins and John Young on *Gemini 10* in July 1966.

Project Apollo and Project Soyuz

The program to fulfill President Kennedy's vision and land a man on the Moon—Project Apollo—was being planned and tested even before the last Gemini flight in November 1966. NASA weighed two options for accomplishing the goal. One was to assemble a large craft in space and send it to the Moon from there. The other was to launch a capsule, or command module, that would carry a smaller lunar lander into space; pilot the combined vehicles into Moon orbit; separate the lander from the capsule for a descent to the Moon's surface; then return the lander to the command module for the flight back to Earth. NASA decided on the second option, using a three-person capsule to be launched from Earth atop a powerful Saturn V rocket.

The Soviets also had resolved to send men to the Moon and had developed a strategy similar to NASA's. The Soviet plan, however, entailed more cumbersome maneuvers for the capsule and the Moon craft, and the overall effort was beset by problems. U.S. intelligence analysts reported as early as 1965 that the Soviets had fallen behind in the race to the Moon and that the Russian program was proving "unsuccessful."

In 1966, with Project Gemini in full swing, NASA readied its first Apollo capsule for a test flight around the Earth. In the rush to meet its deadline, however, NASA apparently accepted a faulty command module, which was beset by technical problems; several last-minute alterations were needed.

Tragedy struck on January 27, when *Apollo 1* astronauts Grissom, White, and Roger Chaffee were training in the command module. A fire erupted, and the flames spread rapidly in the pure-oxygen environment. The three astronauts had difficulty opening the hatch and suffocated in the fumes. The cause of the fire never was ascertained definitively, but it was believed to have been started by an electrical short circuit. As a result of the incident, NASA redesigned the capsule's hatch and ended the use of a pure-oxygen environment on the ground. It was another two years before a modified command module was readied and Project Apollo resumed.

Meanwhile, the Soviet manned-space program, Soyuz, continued to flounder. Russian engineers had developed a modified Soyuz capsule capable of carrying two men to the Moon. In April 1967, however, the capsule experienced difficulties while orbiting the Earth, carrying cosmonaut Vladimir Komarov. First, the automatic altitude control system failed, and then, during the descent to Earth, the capsule became caught in its parachute lines. *Soyuz 1* plummeted to Earth, killing Komarov and causing the Soviets to suspend future flights.

The United States launched its first manned Apollo flight, *Apollo 7*, on October 11, 1968, piloted by astronauts Schirra, Donn Eisele, and Walter Cunningham. Later that month, on October 26, 1968, the Soviets launched *Soyuz 3*, with cosmonaut Georgi Beregovoy aboard. The Russians intended to send two cosmonauts on a flight around the Moon in December 1968, but problems with the launch rocket forced the mission to be postponed.

The United States thus became the first nation to send men around the Moon. In December 1968, *Apollo 8* astronauts Borman, Lovell, and William Anders made ten lunar orbits, broadcasting views from the command module to Earth-bound television viewers on Christmas Day. Lovell observed, "The earth from here is a grand oasis in the vastness of space."

In another key step by the Soviet Union, two manned Soyuz capsules, *Soyuz 4* and *Soyuz 5*, succeeded in docking in space in January 1969, and cosmonauts transferred between them. But a rocket failure the following month was another setback in the Soviet lunar program.

Men on the Moon

The culmination of NASA's efforts since the agency's founding—and the realization of President Kennedy's dream of 1961—came with *Apollo 11.* Launched on July 16, 1969, its command module, *Columbia.* carried Edwin "Buzz" Aldrin, Neil Armstrong,, and Collins, as well as a lunar landing module named *Eagle.*

On July 20, with *Columbia* in lunar orbit (piloted by Collins), Armstrong and Aldrin transferred into the lander, released it from the command module, and descended to the surface of the Moon. "Tranquility Base here," radioed Armstrong. "The *Eagle* has landed."

Then Armstrong slowly backed down the *Eagle*'s ladder and set foot onto the powdery lunar terrain at 10:56 P.M. Eastern Standard Time. Upon stepping onto the surface, Armstrong uttered the historic statement he had prepared before the mission began: "That's one small step for man, one giant leap for mankind." (Armstrong made a small error in the line he had practiced. He had intended to say, "That's one small step for *a* man . . .")

People around the world watched a grainy television image of Armstrong and Aldrin, who joined him outside the lander fifteen minutes later, bounding about the Moon. The two astronauts worked for two hours and thirty-one minutes, Armstrong scooping up specimens and Aldrin hammering core tubes (cylinders used to collect soil samples) into the surface. They also planted a plaque and an American flag.

After spending some time in the *Eagle*—for a total of twenty-one hours on the Moon—the astronauts fired up the lunar lander. The *Eagle* and its passengers rejoined the command module the following day.

On the next Moon mission, Apollo 12, launched on November 14, 1969, astronauts Charles "Pete" Conrad and Alan Bean walked about 1 mile (1.6 kilometers) around three lunar craters, while Richard Gordon remained in the command module. Conrad and Bean collected soil samples and 7 pounds (3.2 kilograms) of rocks, spending a little more than thirty-one hours on the lunar surface.

For the purpose of scientific research, astronauts on missions beginning with Apollo 12 and continuing through Apollo 14–17 left behind a set of instruments called the Apollo Lunar Surface Experiments Package (ALSEP). Using ALSEP, scientists were able to measure and assess various physical properties and phenomena, including the internal structure of the Moon (by detonating small explosives and measuring the seismic shock waves); atmospheric pressure; the behavior of charged particles; the rate at which heat flows from the Moon's interior; the distance from the Earth to the Moon (accomplished by firing a laser at the Earth); and the properties of solar wind, lunar gravity, and the lunar magnetic field. Engineers used signals sent from Earth to control the ALSEP system and run the various experiments. The ALSEP stations continued operating until September 1977.

The successes of the Apollo 11 and Apollo 12 missions were followed by the harrowing and nearly disastrous flight of *Apollo 13*, with astronauts Fred Haise, James Lovell, and John Swigert. The command module, *Odyssey*, was launched on April 11, 1970, atop a Saturn V rocket. The Saturn V's second stage cut off too early, leaving the third stage to work harder; however, this problem was overcome.

THE LUNAR LANDER AND EXPERIMENTS PACKAGE

The landing module (LM) that traveled to the Moon on the Apollo 11 mission, named *Eagle*, consisted of an ascent stage and a descent stage. The two stages remained connected to each other as they landed on the lunar surface.

The ascent stage, which would be used to take the astronauts back to the command module, housed the men in a pressurized compartment with no seats. It had a hatch, through which the astronauts could enter and leave, and triangular windows on either side of the hatch.

The descent stage was shaped like an octagon, and it consisted of an engine and four landing legs with footpads. Attached to one of the legs were a small platform and a ladder, which the astronauts climbed down to reach the lunar surface. As the LM descended to the surface, the descent engine slowed its approach to allow for a soft touchdown. When the astronauts returned to the command module, engines on the ascent stage freed them from the descent stage and placed them back in lunar orbit.

The Apollo 11 astronauts who landed on the moon brought with them the Early Apollo Scientific Experiments Package (EASEP), a predecessor to the Apollo Lunar Surface Experiments Package (ALSEP) used on later lunar missions. The EASAP consisted of two solar panels to provide power, an antenna, and a communications system for sending data to and receiving data from ground stations on Earth.

The scientific instruments in the EASEP included a seismometer to measure ground movement in order to determine the properties of the lunar crust and interior, and a dust collector to gather samples.

The Passive Seismic Experiment Package (PSEP) contained scientific instruments used in lunar-surface experiments by Apollo 11 astronauts Neil Armstrong and Buzz Aldrin in July 1969. (*Science & Society Picture Library/Getty Images*)

On April 13, the *Odyssey* was proceeding toward the Moon when a loud bang shook the command module. There followed a sudden loss of oxygen, and the fuel cells that provided power to *Odyssey* began to falter.

In order to save the astronauts, NASA mission control in Houston ordered Haise, Lovell, and Swigert to activate the lunar lander, *Aquarius*, before the fuel cells gave out completely. This would enable them to use the guidance system necessary to go around the Moon and steer back toward Earth, while using the oxygen supply on *Aquarius*. At the same time, it was vital for the astronauts to conserve energy and reduce their water intake to a mere one-fifth of normal. As *Odyssey* limped back to Earth over the next three days, temperatures in the module dropped to 37 degrees Fahrenheit (3 degrees Celsius), and condensation covered the walls.

The tired and dehydrated crew made it back to Earth with a splashdown in the Pacific Ocean, and they were picked up by the crew of the aircraft carrier USS *Iwo Jima*. Later, a review board blamed the accident on a defective prelaunch test that had failed to detect problems with the oxygen tank fans. When Swigert had turned on the fans, a short circuit had started a fire and caused an explosion, rupturing one of the oxygen tanks and damaging another.

The incident postponed further Apollo missions for nine months. Finally, on July 26, 1971, James Irwin, David Scott, and Alfred Worden headed to the Moon aboard *Apollo 15*.

On the surface of the Moon, Scott and Irwin used a battery-powered rover to travel 5 miles (8 kilometers) and to investigate the Hadley Rille landing site, a steep, V-shaped gorge. During their eighteen hours on the Moon, the astronauts scooped up soil, took core tube samples, and collected rocks, including the first green Moon rocks and a white crystalline rock.

On *Apollo 16*, launched on April 16, 1972, Thomas Mattingly and John Young (with Charles Duke piloting the command module) used a lunar rover to travel more than 16 miles (26 kilometers) on the Moon's surface, exploring mountains and craters. They also collected 213 pounds (97 kilograms) of soil and rocks.

The final manned Moon mission, Apollo 17, was carried out in December 1972. With Ronald Evans in the command module, Eugene Cernan and Harrison Schmitt explored the surface in three separate excursions. They drove the lunar rover a record 21 miles (34 kilometers) and set another record by staying on the ground for seventy-five hours at one time.

Early Space Stations

Meanwhile, the continued failure of the Soviets' N-1 launch rocket caused them to drop their plans for a manned Moon mission and instead focus on building a space station to orbit the Earth. In April 1971, the Soviet Union launched the Salyut 1 space station, the first in a series of Earth-orbiting research facilities.

In June of that year, cosmonauts Georgi Dobrovolsky, Viktor Patsayev, and Vladislav Volkov succeeded in docking their *Soyuz 11* capsule with Salyut. They stayed aboard the space station for four weeks, during which they monitored the Earth's surface and atmosphere, conducted biomedical experiments, observed distant stars, and tended the first space garden. Troubles with the station's operating system forced the cosmonauts to leave earlier than planned, and their capsule lost its oxygen supply on the descent to Earth. All three men died.

The United States launched its own space station, Skylab 1, on May 14, 1973, but it too encountered problems. A failure of the space station's solar panels caused the cooling system to malfunction and the temperature inside the station to rise too high.

The first of three crews to visit Skylab—Charles Conrad, Joseph Kerwin, and Paul Weitz—lifted off eleven days later. Guided by NASA engineers, they made the necessary repairs: They attached an external parasol to cool down the space station, fixed one of the solar panels, and restored power to the batteries. The mission continued for a total of twenty-eight days in space and 404 Earth orbits. During that time, the astronauts took 7,000 photos of the Earth and 30,000 of the Sun.

Three times larger than Salyut, Skylab included a dining room and exercise machines for the well-being of astronauts on extended stays. The last crew to arrive at Skylab, in November 1973, spent a record eighty-four days in space. During their stay, the three astronauts—Gerald Carr, Edward Gibson, and William Pogue—engaged in a series of medical experiments and, using a telescope, took the first photographs of the birth of a solar flare.

The year 1975 brought a historic first in space exploration—and cold war cooperation—as the United States and the Soviet Union undertook a joint mission of docking *Apollo 18* and *Soyuz 19* with each other on July 17. The American crew consisted of Vance Brand, Donald "Deke" Slayton, and Thomas Stafford. The Soviet crew consisted of Valeri Kubasov and Alexei Leonov. After docking, Slayton and Stafford entered the *Soyuz* spacecraft. Later, Leonov entered the *Apollo* capsule, where the astronauts engaged in joint astronomical observations and took photographs of the Earth. The Soviets launched a total of nine Salyut space stations between 1971 and 1982.

The next generation of Soviet space stations, called Mir, began with a launch in February 1986. Modular in design and construction, Mir was larger than its predecessor. With special welding techniques developed for outer space, Mir was enlarged further over the next ten years. Intended as a long-term research base, Mir became the first consistently inhabited space facility. Soviet scientist-cosmonauts engaged in a wide variety of experiments and astrophysical observations, including the detection of a supernova.

In 1993, the United States and Russia agreed on another, more sustained joint project, working to establish an International Space Station with Mir as a training ground. U.S. space shuttles transported supplies to Mir, where American astronauts took up occupancy.

In 1995, a series of launches by the United States and the Soviet Union carried astronauts and cosmonauts to Mir. In one instance, Norman Thagard flew with two cosmonauts aboard the *Soyuz TM-21*. This made him the first American astronaut to fly aboard a Russian spacecraft. Mir remained in operation until March 2001, when it was deemed antiquated and was sent into a lower orbit so it could break up over the South Pacific. In all, the station was occupied for more than twelve of its fifteen years and was visited by astronauts from thirteen different nations.

The Space Shuttle

As the Apollo Project was drawing to a close in 1972, the United States began development of a reusable space shuttle—a major change from the Mercury, Gemini, and Apollo capsules. "All of a sudden," said one member of the astronaut corps, "we had tires, we had wheels, and we had wings, and we had elevons and control surfaces and payload bay doors."

After repeated delays, the space shuttle *Columbia* was launched on April 12, 1981, with a two-man test crew of Crippen and Young. Strapped to rocket boosters during liftoff, the shuttle lost sixteen of its thermal tiles—surface material to protect the spacecraft from the intense heat of reentry. NASA engineers determined that the damage did not risk the safe return of the crew, and *Columbia* orbited the Earth thirty-six times before landing airplane-style at Edwards Air Force Base in California.

NASA called the space shuttle the "space transportation system," or STS. The shuttle's original purpose was to carry material and supplies for a new space station similar in design to Skylab. When plans for the space station were suspended, the shuttle program was reoriented for scientific experimentation and the launching of satellites. Because the shuttle's orbit was too low for most satellites to be released from its cargo bay, rocket boosters were used.

In November 1982, two communications satellites were launched from *Columbia* on mission STS-5. This was the shuttle's first operational mission; the preceding flights had been tests of the worthiness of the spacecraft. It carried a four-man crew.

In June 1983, as part of STS-7, Sally Ride, aboard the space shuttle *Challenger*, became the first U.S. woman to travel into space. The crew also included two physicians, who conducted biomedical experiments to gather information about space sickness. In its cargo bay on mission STS-9, launched in November 1983, *Challenger* carried Spacelab, a reusable workshop and research laboratory used on board the shuttle. More than seventy experiments in life science, space physics, materials technology, and other fields were carried out in Spacelab.

NASA planned to launch fifteen shuttle missions in 1986 and hoped to begin launching thirty per year in 1988. Critics claimed that NASA was emphasizing speed over safety and public relations over a more slow-paced and carefully planned scientific program.

On January 28, 1986, *Challenger* inexplicably exploded seventy-three seconds after launch, killing all seven astronauts aboard, including the first schoolteacher chosen for a spaceflight, Christa McAuliffe.

Investigators later found that faulty seals on the solid-fuel rocket boosters had allowed flames to emerge from one side and penetrate the giant external fuel tank. (The external fuel tank was strapped beneath the shuttle, and attached to the sides of the tank were two solid rocket boosters.) The intense heat compromised a strut holding one of the boosters to the tank, causing the strut to break loose. This, in turn, caused the nose of the booster to shift and pierce the fuel tank. Hydrogen and oxygen poured out of the tank and created a fireball, which caused the shuttle to explode into tiny pieces that plunged into the Atlantic Ocean.

The U.S. space shuttle *Endeavour* carries components of the Japanese Experiment Module (JEM, or Kibo) to the International Space Station in 2009. JEM is used for research in space medicine, biotechnology, physics, materials technology, and communications. (*NASA/ Getty Images*)

After the accident, no shuttles were flown for thirty-two months. A number of improvements were made to the entire shuttle fleet, and the shuttle flight program resumed with the successful mission of *Discovery*, STS-26, in September 1988.

Achievements of the shuttle program have included the launch of the Hubble Space Telescope from *Discovery* in April 1990 (STS-31); of the *Ulysses* solar probe, built by the European Space Agency, from *Discovery* in October 1990 (STS-41); of the Compton Gamma Ray Observatory from the *Atlantis* in April 1991 (STS-37); and of the Upper Atmosphere Research Satellite to measure atmospheric pollution, from *Discovery* in September 1991 (STS-48). The space shuttle program also has launched a number of communications satellites for private corporations and spy satellites for U.S. intelligence agencies.

In addition, the space shuttle program has provided an important venue for core scientific research, especially on Spacelab. For example, Life Sciences 1 mission in June 1991 was the first exclusively dedicated to studying the effects of weightlessness on humans and other living organisms, analyzing how the muscles of rats change in the outer space environment.

The shuttle program suffered its second major disaster on February 1, 2003, when *Columbia* disintegrated over Texas as it was reentering the Earth's atmosphere. All seven crew members were killed. The breakup of the shuttle resulted from an incident that had happened during launch. A piece of insulation foam had broken away from the shuttle's external fuel tank, struck the leading edge of the left wing, and damaged the tiles on the shuttle's surface that were needed to protect it from the intense heat generated during reentry.

In the aftermath of this disaster, the shuttle program was suspended indefinitely. Nevertheless, President George W. Bush committed the United States to resuming space shuttle flights once they were deemed safe and using them to help complete the space station. He also pursued plans to develop a new spacecraft for travel to the Moon and to Mars.

On July 26, 2005, some ten months after the date originally targeted by NASA, the space shuttle flight program resumed as *Discovery* roared into space from Cape Canaveral on mission STS-114. Again, a piece of foam tore away from the fuel tank; fortunately, this one missed striking the shuttle. The mission proceeded successfully, but NASA grounded flights for another year as it addressed the foam and tile problem once more.

In May 2009, the space shuttle *Atlantis* carried out the fifth and final servicing mission to the Hubble Telescope (STS-125). Then, in July, the shuttle *Endeavour* carried supplies and equipment to the International Space Station (ISS; see below). In doing so, it set a new record for the most people in one space transportation device at the same time: thirteen astronauts in the orbiting station and docked shuttle, including astronauts from

Japan and Canada. Two of the astronauts conducted a space walk to install a Japanese experimental facility that housed scientific instruments, such as those to measure the ionosphere.

With the end of the space shuttle program scheduled for 2010, work and planning proceeded on the next major U.S. initiative—the Constellation program. Long-term goals of the project include developing the capabilities and technologies to open the next frontier in space, expanding operational capabilities away from Earth, and pursuing fundamental scientific research.

The Constellation program entails the development of new, more powerful booster rockets—designated Ares I and Ares II—and a next-generation space capsule, called Orion, to take crews and cargo to the ISS. That vehicle is scheduled to be operational in 2014 or 2015. Until then, people and supplies traveling to the ISS likely will do so on Russian spacecraft or perhaps American commercial spacecraft.

The International Space Station and Beyond

The International Space Station was developed as a research facility by the space agencies of the United States, Russia, Japan, and Canada, and by the European Space Agency. Assembly of the space station began in orbit in 1998 and was scheduled to continue into the year 2011. The ISS has been occupied continuously since November 2000 and is expected to remain in use until at least 2015.

The multinational facility has been used to conduct research in biology, physics, astronomy, and meteorology. Scientists aboard the space station have studied the effects of long-term weightlessness on the human body, including muscle atrophy and bone loss, and on the internal functioning of plants and animals.

Physicists, meanwhile, have explored the question of whether fluids that do not mix well on Earth mix better in outer space. A range of experiments has been conducted to gain a better understanding of the structure and properties of these and other materials so they might be processed better on Earth.

Another important investigation has focused on the atmosphere, pollution, and energy. A set of experiments has studied how to control fuel emissions and other polluting agents, contributing to the goal of clean, efficient energy on Earth. Future research will focus on the ozone and water vapor in Earth's atmosphere, along with cosmic rays, cosmic dust, and antimatter and dark matter in the universe. The Alpha Magnetic Spectrometer, scheduled to be carried to the ISS aboard STS-134 in 2010, measures cosmic rays as part of fundamental research in particle physics.

With work on the ISS continuing, the roster of nations taking part in human space exploration has grown. The People's Republic of China joined

EXPERIMENTS ON THE INTERNATIONAL SPACE STATION

Four times larger than Russia's Mir, which represented the previous generation of space research facilities, the International Space Station (ISS)—under construction since 1998—contains six laboratories dedicated to scientific research. Important research has included:

1. The growth and analysis of protein crystals to increase understanding of proteins, enzymes, and viruses and, in turn, help in the development of new drugs capable of treating cancer, diabetes, emphysema, and immune system disorders.

2. The study of long-term exposure to reduced gravity, including changes to the human heart, arteries, veins, and bone density. The Centrifuge Accommodation Module on board has been used to create conditions ranging from zero gravity to double Earth gravity as a way of comparing the gravitational effects on plants and animals. Gravity on the Moon and Mars also has been simulated to prepare astronauts for future space travel.

3. Analysis of the space environment, including the effects of vacuum conditions and the risk of space debris on materials used in building spacecraft. A range of experiments, relying on equipment attached to the exterior of the ISS, has addressed issues in fundamental physics, especially basic forces of nature that are difficult to analyze in the Earth's gravitational sphere.

4. Observations of the Earth to gain a better understanding of hurricanes, volcanoes, the effects of deforestation, the spread of air and water pollution, and other phenomena.

Dutch and Russian astronauts of the European Space Agency perform an experiment aboard the International Space Station in 2004. Like other visitors to the facility, the team carried out an extensive series of experiments in a variety of fields. (*Getty Images*)

the ranks of countries with human spaceflight capability on October 15, 2003, when astronaut Yang Liwei was launched aboard *Shenzhou 5* and spent about twenty-one hours in space.

Several other countries and space agencies have announced or begun human spaceflight programs, among them India, Japan, Iran, Malaysia, and Turkey. As of 2009, individuals who have flown in space have hailed from nearly forty nations.

Further Reading

Beattie, Donald A. *Taking Science to the Moon: Lunar Experiments and the Apollo Program.* Baltimore: Johns Hopkins University Press, 2001.

Bond, Peter. *The Continuing Story of the International Space Station.* New York: Springer, 2002.

Chaikin, Andrew. *A Man on the Moon: The Voyages of the Apollo Astronauts.* New York: Penguin, 2007.

Chien, Philip. *Columbia, Final Voyage: The Last Flight of NASA's First Space Shuttle.* New York: Copernicus, 2006.

DeGroot, Gerard. *Dark Side of the Moon: The Magnificent Madness of the American Lunar Quest.* New York: New York University Press, 2006.

Hansen, James R. *First Man: The Life of Neil A. Armstrong.* New York: Simon and Schuster, 2005.

Russian Federal Space Agency: http://www.roscosmos.ru/main.php?lang=en.

Swanson, Glen E., ed. *Before This Decade Is Out: Personal Reflections on the Apollo Program.* Washington, DC: National Aeronautics and Space Administration, 1999.

Tsymbal, Nikolai, ed. *First Man in Space: The Life and Achievement of Yuri Gagarin.* Moscow: Progress, 1984.

U.S. National Aeronautics and Space Administration: http://www.nasa.gov.

Wolfe, Tom. *The Right Stuff.* New York: Farrar, Straus and Giroux, 1979.

SPACE EXPLORATION, UNMANNED

1946: First scientific exploration in space: the United States launches instruments mounted on a V-2 rocket to measure cosmic radiation

1957: First artificial satellite, Soviet *Sputnik 1*, sent into space; first dog, Laika, lifts off in *Sputnik 2*

1958: The United States sends its first artificial satellite, *Explorer 1*, into space,

1959: Soviet satellite *Luna 1* accomplishes the first flyby of the Moon

1960: The United States launches *TIROS 1*, first in a series of highly successful weather satellites

1962: The United States launches *Telstar 1*, the first satellite to transmit television signals

1966: Soviet *Luna 10*, launched March 31, becomes the first satellite to orbit the Moon; U.S. lunar probe *Surveyor* becomes the first spacecraft to soft-land on the Moon, June 2

1971: U.S. space probe *Mariner 9* orbits Mars, discovers Olympus Mons, an extinct volcano

1975: Soviet *Venera 9* orbits Venus and sends a lander to the surface

1986: *Giotto*, launched by the European Space Agency, investigates Halley's Comet

1990: The United States launches the Hubble Telescope from the space shuttle *Discovery*

1995: U.S. space probe *Galileo*, launched by the space shuttle *Atlantis*, orbits Jupiter

1997: *Mars Pathfinder* completes a soft landing on the Martian surface and releases the rover *Sojourner* to investigate

2003: The United States sends Mars Exploration Rovers (MERs) *Spirit* and *Opportunity* to the planet's surface

2004: U.S. interplanetary spacecraft *Cassini-Huygens* begins orbiting Saturn; flies close by the moon Phoebe; releases a probe to the surface of the moon Titan

2006: The United States launches *New Horizons*, to study Pluto

2007: China launches the *Chang'e 1* orbiter to study the Moon's geological features

2009: U.S. *Lunar Reconnaissance Orbiter* orbits and studies the Moon; findings indicate that the Moon could contain layers of water, in the form of dirty ice, beneath its dry soil

Unmanned space exploration was made possible in the second half of the twentieth century by the development of rockets capable of sending heavy payloads into space, the cold war competition for global influence between the United States and the Soviet Union, the desire to further scientific research and technological development, and the sheer allure of outer space.

The first Earth-orbiting satellites, developed in the late 1950s and capable of little more than measuring radiation, have evolved into complex devices built to transmit television signals, detect military operations, survey weather developments, measure infrared signals, inventory the Earth's resources, and peer into deep space. In a few short decades, unmanned space exploration moved far beyond Earth's orbit, with probes sent to the Moon, Mars, Mercury, the Sun, and Venus, and to the fringes of the solar system and beyond.

First Artificial Satellites

The first man-made object to reach outer space was a V-2 rocket, developed and utilized as a ballistic missile by Germany during World War II. The first scientific exploration in space was a cosmic radiation experiment conducted by the United States with devices aboard a V-2 rocket, launched in May 1946. Later that year, fruit flies became the first living beings sent into outer space, also aboard a U.S. V-2 rocket.

The important advance of controlled orbital spaceflight came on October 4, 1957, with the successful launch by the Soviet Union of an artificial satellite, *Sputnik 1*. Carried aloft by an R-7 rocket, the 184-pound (83-kilogram) satellite—about the diameter of a beach ball—orbited the Earth at an altitude of 150 miles (240 kilometers). *Sputnik*'s transmitters broadcast a radio signal in the form of beeps that allowed scientists to measure the electron density in the ionosphere, along with the temperature and atmospheric pressure.

Barely a month later, on November 3, 1957, the Soviets followed with the launch of *Sputnik 2*, a larger satellite consisting of three parts: a top section containing instruments for measuring radiation; a middle section housing a radio transmitter; and a lower section that held a dog, Laika. She had undergone extensive training to acclimate to the compartment and the rigors of space travel. Laika died a week after liftoff when her supply of oxygen ran out.

The Sputnik program had grown out of an agreement between the Soviet Union and the United States to use satellites in scientific experi-

SPUTNIK 1

The world's first artificial satellite—*Sputnik 1*, launched by the Soviet Union on October 4, 1957—was the brainchild of rocket designer Sergey Pavlovich Korolyov, who was the country's chief space engineer, Korolyov originally had wanted to place a 1-ton satellite packed with scientific equipment into Earth's orbit. But problems with that spacecraft caused him to postpone a launch attempt (it would achieve success as *Sputnik 3* in 1958) and opt for a simpler design that would enable the Soviets to send a satellite into space ahead of the Americans.

Sputnik 1 was a small aluminum ball, measuring only 23 inches (58 centimeters) in diameter. It had two antennae, a radio transmitter, and a temperature regulation system. It also carried three silver-zinc batteries. Two of the batteries powered the radio transmitter. The other battery powered the temperature regulation system, which consisted of a fan, a dual thermal switch, and a thermal control switch to keep the satellite from overheating.

The satellite emitted a simple "beep, beep" radio signal on two wavelengths, which the Soviets hoped would be heard by amateur radio operators worldwide as proof that *Sputnik 1* was orbiting Earth. Indeed, anyone possessing a short-wave receiver could detect the satellite as it passed overhead. Soviet scientists analyzed *Sputnik 1*'s radio signals to gauge the electron density of Earth's ionosphere, while information on temperature and pressure was encoded in the duration of the beeps.

News reports from the Soviet Union were muted in the immediate aftermath of the launch. But well before *Sputnik 1* reentered the Earth's atmosphere and burned up, on January 4, 1958, newspapers around the globe were hailing the Soviet feat with such headlines as "Space Age Is Here" and "Russia Wins Race Into Outer Space."

A stray dog named Laika paved the way for human space travel aboard the Soviet space-craft *Sputnik 2* on November 3, 1957. Laika proved that a living passenger could survive the launch into space, but she later died in orbit. *(AFP/Stringer/ Getty Images)*

ments developed for the International Geophysical Year. The success of the Sputnik program, however, far exceeded this goal. It was an important moral and ideological victory for the Soviet Union in the cold war, allowing the Russians to portray their communist nation as being technically, educationally, and even morally (in the sense of a society dedicated to serious rather than frivolous employment) more advanced than America's capitalist one.

Under pressure to respond, the United States prematurely attempted to launch a test satellite aboard a Vanguard rocket in December 1957. The rocket failed immediately upon takeoff, crashed onto the launchpad, and exploded. (Due to secrecy on the part of the Russian government, the exact number of failed Soviet launches has never been disclosed.)

Finally, on January 31, 1958, a four-stage Jupiter rocket propelled the U.S. *Explorer 1* satellite into space from Cape Canaveral, Florida. During the satellite's 111 days in space, an onboard detector discovered a belt of radiation around the Earth. It was named the Van Allen belt in honor of James Van Allen, who had designed the measuring instrument.

On May 15, 1958, the Soviets launched *Sputnik 3*, an orbiting geophysical research station. Its instruments, powered, in part, by solar panels, measured meteoroids, magnetic fields, and the radiation belt. *Sputnik 4* followed on May 15, 1960, carrying a Vostok space capsule intended for use in the country's manned program. Later that year, the Soviets sent two dogs into space aboard *Sputnik 5* and brought them safely back to Earth—a crucial step toward sending human beings into space.

However, the Soviet space program suffered a tragic setback in October 24, 1960, when an unmanned rocket exploded on launch at the Baikonur Cosmodrome in Kazakhstan, killing up to 100 workers on the ground. Another explosion at the site in June 1963 took seven lives.

Meanwhile, in July 1958, President Dwight D. Eisenhower created a new government agency to direct the American space initiative: the National Aeronautics and Space Administration (NASA). Eisenhower's primary purpose was twofold: to develop satellites capable of spying on the Soviet Union and to avert a communist propaganda victory by sending a man into space before the Soviets did. A well-funded federal civilian agency was deemed essential to maintaining a large-scale, competitive U.S. space program.

To test the effects of high-gravity acceleration and prolonged weight-lessness, critical factors for human spaceflight, on January 21, 1960, the United States launched a rhesus monkey named Little Sam into Earth orbit. The primate was returned safely to Earth; the capsule was recovered as well. (Little Sam lived until 1982.)

In January 1961, in preparation for Alan Shepard's historic first flight aboard a Mercury capsule in May, a chimpanzee named Ham was catapulted into space. Ham carried out simple maneuvers, pulling levers in response to flashing lights (as he had been trained to do on Earth) before landing unharmed sixteen minutes later. (Ham lived until 1983.)

The Soviet *Sputnik 7* spacecraft, launched on February 4, 1961, and *Sputnik 8*, launched on February 12, 1961, carried Venera satellites that would be launched to explore Venus. *Sputnik 7* proved to be a failure, but *Sputnik 8* succeeded in ejecting the probe into the solar system. *Sputnik 9* and *Sputnik10*, the Soviets' last tests before sending cosmonaut Yuri Gagarin into space on April 12, 1961, each carried a space dummy and a dog on one Earth orbit; both missions were successful.

Television, Military, Spy, and Weather Satellites

Unmanned space exploration took an important new turn on July 10, 1962, when the United States launched *Telstar 1*, the first space satellite to transmit television signals. Designed by the American Telephone and Telegraph Company (AT&T), *Telstar 1* was placed in an elliptical Earth orbit so that its signals could be distributed to television stations on both sides of the Atlantic Ocean, including ones in the United States, Great Britain, and France.

Telstar 1's low altitude, however, limited its use to just 102 minutes per day. Moreover, the day before the satellite's launch, the United States detonated a high-altitude thermonuclear bomb. The increase in radiation from that and subsequent nuclear test explosions damaged *Telstar 1*'s transistors, and it went permanently out of service in February 1963. Three months later, it was replaced by *Telstar 2*.

In 1978, the Public Broadcasting System (PBS) became the first television network to use satellites to send signals to its affiliate stations. Until the 1990s, satellite television signals were too weak to be picked up on Earth except by large, parabola-shaped "dish" antennas.

Today, however, digital broadcast satellites can send signals directly to houses outfitted with antenna dishes as small as 15 inches (38 centimeters) in diameter. These satellites also can transmit hundreds of channels simultaneously and, unlike the *Telstar* satellites, use geostationary orbits that keep them in a fixed position relative to the ground and thus able to operate around the clock.

Satellites also have been used by a number of countries for defense-related purposes. On November 6, 1970, the United States launched its first satellite as part of the Defense Support Program (DSP), to send data continuously to the Missile Warning Center in Colorado. Sensors aboard the satellite were designed to detect nuclear detonations and the launching of intercontinental ballistic missiles.

Over the years, DSP satellites have undergone major improvements and enhancements. They now have more sensors, can withstand laser jamming, and can maneuver to escape an attacking satellite. In 1991, a DSP satellite was used to detect Iraqi ballistic missiles being launched against U.S. troops during Operation Desert Storm.

Far more elaborate was the Strategic Defense Initiative (SDI), an elaborate antiballistic missile system—part of it based in space—proposed by President Ronald Reagan's administration in 1983. Although the Star Wars program, as it was dubbed, never came to complete fruition (or full funding), it did serve as a starting point for ongoing research and development in space-based missile defense.

In the arena of national intelligence, the first U.S. reconnaissance (spy) satellites, code-named Corona, were launched in 1959 and 1960. The satellites carried a camera and sent the film back to Earth in canisters, which were retrieved in midair as they parachuted down. The Soviets launched their first successful camera-toting spy satellite, *Zenit*, in April 1962. Since then, hundreds of spy satellites have been used by the United States, Russia, China, and Israel, and, jointly, by France, Spain, and Italy.

Spy satellites typically orbit the Earth at an altitude of 100 miles (160 kilometers). The most recent ones carry high-resolution, multispectral digital photography systems, which take visible light and infrared pictures. These satellites can discern objects as small as a person and can be used in battlefield situations.

Another important use of satellites is to collect data on meteorology. The satellite *Explorer 6*, sent aloft in August 1959, radioed the first pictures of clouds. The first operational weather satellite, launched by the United States on April 1, 1960, was called the *Television and Infrared Observation Satellite*, or *TIROS 1*. The cameras aboard *TIROS 1* could record cloud patterns, but the satellite operated for only eighty-nine

Satellite television transmission and high-speed data communications began with the U.S. launch of *Telstar 1* in July 1962. The multifaceted sphere, measuring 3.3 cubic feet (1 meter) in diameter, provided the first transatlantic television feed. *(Science & Society Picture Library/ Getty Images)*

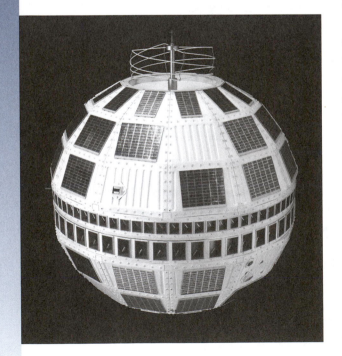

days. The Soviets launched their first weather satellite in 1962, followed by the European Space Agency (ESA) in 1977, and China in 1988.

Today, there are more than 200 weather satellites orbiting the Earth, sixty of which originated in the United States. These satellites photograph clouds; record atmospheric and water temperatures; track hurricanes; determine if hailstorms and tornadoes are forming; measure land and ocean wind speeds, rainfall, snow cover, and ground moisture; and map ocean currents.

Infrared, X-ray, and Remote-Sensing Satellites

Infrared satellites carry special telescopes to detect objects in space that, while too cool to produce much visible light, produce infrared light. Infrared light is a form of electromagnetic energy with wavelengths longer than those of visible light, making it invisible to the human eye.

The telescopes on infrared satellites can detect dust grains around newly forming stars, as well as gas and dust from dying stars. And because infrared telescopes can penetrate cosmic dust, they can be used to view the Milky Way and other galaxies, providing valuable information to astronomers.

The United States, in cooperation with Great Britain and the Netherlands, launched the Infrared Astronomical Satellite (IRAS) in January 1983. In November 1995, the ESA sent the Infrared Space Observatory into orbit.

X-ray observatory satellites comb outer space for the source of X-rays and measure their strength, both vital information for astrophysicists. The United States launched the first such satellite, *Uhuru*, in 1970. It discovered X-rays pulsating from an object named Centaurus X-3 and led scientists to theorize that, because gas was being heated to millions of degrees and releasing X-ray energy, this was a neutron star absorbing gas from a neighboring star.

X-ray satellites also have been launched by Japan, Russia, and the ESA. In 2007, the orbiting X-ray telescopes XMM-Newton and Chandra discovered a pair of galaxy clusters merging into one, affirming that galaxy clusters can collide faster than previously thought.

Remote-sensing satellites carry devices designed to take images of visible and infrared electromagnetic wavelengths. These satellites also may include synthetic aperture radar, which beams radio waves toward the ground and then records their reflection. Remote-sensing technology also can penetrate cloud cover, vegetation, and even soil. Remote-sensing satellites chart previously hidden geographical features, show how land use is changing, uncover objects for archaeologists, measure pollution, and contribute to hurricane and flood relief by revealing changes brought about by such disasters.

The first satellite dedicated to remote sensing was *Landsat 1*, launched by the United States in 1972; the last satellite in the program, *Landsat 7*, was launched in 1999. The Landsat satellites, some of which are still functioning, photograph the Earth's surface every sixteen days. Other such satellites have been sent into space by Canada, China, Japan, Russia, and the ESA.

The Hubble Telescope

Among the most publicized and scientifically fruitful unmanned space instruments has been the Hubble Telescope, named for U.S. astronomer Edwin Hubble (1889–1953). Hubble proved that other galaxies were moving away from our own Milky Way, a conclusion important to the big bang theory, which seeks to explain what happened at the beginning of the universe. (According to this theory, the universe was extremely compact, dense, and hot until a cosmic explosion 10 billion to 20 billion years ago caused it to begin expanding, cooling, and taking the form we know today—a form that continues to change.)

The Hubble Telescope has produced astonishing photographs of distant space objects—such as this column of molecular hydrogen gas and dust—and has led scientists to important new understandings of the universe and astrophysical phenomena. *(Science & Society Picture Library/ Getty Images)*

The Hubble Telescope was launched by the United States from the space shuttle *Discovery* on April 24, 1990, and it orbits the Earth at an altitude of 320 miles (515 kilometers). The telescope, whose orientation is controlled from the ground, has two cameras to record its findings.

Already late and over budget at the time of its launch, Hubble was immediately beset by problems. First, it was discovered that the telescope's main mirror had been improperly designed and had to be replaced, at a cost of more than $1 billion; astronauts aboard the space shuttle *Endeavour* made the change during a spacewalk in early December 1993. The telescope also was serviced or repaired on subsequent shuttle missions in 1997, 1999, 2002, 2005, and 2009.

A collaboration between NASA and the ESA, Hubble includes a high-resolution spectrograph for recording ultraviolet, visible, and near-infrared wavelengths, which can reveal the temperature, chemical makeup, and motion of planets, dust clouds, and stars. In addition, Hubble contains a faint-object camera designed to detect extremely distant and dim objects, and a Near-Infrared Camera and Multi-Object Spectrometer (NICMOS) that is used to detect cool-temperature objects and those that emit infrared light.

In May 2009, astronauts aboard the space shuttle *Atlantis* made several repairs to the Hubble Telescope that were expected to extend its life. The Hubble Telescope will remain in service at least until NASA launches its next-generation space observatory: the James Webb Space Telescope, an infrared scanning instrument scheduled to become operational in 2013. (Webb was head of NASA from 1961 to 1968.)

The Moon

The first successful flyby of the Moon—within 3,100 miles (5,000 kilometers) of the surface—was accomplished by a Soviet satellite, *Luna 1*, in January 1959. This was followed in September by the flight of *Luna 2*, a satellite that became the first Earth object to strike the Moon when it was deliberately crashed into the surface east of Mare Serenitatis (the Sea of Serenity). Before its demise, *Luna 2* sent back information confirming that the Moon lacks a magnetic field and radiation belts. Then, in October 1959, *Luna 3* took the first hazy photographs of the dark side of the Moon.

Following several failed attempts to soft-land a satellite on the Moon, the Soviets succeeded on February 3, 1966, with *Luna 9*, which sent photographs from the surface.

In April 1966, *Luna 10* became the first satellite to orbit the Moon, providing scientific measurements—and the Soviet government with a major propaganda victory in the cold war. *Luna 17* landed on the Moon in November 1970 and released an eight-wheeled rover that rode across the surface, performed soil tests, measured X-rays, and calculated the exact distance between the Moon and the Earth.

The United States also sent space probes to the Moon as part of its Ranger and Surveyor programs. Like the Soviet Luna program, Ranger and Surveyor included failures as well as successes. The Ranger spacecraft were designed to crash on the lunar surface, and, in July 1964, *Ranger 7*—making the first successful flight in the program—transmitted photographs of the approaching terrain for twenty minutes before impact.

The first U.S. soft landing on the Moon was accomplished by *Surveyor 1* in June 1966; this feat was replicated by *Surveyors 3, 5, 6,* and *7* through early 1968. *Surveyor 6* was the first space vehicle to lift off the surface of the Moon as well as land on it. The Surveyor satellites that succeeded in landing took photographs and employed instruments to sample the lunar surface—providing important data that confirmed the texture of the soil would support astronauts on foot.

Another important breakthrough for the United States came in January 1998, when it placed the *Lunar Prospector* in low-polar orbit around the Moon, where the spacecraft remained until being intentionally crashed into the surface in July 1999. The mission yielded a detailed map of the Moon's surface composition, along with information about the planet's origins and resources. Scientific research on the mission also included the discovery of ice in the polar craters of the Moon and the mapping of its gravity field.

The United States sent the *Lunar Reconnaissance Orbiter* (LRO) around the Moon in June 2009 as part of the American Vision for Space Program. The goals of that program include sending astronauts back to the Moon as a follow-up to the lunar landing missions of the late 1960s and early 1970s, creating a three-dimensional map of the Moon's surface, and surveying lunar resources.

With the winding down of the cold war in the early 1990s, other countries began sending probes to the Moon. Japan launched its *Hiten* spacecraft into Earth orbit in January 1990; the *Hiten*, in turn, launched a smaller satellite, the *Hagoromo*, into lunar orbit. When the transmitter aboard the *Hagoromo* failed, in October 1991, Japanese space scientists succeeded in redirecting the *Hiten* to the Moon. Eighteen months later, it was deliberately crashed on the lunar surface. In September 2007, the Japanese launched the *Kaguya* lunar probe, which orbited and surveyed the Moon for two years.

The People's Republic of China joined lunar exploration by satellite in October 2007 with its *Chang'e 1* orbiter, which was named for a Chinese Moon goddess. For the first mission in the Chinese Lunar Exploration Project, *Chang'e 1* assembled a three-dimensional image of the Moon's geological features, mapped the chemical elements on the surface, measured the depth of lunar soil, and studied solar wind. *Chang'e 2* was scheduled for 2010 or 2011.

India's first lunar mission came with the October 2008 launch of the *Chandrayaan-1* satellite, which orbited the Moon and released an impact probe to the surface that November. The probe struck the lunar south pole in an experiment to determine whether ice was present. Among the scientific instruments aboard *Chandrayaan-1* were a mapping camera, a spectral imager, and a gamma ray spectrometer.

The Sun and Mercury

Between 1960 and 1968, the United States sent several small unmanned space probes to orbit the Sun as part of the Pioneer program. *Pioneer 5*, launched in March 1960, carried high-energy particle detectors and a magnetic-field detector and measured how magnetic fields were changed by solar flares. *Pioneers* 6 through 9 measured the structure and flow of solar wind; the spacecraft were positioned in orbit in such a way that astronomers could use the data they collected to forecast solar storms up to two weeks before they occurred. NASA scientists remained in contact with several of the Pioneer probes into the early 1990s, and with *Pioneer 6* until 1997.

The innermost of the solar system's planets, Mercury, has been little explored. The U.S. *Mariner 10*, which flew by Venus in February 1974, came close to Mercury that March, at a distance of about 430 miles (700 kilometers). After looping around the Sun, it made its second flyby that December and its last in March 1975. *Mariner 1* mapped a little less than half of Mercury's surface and discovered that the planet's atmosphere consists mainly of helium. It also found that Mercury has a magnetic field and an iron-rich core.

In January 2008, a NASA spacecraft known as the Mercury Surface, Space Environment, Geochemistry, and Ranging (MESSENGER) probe made another flyby of Mercury and discovered great variability in the planet's magnetic field. It also produced images of Mercury's previously unrecorded surface and detected magnesium in the planet's atmosphere.

Venus

Venus became the object of exploration when, in 1961, the Soviet Union began its Venera program, with the goal of landing a probe on the planet. Of the eight initial Venera craft, two descended toward the planet's surface and sent back data that revealed the atmospheric pressure was ninety times greater than Earth's, surface temperatures exceeded 9,000 degrees

Fahrenheit (4,982 degrees Celsius), and 97 percent of the atmosphere was carbon dioxide.

In October 1975, the Soviet Union succeeded in landing two probes on the Venusian surface. *Venera 9*, launched on June 8, 1975, consisted of an orbiter and a lander. The orbiter had engines to break its speed and help it to circle the planet. The lander included parachutes to slow its descent and a "crush ring" to absorb the shock of impact with the surface, and was encased in a sphere built to protect it from heat and atmospheric pressure. The lander touched down on the Venusian surface on October 22 and transmitted data, including one photograph, for fifty-three minutes.

Venera 10, launched on June 14, 1975, also landed a surface vehicle on October 25; it provided several photos of Venus's surface. Other Venera satellites, some landers and some orbiters, followed. The last in the program was *Venera 16*, which orbited Venus and mapped the planet's northern hemisphere in October 1983.

In December 1978, the U.S. probe *Pioneer Venus 1* orbited Venus and mapped nearly the entire planet with its radar. Also arriving that month was *Pioneer Venus 2*, which consisted of four separate atmospheric probes. One of the probes used a parachute to slow its descent, while the three remaining probes plunged straight through Venus's atmosphere.

A more extensive mapping of Venus was accomplished by the Magellan mission in 1989 and 1990. NASA's first interplanetary probe since Pioneer in 1978, the probe *Magellan* was launched from the space shuttle *Atlantis* on May 4, 1989, and propelled by a solid-fuel rocket. By August 1990, the spacecraft had arrived at Venus and begun an elliptical orbit. Circling the planet, *Magellan* mapped the surface with radar. Before the mission ended in October 1994, the probe sent back images of 98 percent of the surface.

In November 2005, the European Space Agency launched *Venus Express*, its first probe of that planet. Arriving at Venus in April 2006, the spacecraft deployed a variety of scientific instruments: a magnetometer to measure the planet's magnetic field; three spectrometers, to measure the atmosphere, analyze radiation, and observe the electromagnetic spectrum; and a transmitter to send radio waves and measure them as they travel through the atmosphere or bounce off the surface. Initial findings from these experiments indicate that Venus once had oceans and that it currently experiences lightning more frequently than does Earth.

Mars

The first spacecraft to fly by Mars was the U.S. probe *Mariner 4*. It came within 6,200 miles (10,000 kilometers) of the planet on July 14, 1965.

NASA engineers demonstrate the Mars Exploration Rover (MER), a six-wheeled robotic device deployed to the planet's surface to search for, collect, and analyze rocks, minerals, and soil. (*Robyn Beck/AFP/ Getty Images*)

Images from the vehicle showed the surface of Mars to be barren and cratered, with an atmospheric pressure too low to allow for liquid water on the surface. In 1969, *Mariner 6* and *Mariner 7* traveled closer to the planet and produced sharper, but similar, images.

Then, in November 1971, *Mariner 9* became the first space probe to orbit Mars. A dust storm impeded the transmission of images at first, but *Mariner 9* eventually sent more than 7,300 photos, which revealed two previously unknown geological features: Olympus Mons, an extinct volcano reaching a height of 78,000 feet (24,000 meters), and a long valley that was named Valles Marineris.

Two more American spacecraft, *Viking 1* and *Viking 2,* went into Mars orbit in 1976 and sent landers to the surface. The orbiters took tens of thousands of photos and detected water vapor in the Martian atmosphere. The landers transmitted panoramas of the landscape and collected vital information about the planet's climate and seismic activity.

The major breakthrough in Martian exploration came on July 4, 1997, when the U.S. spacecraft *Pathfinder* landed on the planet's surface. The probe had slowed its descent by using a parachute and braking rockets, and cushioned its landing through the use of airbags. *Time* magazine reported,

> Across the U.S. and much of the world, the ship's successful arrival was greeted with the most attention accorded an otherworldly landing since, perhaps, Apollo 11 touched down on the moon 28 years ago. At the Pasadena convention center, near NASA's Jet Propulsion Laboratory, where the Pathfinder mission was being run, a standing-room-only crowd of more than

2,000 people whooped and wept as the pictures from Pathfinder streamed onto a 25-ft. screen. On the Internet, NASA sites that promised to post the pictures as soon as they became available recorded a staggering 100 million hits on Friday alone.

Once on Mars, *Pathfinder* released a six-wheeled robotic rover called *Sojourner*. Roaming the rocky surface, *Sojourner* sent 550 photographs back to Earth—these were in addition to the 16,500 sent by *Pathfinder*—and analyzed chemical properties at some sixteen locations on Mars.

In September 1997, the *Mars Global Surveyor*, another U.S. probe, reached the Red Planet (so called because of its reddish appearance, caused by iron dioxide present on its surface), went into orbit, and began sending data back to NASA scientists. Laser beams sent from the spacecraft to the surface revealed topographical details, including the existence of vast plains in the northern hemisphere. A thermal emission spectrometer recorded temperatures and, by detecting chemicals, enabled a mineral map to be made of the entire planet. The *Surveyor* also produced more than 25,000 photographs, which have revealed sand dunes and gullies, perhaps caused by now-extinct water flows.

In 2003, as part of its Mars Exploration Rover (MER) program, the United States sent two more robotic rovers to the Martian surface, *Spirit*

SOJOURNER

On July 6, 1997, two days after the *Mars Pathfinder* spacecraft landed in the Ares Valley region of the Red Planet, *Sojourner*, a robotic rover on wheels, was released from *Pathfinder* and began exploring the planet. *Sojourner* was named for Sojourner Truth, the nineteenth-century African American woman who advocated against slavery and for women's rights.

The rover was designed by a team of National Aeronautics and Space Administration (NASA) scientists and engineers led by Jacob Matijevic and Donna Shirley. Measuring only 10 inches (25 centimeters) high, 2 feet (0.6 meters) long, and 1.5 feet (0.45 meters) wide, and weighing 22 pounds (10 kilograms), *Sojourner* was powered by a flat solar panel and rolled about on six wheels. The robotic device did more than react to commands from Earth: It had laser eyes and automatic programming that allowed it to avoid unexpected obstacles in its path.

Sojourner moved slowly—only 1.5 feet (0.46 meters) per minute—and it stopped frequently to survey the terrain. While on Mars, the rover traveled a total of about 325 feet (100 meters) and performed chemical analyses of rocks and soil at sixteen sites near the landing site. It also sent back 550 close-up images of the Martian landscape and millions of measurements of atmospheric pressure, temperature, and wind.

Sojourner ceased operating September 27, 1997, having well exceeded its expected life span of seven days. It remains on the planet's surface.

(*MER-A*) and *Opportunity* (*MER-B*). The primary scientific objective of the mission was to collect more information about the planet's geology, especially anything it might reveal about water activity. The rovers continued in operation into 2009.

The Outer Planets and Beyond

Jupiter has been the object of eight space probes, all of them American and only one of which orbited the planet. The first, *Pioneer 10*, was launched in March 1972 and began its flyby of Jupiter in late November 1973. The probe encountered intense radiation as it flew within 81,000 miles (130,000 kilometers) of the planet's chemical clouds and confirmed what most scientists had suspected: Jupiter's distinctive red spot was a giant storm. *Pioneer 11*, which passed within 21,000 miles (34,000 kilometers) of Jupiter in December 1974, made the first investigations of the planet's expansive polar regions.

The *Voyager 1* and *Voyager 2* planetary probes—the last spacecraft in NASA's Mariner series and the first to reach the outermost planets—made their closest approaches to Jupiter in March and July 1979, respectively. Important discoveries about Jupiter by the Voyager probes included three new moons, a ring system, and evidence of volcanic activity on one of the planet's moons (Io).

In 1992, the spacecraft *Ulysses* investigated Jupiter's magnetic field, then continued its scheduled journey farther into space. In 1995, *Galileo*—launched by the shuttle *Atlantis* in October 1989—became the first spacecraft to orbit Jupiter. It surveyed the planet and its moons for eight years, and it revealed that three Jovian moons have very thin atmospheres and might contain liquid water beneath their surfaces. In 1995, *Galileo* sent a small probe into Jupiter's atmosphere; in the one hour before it was destroyed by the heat and intense atmospheric pressure, the probe sent back considerable data about the planet's atmosphere.

The year 2000 brought a flyby of Jupiter by the *Cassini-Huygens* spacecraft, a joint effort by NASA and the ESA. This flyby yielded some of the most extensive images of the planet to date—about 26,000 photos in all—including features as small as 40 miles (64 kilometers) in diameter. And, in September 2006, another planetary probe en route to the edge of the solar system and beyond, *New Horizons*, flew close enough to get a boost (or "assist") from the planet's gravitational field. (The satellite came within about 1.7 million miles, or 2.3 million kilometers, of the planet.)

The first space probe to visit Saturn was *Pioneer 11*, which had investigated Jupiter in late 1974. In September 1979, *Pioneer 11* passed within 13,000 miles (21,000 kilometers) of Saturn, later crossing the orbit of Neptune and becoming the first spacecraft to leave the solar system. The first high-resolution images of Saturn came from the flyby of *Voyager 1* in 1980, which also passed near one of the planet's moons, Titan, and examined its atmosphere. Additional images of Saturn were taken in August 1981 by *Voyager 2*, which used a radar system to measure the temperature and density of the upper atmosphere.

In July 2004, the *Cassini-Huygens* spacecraft—consisting of the *Cassini* orbiter and *Hugyens* probe—reached Saturn and began orbiting. On July 11, the piggybacked vehicle flew close by the moon Phoebe and returned a series of close-up photos. In December, *Cassini* released *Huygens* to land on the surface of Titan, the largest of Saturn's moons. The probe transmitted photos showing what might be a shoreline and islands, and revealed clouds of methane. The probe continued to send back data for more than an hour after landing. Before the *Cassini-Hugyens* mission ended in 2008, it confirmed the existence of four previously unknown moons of Saturn.

The planets Uranus and Neptune have been visited by only one spacecraft, *Voyager 2*. The spacecraft made its closest approach to Uranus in January 1986, coming within 50,600 miles (81,500 kilometers); notable discoveries included a magnetic field and ten previously unknown moons. In 1989, *Voyager 2* came within 3,000 miles (4,800 kilometers) of Neptune's north pole, revealing four planetary rings, six moons, and the existence of auroras.

The *New Horizons* probe, meanwhile, launched by the United States in January 2006, is on course to visit the dwarf planet Pluto and its three known moons. The probe is scheduled to arrive at Pluto in July 2015 and then continue on to study the Kuiper Belt, a region beyond the solar system that contains frozen objects called "ices," made largely of methane, ammonia, and water.

Aside from planetary probes, *Giotto*, a spacecraft launched by the European Space Agency on July 2, 1985, made a flyby of Halley's Comet on March 14, 1986. *Giotto* entered the comet's atmosphere, passed within 400 miles (644 kilometers) of the comet and 640 miles (1,030 kilometers) of its nucleus, and survived despite being hit by several particles. *Giotto* transmitted the first close-up images of Halley's Comet and the first images ever of a comet's nucleus. Scientists then were able to set *Giotto* on a different course, using a gravitational slingshot through the Earth's atmosphere to propel it to Comet Grigg-Skjellerup, which it passed in July 1992.

NASA initiated a new phase in deep space exploration in March 2009 with the launch from Cape Canaveral of the new Kepler Space Telescope, designed to identify planets such as Earth that orbit suns other than ours. The $600 million device, which was sent into orbit around the Sun, can observe distant stars in the Milky Way Galaxy and measure the size and orbit of every planet that passes in front of them. By the year 2013, according to one scientist involved with the project, Kepler likely will have located hundreds of planets, perhaps thousands, that may be home to intelligent life.

Further Reading

Brunier, Serge. *Space Odyssey: The First Forty Years of Space Exploration.* Cambridge, UK: Cambridge University Press, 2002.

Cadbury, Deborah. *Space Race: The Epic Battle Between America and the Soviet Union for Dominion in Space.* New York: HarperCollins, 2006.

Godwin, Robert. *The Lunar Exploration Scrapbook: A Pictorial History of Lunar Vehicles.* Burlington, Canada: Apogee, 2007.

Harland, David M. *Jupiter Odyssey: The Story of NASA's Galileo Mission.* New York: Praxis, 2000.

Mishkin, Andrew. *Sojourner: An Insider's View of the Mars Pathfinder Mission.* New York: Berkeley, 2003.

Winchester, Jim, ed. *Space Missions: From Sputnik to SpaceShipOne, The History of Space Flight.* San Diego, CA: Thunder Bay, 2006.

SPEKE, JOHN HANNING (1827–1864)

1827:	Born on May 4 in Jordans, England
1844:	Begins serving in the army of the East India Company
1854:	Joins an expedition to East Africa under Richard Burton to explore Somaliland
1856:	Begins a second expedition to East Africa under Burton to find the source of the Nile River
1858:	With Burton, discovers Lake Tanganyika
1859:	Announces to the Royal Geographical Society that Lake Victoria is the source of the Nile
1862:	Discovers the place where the Nile leaves Lake Victoria and names it Ripon Falls
1863:	Publishes *Journal of the Discovery of the Source of the Nile*
1864:	Dies on September 18 from gunshot wounds suffered while partridge hunting

English explorer John Hanning Speke discovered Lake Victoria in eastern equatorial Africa and correctly identified it as the principal source of the Nile River.

He was born on May 4, 1827, in Jordans, Somerset, England, to William Speke and Georgina Elizabeth Hanning. John's father was a captain in the British army, and he directed his son toward a military career. In 1844, John Speke began serving in the army of the East India Company and was active in the Punjab campaign, which included battles at Ramnagar, Sadullapur, and Chilianwala, and in Gujarat.

English explorer John Hanning Speke reached Lake Victoria in 1858 and correctly identified it as the source of the Nile River. He also collected a wealth of scientific information on the geography, climate, flora, and fauna of East Africa. (*Apic/ Hulton Archive/ Getty Images*)

In 1854, Speke joined an expedition to East Africa under the explorer Richard Burton, with the purpose of traversing Somaliland (now Somalia). Both Burton and Speke were attacked by tribesmen and severely wounded. Speke nearly died, but recovered and went on to serve in the Crimean War (1853–1856). Burton also recovered, returned to England, and fought in the Crimean War.

Lake Tanganyika and Lake Victoria

Despite friction between the two men over what Speke believed was Burton's questioning of his bravery in Somaliland, the two men teamed up in 1856 for another expedition to East Africa. Their shared goal was the discovery of a vast inland "sea" called Ujiji (Lake Tanganyika, which lies between the Democratic Republic of the Congo and Tanzania) and the source of the Nile River (found to be at Lake Victoria, on the borders of Kenya, Tanzania, and Uganda).

Traveling inland from Zanzibar in June 1857, the two Englishmen were beset by tropical disease throughout the journey. In addition, Speke temporarily lost his hearing after a beetle crawled inside his ear and had to be removed with a knife.

Speke and Burton reached their destination, Lake Tanganyika, in February 1858. Speke had been nearly blinded by an illness and could not clearly see the body of water they had discovered. (He later regained his sight.) After exploring the lake for three months, and with Burton now ill, the two men prepared to head back to the East African coast—only to be told of a large lake to the north.

On July 9, with Burton still too sick to make the journey, Speke set out in search of the lake. Several weeks later, in August, he discovered the lake and named it Victoria Nyanza (Lake Victoria). He believed it was the source of the Nile River, but he had lost most of his survey equipment and was unable to determine the depth or size of the lake or to make other investigations. Burton rejected Speke's claim, insisting that the source of the Nile was Lake Tanganyika.

Speke returned to England in May 1859, about two weeks ahead of Burton. During those two weeks, Speke delivered a speech to the Royal Geographical Society and published an article in *Blackwood's Magazine* in which he told of the expedition and announced that he had found the source of the Nile.

Burton was furious. By reporting on the mission first, he believed that Speke had violated an agreement between the two men to make a joint announcement of their findings. He also was angry that Speke had advanced his claim for Lake Victoria as the source of the Nile without Burton having an opportunity to argue for Lake Tanganyika. The subsequent split between the two explorers was deep and permanent.

Ripon Falls and the Source of the Nile

Under the sponsorship of the Royal Geographical Society, Speke returned to Africa in 1860 with James Augustus Grant, a friend and an officer in the British army, for the purpose of confirming Lake Victoria as the source of the Nile. On September 25, 1860, Speke's party of 217, including porters and armed men, departed Zanzibar. The expedition was soon halted, however, as disputes among his interpreters caused negotiations with local tribes to break down and prevented him from gaining assurances of safe passage. Grant, meanwhile, had embarked on a more northerly route, only to have his caravan attacked and his supplies stolen.

Together, the two men resumed their journey in September 1861. Grant became ill in January 1862, and Speke continued north into Uganda without him. In February, Speke arrived at the palace of King Mutesa and negotiated with the ruler to obtain permission to travel onward.

Finally, in July 1862, Speke reached the Nile River on the northwest shore of Lake Victoria, in Uganda. On July 28, he found the site at which the Nile River exits the lake and named it Ripon Falls (after Lord Ripon, the British undersecretary of state for war who had been instrumental in arranging the expedition).

Speke began following the river downstream (north) from the lake, but he was forced away from the water by hostile local tribes. He later returned to the Nile, rejoined Grant, and reached Gondokoro, a trading depot in southern Sudan, in February 1863. From Khartoum, which was farther north, Speke sent a telegram to London in which he declared, "The Nile is settled."

In carrying out the expedition, Speke and Grant became the first Europeans to cross equatorial eastern Africa. In doing so, they explored 500 miles (800 kilometers) of territory never before seen by Europeans. But because Speke had been unable to follow the river downstream the entire distance from Ripon Falls to Gondokoro, some questioned whether he had really found the source of the Nile. His old companion and nemesis, Burton, expressed particular skepticism, insisting that there was no proof that the river that intersected with Lake Victoria was indeed the Nile.

SPEKE'S SCIENTIFIC FINDINGS

In 1863, John Hanning Speke published *Journal of the Discovery of the Source of the Nile*, in which he provided a vivid account of the adventure he experienced in East Africa. He also presented a wealth of scientific findings in four categories: "Geography," "Atmospheric Agents," "Flora," and "Fauna."

Under Geography, he wrote:

The continent of Africa is something like a dish turned upside down, having a high and flat central plateau, with a higher rim of hills surrounding it.

Under Atmospheric Agents, he displayed a chart showing "the number of days on which rain fell (more or less) during the march of the East African Expedition from Zanzibar to Gondokoro." About the winds, he observed:

In the dryer season they blow so cold that the sun's heat is not distressing; and in consequence of this, and the average altitude of the plateau, which is 3,000 feet [900 meters], the general temperature of the atmosphere is very pleasant, as I found from experience; for I walked every inch of the journey dressed in thick woolen clothes, and slept every night between blankets.

Under Flora, Speke noted:

There exists a regular gradation of fertility, surprisingly rich on the equator, but decreasing systematically from it.

And under Fauna, he observed:

One thing only tends to disorganize the country, and that is war caused, in the first instance by polygamy, producing a family of half-brothers, who, all aspiring to succeed their father, fight continually with one another, and make their chief aim slaves and cattle.

Back in London, Speke appeared again before the Royal Geographical Society—this time, to announce that he had found the source of the Nile—and was widely celebrated. In December 1863, he published a book on the expedition, *Journal of the Discovery of the Source of the Nile*, which was widely read but poorly edited, and its accuracy was questioned. The following year, Speke published a second work, *What Led To the Discovery of the Source of the Nile*.

Burton, meanwhile, still insisted that Lake Tanganyika, not Lake Victoria, was the true source of the Nile. The two rivals were scheduled to debate the issue on the morning of September 16, 1864, at a meeting of the British Association for the Advancement of Science, when tragedy struck. On the afternoon before the debate, Speke went hunting for partridges in the Wiltshire countryside. As he was climbing over a wall, his gun fired accidentally, leaving a wound in his left side. When a friend approached him, Speke said weakly, "Don't move me."

Within fifteen minutes, the man who had correctly concluded that Lake Victoria was the source of the Nile was dead, at the age of thirty-eight. In his honor, a red granite obelisk was erected in London's Kensington Gardens. According to a contemporary observer, "Speke's nature displayed a truly remarkable blend of indomitable determination with the spirit of perennial youth."

Further Reading

Carnochan, W.B. *The Sad Story of Burton, Speke, and the Nile; Or, Was John Hanning Speke a Cad?* Stanford, CA: Stanford General, 2006.

Maitland, Alexander. *Speke.* London: Constable, 1971.

Speke, John Hanning. *Journal of the Discovery of the Source of the Nile.* 1863. Mineola, NY: Dover, 1996.

See also: Burton, Richard Francis; Royal Geographical Society.

STANLEY, HENRY MORTON.

See Livingstone, David

STARK, FREYA (1893–1993)

- 1893: Born on January 31 in Paris
- 1927: Travels to Lebanon and is enchanted by the Middle Eastern desert
- 1929: Undertakes solo expedition through Persia to the Caspian Sea
- 1932: Publishes *Baghdad Sketches*
- 1934: Publishes *The Valleys of the Assassins*
- 1936: Awarded the Mungo Park Medal by the Royal Geographical Society; publishes *The Southern Gates of Arabia*
- 1951: Publishes *Beyond Euphrates*
- 1972: Named a dame of the British Empire
- 1993: Dies at age 100 on May 9 at her home in Asolo, Italy

An English travel writer and explorer, Freya Madeleine Stark journeyed throughout the Middle East, including areas where few Western men, and fewer Western women, had ever traveled before. Her observations of the land, peoples, and everyday life—recorded in some two dozen books—are known for their poetic beauty and incisive analysis.

Born on January 31, 1893, in Paris to British painters who moved frequently, Stark was raised in several locations, including rural England and London. She spent much of her youth in northern Italy, however, and was educated by tutors at her grandmother's house in Genoa. Because of her travels and education, she could speak English, French, German, and Italian.

At age nine, she read *The Book of the Thousand Nights and a Night* (1885), also known as *The Arabian Nights*, and was captivated by its tales of Arabia and Persia. The book stimulated her interest in the Middle East and a desire to travel to the region. So, too, did the frequent relocations by her family. As she later said,

> I loved languages . . . and I loved to travel. My sister and I were brought up to travel; we wandered about [and] I always had a feeling for learning languages, and Arabic covers the greatest number of countries with the most interesting history that was within my reach. I never thought of Far Eastern languages, but I could learn Arabic, and it covers the greatest area. And, strangely, I thought when I was about 20 that the countries where oil was being found were going to be the most interesting in my life.

Dame Freya Stark lived and traveled throughout the Middle East from the 1920s to 1950s. In many areas, she was one of the first Western women to do so. Her more than thirty books about the region, the people, and her experiences are considered classics. *(Hulton Archive/Stringer/ Getty Images)*

Stark studied literature at Bedford College in London and then served as a battlefield nurse during World War I. She completed a course in Arabic at the School of Oriental and African Studies at the University of London and in 1927 decided to travel to Lebanon. Once there, she immediately fell in love with the desert. "I never imagined that my first sight of [it] would come as such a shock of beauty and enslave me right away," she wrote.

In 1929, Stark undertook difficult solo expeditions from Baghdad to Lorestan Province (in western Persia, now Iran) and to the mountains of Mazandaran Province on the Caspian Sea, where she nearly died of malaria and dysentery. Over the next twelve years, she traveled extensively in Arabia, Iraq, Lebanon, Persia, and Syria. She mapped a remote part of the Elburz Mountains in Persia and explored remote southern Arabia, where few Westerners had ever before ventured.

During World War II, Stark joined Britain's Ministry of Information and took part in Arabic radio broadcasts aimed at getting nations in the Middle East to support the Allies or at least convincing them to remain neutral. She was particularly influential in Yemen, where she traveled with a projector and films that she showed to audiences as part of an Allied propaganda campaign.

In Cairo, Egypt, she founded a secret anti-Fascist society called the Brothers of Freedom, which advocated in the Middle East for democracy and religious tolerance. She later recalled,

> We started with 12 friends and gradually spread. . . . In a year or two we had over 100,000 people in the committees who wanted to help us.

Beginning in the 1950s, even as she spent much of her time writing, Stark continued to travel and explore. She kept on doing so into her later years. For example, she voyaged down the Euphrates River on a raft in her eighties.

Stark wrote twenty-four books about her travels, all published by the John Murray company in London, as well as an autobiography and eight volumes of letters, which reveal the wealth of her friendships and the excitement of her adventures. Stark's books are known for their spirit, lucidity, and fascination with landscapes. In *Baghdad Sketches* (1932), for example, she wrote,

> I like these slow yellow streams. As they silt up or shift in their lazy beds, they remove cities boldly from one district to another. They are as indolent, and wayward, powerful, beneficent and unpitying as the Older Gods whom no doubt they represent; and there is no greater desolation in this land than to come upon their dry beds, long abandoned, but still marked step-by-step with sand-colored ruins of the desert.

Freya Stark was awarded the Mungo Park Medal for exploration by the Royal Scottish Geographical Society in 1936. In 1972, she was named dame of the British Empire (the equivalent of knight). She died on May 10, 1993, at her home in Asolo in northeast Italy; she was 100 years old.

Further Reading

Geneisse, Jane. *Passionate Nomad: The Life of Freya Stark*. New York: Modern Library, 2001.

Moorehead, Caroline. *Freya Stark*. New York: Viking, 1985.

Moorehead, Lucy, ed. *Letters of Freya Stark*. 8 vols. Salisbury, UK: Compton Russell, 1974–1982.

Stark, Freya. *The Freya Stark Story*. New York: Coward-McCann, 1953.

See also: Royal Geographical Society.

THOMAS, ELIZABETH MARSHALL (1931–)

1931: Born on September 13 in Boston
1950: Visits the Kalahari Desert in southwestern Africa with her family
1959: Publishes *The Harmless People*, a study of the Bushmen in Africa
1965: Publishes *The Warrior Herdsmen*, about the Dodoth people of Uganda
1993: *The Hidden Life of Dogs* becomes a best seller
2006: Publishes *The Old Way: A Story of the First People*, about the Bushmen

An American anthropologist and author best known for her books about dog and cat behavior, Elizabeth Marshall Thomas also explored remote areas of sub-Saharan Africa in researching her compelling studies of the Bushmen and Dodoth peoples.

She was born Elizabeth Marshall in Boston on September 13, 1931, to Laurence Marshall, a civil engineer and cofounder of the Raytheon Company (then called the American Appliance Company), and Lorna McLean, an English teacher and ballerina. She attended Abbot Academy, a girls' boarding school in Andover, Massachusetts. Following her graduation from the academy in 1949, Elizabeth attended Smith College in Northampton, Massachusetts.

Her father interrupted her schooling the following year to take the family on a trip to the Kalahari Desert in Botswana (at that time, the Bechuanaland Protectorate) in southwestern Africa. He was seeking adventure and a different kind of educational experience for himself and his family. Without formal academic training, the Thomases plunged into an anthropological study of the Bushmen. At the time, the Bushmen had little contact with the modern outside world and followed traditional lifeways, subsisting as hunters and gatherers.

From 1950 to 1955, Elizabeth Marshall made several journeys to Botswana to study the Bushmen, spending a full year with them in 1952. She also resumed her college studies, transferring from Smith College to Radcliffe College in Cambridge, Massachusetts. During her junior year, she wrote a short story about the Bushmen titled "The Hill People," which won a fiction contest held by *Mademoiselle* magazine. After getting her degree from Radcliffe in 1954, Marshall married Stephen Thomas; the couple would have two children.

Further research among the Bushmen resulted in Elizabeth Marshall Thomas's first book, *The Harmless People* (1959), an anthropological study of life in the tribe written in unusually vivid, nonscientific prose. The book found a wide audience. Thomas updated the work in the 1980s to consider the effect of modern influences, especially alcohol and a wage-labor system, on Bushman society.

Thomas journeyed again to Africa in 1960, this time to study the Dodoth people in Uganda. Unlike the Bushmen, the Dodoth were warriors who raised cattle. Based on that expedition and her studies of Dodoth life, Thomas wrote *The Warrior Herdsmen*, published in 1965.

According to a reviewer for *The New York Times*, the book contained "few ethnographic facts of the more conventional sort" but was "more like the personal journal of an exciting adventure." Nevertheless, the reviewer continued, it conveyed an "underlying anthropological understanding," showing that "the Dodoth are real people of the twentieth century caught up in the trials and tribulations of emergent Africa."

Thomas's first novel about indigenous cultures, *Reindeer Moon* (1987), tells the story of a teenage girl who lived in a hunter-gatherer tribe of Siberia about 20,000 years ago. *The Animal Wife* (1990) is a companion novel set in the same location and time period.

At the same time that she was conducting her anthropological studies and writing works of fiction and nonfiction based on them, Thomas also was pursuing a passion she had had since childhood: animals and animal behavior. Objects of her study included elephants at zoos in the United States and in the wilds of Namibia (in southwestern Africa). With scientist Katy Payne, she discovered that elephants communicate by using sounds too low for human beings to hear. Thomas also studied wolf packs on Baffin Island, off the northeastern coast of Canada, and she found that they exhibit an orderly social structure.

Thomas began making a rigorous study of a friend's husky, Misha, following the dog as it wandered about. Then, she studied Misha's interactions with her own dogs and the offspring of these dogs. From her investigation came the book *The Hidden Life of Dogs* (1993), which reached *The New York Times* best-seller list—and remained on it into 1994.

In this book, Thomas sought to answer the basic question, "What do dogs want?" Misha's primary mission, she concluded, was to establish dominance over other dogs. Her portrayal of the canine world in human terms—with references to "depression," "marriage," and the like—was vivid and appealing to readers but objectionable to some dog experts. Behavioral scientists criticized her for anthropomorphizing dogs and argued that her understanding of dog consciousness was actually an understanding of the human reaction to dog consciousness.

Thomas followed her best seller about dogs with a book about cats, *The Tribe of the Tiger: Cats and Their Culture* (1994). In this work, she discusses cats as house pets, as well as her own encounters with lions and tigers in Africa. Her subsequent works about animals have included *The Social Lives of Dogs: The Grace of Canine Company* (2000) and *The Hidden Life of Deer: Lessons from the Natural World* (2009). Despite the popular format of these books, Thomas tries to provide readers with behavioral insights based on rigorous study and scientific observations.

In *The Old Way: A Story of the First People* (2006), Thomas returns to the Ju/Wasi Bushmen of southwestern Africa. This book encompasses an autobiographical account of her travels, a family memoir, and updated observations and reflections on native customs.

Further Reading

Thomas, Elizabeth Marshall. *The Hidden Life of Dogs.* Boston: Houghton-Mifflin, 1996.

——. *The Old Way: A Story of the First People.* New York: Farrar, Straus and Giroux, 2006.

——. *Warrior Herdsmen.* New York: W.W. Norton, 1981.

V

VAN DER POST, LAURENS (1906–1996)

1906: Born on December 13 in Philippolis, South Africa

1926: Publishes a magazine critical of racial segregation in South Africa

1939: Joins the British Army in World War II

1943: Taken prisoner by Japanese troops in Indonesia

1952: Publishes *Venture to the Interior,* a best seller about his travels in Nyasaland (Malawi)

1955: Undertakes expedition into the Kalahari Desert in southwestern Africa to study the Bushmen

1977: Takes Prince Charles of England on safari in Kenya, Africa, and organizes the World Wilderness Congress to serve as an international environmental forum

1981: Knighted by Queen Elizabeth II

1996: Dies on December 16 in London

Afrikaner writer, journalist, World War II hero, explorer, and conservationist Laurens van der Post also was a political advisor to Great Britain, a friend and follower of Swiss psychologist Carl Jung, and an opponent of apartheid who introduced the Bushmen of the Kalahari Desert to the outside world in a series of popular books and television documentaries.

Van der Post was born on December 13, 1906, at Philippolis in the Orange River Colony (now the Orange Free State province of the Republic of South Africa). His father, of Dutch descent, was Christian Willem Hendrik van der Post, a prominent South African political leader and lawyer. His mother, of German descent, was Lammie van der Post. Laurens was the thirteenth of fifteen children.

Youth and Early Career

As a child, Laurens van der Post worked on his father's farm, enjoyed reading books, and attended Grey College in Bloemfontein from age eleven. In 1925, he became a cub reporter for the *Natal Advertiser* in Durban. The following year, he began publishing with two other writers a satirical magazine that advocated the integration of the white and black races in South Africa.

REMOVAL OF THE BUSHMEN

Although the Bushmen of southern Africa had been protected from encroachment since 1961, when the British colonial authority of Bechuanaland (today Botswana) created the Central Kalahari Game Reserve on their ancestral land, the government of Botswana began an aggressive relocation program in the mid-1990s .

The goals of the program, officials maintain, are to protect wildlife on the reserve and to integrate native Bushmen into the country's social and economic life. In fact, the government claims, it has become clear that the Bushmen are ready to give up their traditional role as hunters and gatherers to become farmers and herdsmen.

Opponents criticize the policy as one of forced relocation. Survival International, a group based in Great Britain that supports tribal communities in the fight to hold onto their lands, claims that the Botswana government seeks the removal of the Bushmen in order to mine for diamonds on the reserve. Moreover, Survival International charges, the Bushmen have been "tortured, beaten up or arrested for supposedly over-hunting or hunting without correct licenses." The government also has been accused of reducing the Bushmen's water supply by destroying a water pump on the reserve and draining natural bodies of freshwater.

In December 2006, a court in Botswana ruled that the government had indeed persecuted the Bushmen, who had been "forcibly and wrongly deprived of their possessions." By that time, however, few if any Bushmen remained on the reserve.

More than 1,000 Bushmen expressed the intention of returning to their homeland, even though the government was not compelled to restore services in the area. In April 2008, the United Nations Human Rights Council issued a criticism of the Botswana government for blocking the Bushmen's return.

Authorities shut down the magazine after three issues. Van der Post later said that he had grappled with two problems in his youth:

> One was that my people [the Dutch] had been conquered by the British just a few years before I was born. . . . Though I like the English without reservation, I had inherited this bitterness. The second problem was the fact that I loved the black peoples of Africa. . . . It was a great shock to me, when I was sent away . . . [to Grey College] to find that I was being educated into something which destroyed the sense of common humanity I had shared with the black people.

After several months at sea, marrying, and starting a family in England, Van der Post returned to South Africa in 1929 and worked as a journalist for the *Cape Times*, a newspaper in Cape Town. Again, he criticized racial segregation, writing in one article, "The future of civilization of South Africa is, I believe, neither black or white but brown."

Back in England in the early 1930s, Van der Post began socializing with the Bloomsbury Group, a collection of prominent intellectuals and writers that included John Maynard Keynes, E.M. Forster, Virginia Woolf, and Leonard Woolf. In 1934, the Woolfs published Van der Post's first novel, *In a Province*, about the damage being done to South Africa by its racial and ideological divisions.

By this time, Van der Post had taken to heavy drinking in the face of personal problems. He was especially torn between the loyalty he felt for his wife and family and the love he felt for an English actress with whom he was having an affair.

With the outbreak of World War II in 1939, Van der Post joined the British army and soon rose to the rank of captain with the Intelligence Corps in East Africa. In early 1942, he was transferred to the Dutch East Indies (now the Republic of Indonesia), where, it was felt, he could help the Allied war effort due to his ability to speak both English and Dutch. As a military commander, he succeeded in evacuating from Java Allied personnel who had been captured by the Japanese.

In April, however, Van der Post himself was taken prisoner. He spent the rest of the war at two prison camps in Japan, Sukabumi and Bandung, where he dedicated himself to lifting the morale of fellow prisoners. He later wrote three books about his wartime experiences: *A Bar of Shadow* (1954), *The Seed and the Sower* (1963), and *The Night of the New Moon* (1970).

Studies of African Tribes

With the end of World War II, Van der Post remained in Indonesia, where he worked for two years to help reconcile differences between Indonesian nationalists and the Dutch colonial authority. The effort failed, and Van der Post left as British troops withdrew. He returned to England in 1947, by which time, a revolution was under way in Indonesia.

Between 1948 and 1965, Van der Post tended his farm in South Africa while writing books and engaging in several explorations of southern Africa. In 1951, he published a best-selling work called *Venture to the Interior*, about his travels in Nyasaland (then a British protectorate, today the country of Malawi).

This work reflected the influence of Jung, who posited two aspects of the human unconscious: the personal unconscious (the repressed thoughts and feelings accumulated during an individual's life) and the collective unconscious (the inherited memories, symbols, experiences, and feelings common to people in all cultures). Accordingly, Van der Post maintained in *Venture to the Interior*, everyone's personality is divided between primitive and civilized components; the former is instinctive and subjective, the latter objective and rational. His own journey in Africa, he observed, was more than geographical; it was a journey into the "inward, nebulous, subconscious, disquieting, where Africa becomes a spiritual continent."

In the early 1950s, Van der Post undertook an extensive study of the Bushmen of the Kalahari Desert in the Bechuanaland Protectorate (now Botswana), in southwestern Africa. In 1954, he lectured at the Jung Institute in Zurich, Switzerland.

In 1955, he published the book *The Dark Eye in Africa*, in which he asserted that the white oppression of blacks comes from a desire to suppress what he called the "instinctive man" (as opposed to the rational man), which he said resides in the "dark brother." That same year, he returned to Bechuanaland for an expedition sponsored by the British Broadcasting Company (BBC), which yielded a six-part television documentary in 1956 and led to his writing the book *The Lost World of the Kalahari* (1958).

By this time, Van der Post was considered a leading expert on the Bushmen. He would write several more books about them, including two novels set near the Kalahari. His writing emphasized the outside pressures being faced by the Bushmen; the response to his observations prompted the British colonial government in 1961 to establish the Central Kalahari Game Reserve, where the Bushmen were to live undisturbed. By the 1990s, however, the Bushmen were being forced out of their homeland by the government, and Van der Post joined the fight against the relocation program. Ironically, the Bushmen were being removed in part as a result of the expanding cattle ranching he had promoted back in the 1950s.

Van der Post also cultivated relationships in the high echelons of the British government, advising officials on issues of conservation and South African policy. In 1977, he took Prince Charles of England on an African safari in Kenya, and, with the South African conservationist Ian Player, he organized the World Wilderness Congress in Johannesburg, South Africa, to serve as an international environmental forum. Two years later, he advised Britain's Prime Minister Margaret Thatcher on South African issues. In 1981, he was knighted by Queen Elizabeth II.

Van der Post died in London on December 16, 1996, leaving extensive research and writings about the Bushmen and environmental issues. He had published a total of twenty-six books, many of them anthropological studies based on personal experiences and adventures. Aside from *The Lost World of the Kalahari*, his major works on the Bushmen include *The Heart of the Hunter* (1961) and *Testament to the Bushmen* (1984).

In the years since his death, Van der Post has been accused of fabricating certain information in his memoirs and other books. For example, some have challenged his claims to have explored territory previously unseen by white men. In his writings, however, Van der Post expressed the noblest sentiments about Africa and life in general. He once observed,

I've always said that there are two great sources of corruption. Corruption by power, and corruption by suffering. We have got to hold out against powerful men and societies who dominate vulnerable and less-powerful people—and other forms of life. And we must take an equally strong stand against becoming bitter, and vengeful, and cynical, and even anarchical because of what others have inflicted on us. It is the hallmark of a truly integrated person that he will not allow his suffering to turn him sour. The history of Africa has never been a pleasant one, but I believe that there is a place in Africa for anybody to live in dignity and love.

Further Reading

Jones, J.D.F. *Storyteller: The Many Lives of Laurens van der Post*. London: John Murray, 2001.

Van der Post, Laurens. *About Blady: A Pattern Out of Time*. New York: William Morrow, 1991.

———. *Venture to the Interior*. New York: William Morrow, 1951.

WALLACE, ALFRED RUSSEL (1823–1913)

1823: Born on January 8 in Usk, Wales

1848: With naturalist Henry Walter Bates, undertakes an expedition to the Amazon River basin in South America

1853: Publishes *A Narrative of Travels on the Amazon and Rio Negro*

1858: Writes an essay in which he formulates the theory of evolution based on natural selection

1881: Becomes president of the Land Nationalisation Society, which he founded to promote equal access to English real property (land and that which is attached to it, such as buildings)

1890: Named by the Royal Society of London for the Improvement of Natural Knowledge as the first recipient of the Darwin Medal, issued for "his independent origination of the theory of evolution through natural selection"

1913: Dies November 17 in Broadstone, England

A British naturalist and geographer who wrote on issues as disparate as politics, spiritualism, and the environment, Alfred Russel Wallace was the first to formulate the theory of evolution by natural selection, even before Charles Darwin published his own conclusions on the subject.

Born on January 8, 1823, in Usk, Monmouthshire, Wales, to Thomas Vere Wallace and Mary Anne Greenell, Alfred was the eighth of nine children. He attended grammar school at Hertford in England. At age fourteen, he left school for London, where he learned surveying from his brother William.

Despite his limited formal education, Alfred was an avid reader and enjoyed studying maps. He pursued an education on his own, reading and attending lectures, and worked briefly as a watchmaker. In 1839, William took him to Hertfordshire to work as his assistant in the surveying business. Alfred's curiosity also extended to astronomy, agriculture, and botany, all of which he studied zealously.

During the course of his surveying, Alfred Russel Wallace witnessed firsthand the plight of farmers in the wake of the passage of enclosure laws, which restricted their access to land. Beginning in 1750, such laws allowed the closing off by wealthy landowners of fields and common lands where farmers traditionally had grazed their animals. An enclosure law passed in 1845 strengthened the practice, which Wallace addressed in an essay titled "The South-Wales Farmer." (The essay was published years later.)

Meanwhile, in 1843, Wallace had become a master in the Collegiate School at Leicester. There, he began experimenting with phrenology, hypnotism, and telepathy, interests he would pursue later in life, much to the chagrin of those who considered them foolish eccentricities. While at Leicester, Wallace met the naturalist Henry Walter Bates, who introduced him to the study of entomology.

South America and the Malay Archipelago

Wallace returned to surveying in 1846. Two years later, he convinced Bates to accompany him on an expedition to the Amazon basin in South America to collect insects, animals, and plants. For reasons unknown, the two naturalists parted company in 1850. Wallace remained in South America until 1852; Bates stayed for eleven years.

While in South America, Wallace surveyed a large part of the Amazon River. He determined that numerous details on existing maps were incorrect, including the locations of islands, the existence of parallel channels, and the width of the river at various locations. He studied the habitats and languages of the various peoples he encountered; collected a wide variety of insect and bird specimens; and compiled detailed notes on his observations and discoveries.

In his published account of the expedition, *A Narrative of Travels on the Amazon and Rio Negro* (1853), Wallace reported at least one important scientific observation: the Amazon River limited the range of animal species in the immediate vicinity. For example, on one side of the river, he found a butterfly with sky-blue wings; on the other side, he found a similar species with indigo-colored wings. Neither species commingled with the other, which later prompted Wallace to consider the relationship between geographic influence and evolution.

The expedition to South America was dogged by tragedy. In 1851, Wallace's younger brother, Herbert, who had joined him on the trip, died of yellow fever. Then, on the return trip to England, the ship on which Wallace was traveling, the *Helen*, caught fire at sea, forcing him, the other passengers, and the crew into open boats. All of the notes and specimens he had not previously sent to England were lost.

On his next expedition, from 1854 to 1862, Wallace journeyed to the Malay Archipelago, where he traveled among the islands, collected biological specimens, and wrote scientific articles. He discovered that the archipelago is divided by a strait (today called "Wallace's Line") and that, as in the Amazon basin, geography shaped life-forms. West of the strait, he found the flora and fauna to be Asian in its physical attributes; east of the strait, he discovered the native species to be Australian.

Theory of Evolution Through Natural Selection

In 1853, after returning from his trip to South America, Wallace wrote a paper, "On the Habits of Butterflies of the Amazon Valley," that clearly anticipated the theory of evolution through natural selection. For instance, he wrote of the *Heliconia* species,

> [They] are exceedingly productive in closely allied species and varieties of the most interesting description and often have a very limited range. . . . [As] there is every reason to believe that the banks of the lower Amazon are among the most recently formed in South America, we may fairly regard those insects, which are peculiar to that district, as among the youngest of species, *the latest in the long series of modifications which the forms of animal life have undergone.* [Italics added.]

After expeditions in the Amazon basin and Malay Archipelago to collect animal and plant specimens, Alfred Russel Wallace began formulating the theory of evolution by natural selection—independently from Charles Darwin—in the mid-1850s. *(Granger Collection, New York)*

Wallace later claimed that the theory of evolution through natural selection came to him while he was suffering a severe case of malaria in 1858. Gripped by fever in the Molucca Islands, he began thinking about the theory of philosopher Thomas Malthus that war, famine, disease, and infertility are natural checks on the growth of human population. Likewise, Wallace thought, such elements also must control the growth of animal populations.

Based on this thinking, Wallace wrote an essay—titled "On the Tendency of Varieties to Depart Indefinitely from the Original Type: Instability of Varieties Supposed to Prove the Permanent Distinctness of Species." In this work, he maintained that the life of wild animals is a struggle for existence based on self-preservation and the survival of infant offspring.

In June 1858, Wallace sent the paper to his friend and fellow naturalist Charles Darwin, to ask his opinion and in case it might help Darwin in his own work on the origin of species. Darwin was stunned, as Wallace's essay contained the very ideas he had formulated on the subject. In short, the two men had reached the same conclusion independently.

Facing a dilemma, Darwin decided to submit extracts of his own previous writings, along with Wallace's paper, to the prestigious Linnean Society of London. The writings of both men were read at a meeting of the society on July 1 and published as a single paper in the society's journal under the names of Darwin and Wallace.

ALFRED RUSSEL WALLACE AND
THE GEOGRAPHICAL DISTRIBUTION OF ANIMALS

In several books and essays, Alfred Russel Wallace emphasized a key aspect of his theory of evolution: Changes in species are directly related to changes in geography, climate, and vegetation. In *The Geographical Distribution of Animals* (1876), he wrote:

Naturalists have now arrived at the conclusion, that by some slow process of development or transmutation, all animals have been produced from those which preceded them; and the old notion that every species was specially created as they now exist, at a particular time and in a particular spot, is abandoned as opposed to many striking facts, and unsupported by any evidence. This modification of animal forms took place very slowly, so that the historical period of three or four thousand years has hardly produced any perceptible change in a single species. Even the time since the last glacial epoch, which on the very lowest estimate must be from 50,000 to 100,000 years, has only served to modify a few of the higher animals into very slightly different species. The changes of the forms of animals appear to have accompanied, and perhaps to have depended on, changes of physical geography, of climate, or of vegetation; since it is evident that an animal which is well adapted to one condition of things will require to be slightly changed in constitution or habits, and therefore generally in form, structure, or colour, in order to be equally well adapted to a changed condition of surrounding circumstances. Animals multiply so rapidly, that we may consider them as continually trying to extend their range; and thus any new land raised above the sea by geological causes becomes immediately peopled by a crowd of competing inhabitants, the strongest and best adapted of which alone succeed in maintaining their position.

History would give credit largely to Darwin, in part because his landmark book on the subject, *On the Origin of Species* (1859), articulated the theory in detail and triggered widespread hostile reaction. Wallace would become one of the forgotten men of modern biological science despite the essential similarity—and originality—of his theory.

Wallace returned to England from Southeast Asia in 1862, by which time he had gained prominence as a natural scientist and geographer. Four years later, he married Annie Mitten, the daughter of a botanist, with whom he would have three children.

In 1869, he published a well-received account of his experience in Southeast Asia, *The Malay Archipelago: The Land of the Orang-Utan and the Bird of Paradise*, which he followed in 1870 with *Contributions to the Theory of Natural Selection*. His *Geographical Distribution of Animals* (1876), which was published in two volumes, and *Island Life* (1880) placed the geographic dispersal of living and extinct animals in an evolutionary context.

Over the years, Wallace moved frequently in England, living in London, in Grays in Essex, and in Parkstone and Broadstone, both in Dorset. He earned some money from his books and by selling specimens he had collected during his expeditions to museums, but he never held a salaried position, and he invested his money carelessly. As a consequence, he sank into poverty. In 1881, he was rescued by a small pension that was granted to him by the British government at the behest of two friends, Darwin and naturalist Thomas Huxley.

Also in 1881, Wallace was elected president of the new Land Nationalisation Society, which enabled him to address some of the social and economic issues facing England, including trade policy and land reform. Returning to the plight of farmers, which he had been exposed to as a young surveyor, Wallace advocated the view that the government should help those disposed of land to rise out of poverty by buying arable acreage and renting it to small farmers. In 1886, he made his last trip outside England, a ten-month lecture tour of the United States.

Wallace spent his later years immersed in the spiritualist world of mediums, criticizing the many scientists and others who dismissed such interests as quackery. He asked,

> Now what do our leaders of public opinion say when a scientific man of proved ability again observes a large portion of the more extraordinary phenomena, in his own house, under test conditions, and affirms their objective reality; and this not after a hasty examination, but after four years of research?

In 1890, Wallace was named the first recipient of the biennial Darwin Medal, awarded for important work in Darwinian science by the Royal Society of London for the Improvement of Natural Knowledge. In 1892, he received the Linnean Society's Gold Medal and the Royal Geographical Society's Founder's Medal. During his lifetime, he published a total of twenty-one books, in addition to numerous articles and essays.

Alfred Russel Wallace died on November 17, 1913, in Broadstone, southwest England, where he was buried. Two years later, a commemorative marble medallion in his honor was unveiled in London's Westminster Abbey.

The first scientific paper on the theory of evolution by natural selection, "On the Tendency of the Species to Form Varieties," coauthored by Charles Darwin and Alfred Russel Wallace, was published on August 20, 1858. (*Granger Collection, New York*)

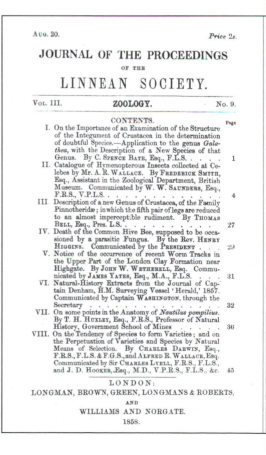

AUG. 20.   Price 2s.

JOURNAL OF THE PROCEEDINGS
OF THE
LINNEAN SOCIETY.

VOL. III.   ZOOLOGY.   No. 9.

CONTENTS.   Page

I. On the Importance of an Examination of the Structure of the Integument of Crustacea in the determination of doubtful Species.—Application to the genus *Galathea*, with the Description of a New Species of that Genus. By C. SPENCE BATE, Esq., F.L.S.   1

II. Catalogue of Hymenopterous Insects collected at Celebes by Mr. A. R. WALLACE. By FREDERICK SMITH, Esq., Assistant in the Zoological Department, British Museum. Communicated by W. W. SAUNDERS, Esq., F.R.S., V.P.L.S.   4

III. Description of a new Genus of Crustacea, of the Family Pinnotheridæ; in which the fifth pair of legs are reduced to an almost imperceptible rudiment. By THOMAS BELL, Esq., Pres. L.S.   27

IV. Death of the Common Hive Bee, supposed to be occasioned by a parasitic Fungus. By the Rev. HENRY HIGGINS. Communicated by the PRESIDENT   29

V. Notice of the occurrence of recent Worm Tracks in the Upper Part of the London Clay Formation near Highgate. By JOHN W. WETHERELL, Esq. Communicated by JAMES YATES, Esq., M.A., F.L.S.   31

VI. Natural-History Extracts from the Journal of Captain Denham, H.M. Surveying Vessel 'Herald,' 1857. Communicated by Captain WASHINGTON, through the Secretary   32

VII. On some points in the Anatomy of *Nautilus pompilius*. By T. H. HUXLEY, Esq., F.R.S., Professor of Natural History, Government School of Mines   36

VIII. On the Tendency of Species to form Varieties; and on the Perpetuation of Varieties and Species by Natural Means of Selection. By CHARLES DARWIN, Esq., F.R.S., F.L.S. & F.G.S., and ALFRED R. WALLACE, Esq. Communicated by Sir CHARLES LYELL, F.R.S., F.L.S., and J. D. HOOKER, Esq., M.D., V.P.R.S., F.L.S., &c.   45

LONDON:
LONGMAN, BROWN, GREEN, LONGMANS & ROBERTS,
AND
WILLIAMS AND NORGATE.
1858.

Further Reading

Camerini, Jane R., ed. *The Alfred Russel Wallace Reader: A Selection of Writings from the Field.* Baltimore: Johns Hopkins University Press, 2002.

Fichman, Martin. *An Elusive Victorian: The Evolution of Alfred Russel Wallace.* Chicago: University of Chicago Press, 2004.

Raby, Peter. *Alfred Russel Wallace: A Life.* Princeton, NJ: Princeton University Press, 2001.

Smith, Charles H., and George Beccaloni, eds. *Natural Selection and Beyond: The Intellectual Legacy of Alfred Russel Wallace.* New York: Oxford University Press, 2008.

See also:
Bates, Henry Walter; Darwin, Charles.

WASHBURN, BRADFORD (1910–2007)

1910: Born on June 7 in Cambridge, Massachusetts

1921: Climbs the highest peak in the northeastern United States, Mount Washington in New Hampshire

1933: Receives an undergraduate degree from Harvard University

1937: Explores Mount Lucania in Canada, the highest unexplored peak in North America

1939: Becomes director of the New England Museum of Natural History

1951: Makes the first-ever ascent of Mount McKinley, in Alaska, by way of the mountain's West Buttress

1974: Compiles a map of the inner part of the Grand Canyon, in Arizona

1978: Completes a map of the center section of the Grand Canyon

2007: Dies on January 10 in Lexington, Massachusetts

An American mountaineer, photographer, and cartographer, Bradford Washburn also was the director of the New England Museum of Natural History; the founder and longtime director of the Boston Museum of Science; and the leader of a project in the 1970s to map the Grand Canyon in Arizona.

Bradford Washburn was born on June 7, 1910, to Henry and Edith Washburn in Cambridge, Massachusetts. His father was dean of the Episcopal Theological School, and his mother was an amateur photographer. He later said that his mother was the first to put a camera in his hands, and added: "It is probably fair to say that my mother contributed to my sense of adventure and that my father contributed to my appreciation for detail and accuracy."

From boyhood, Washburn climbed mountains. At age eleven, he scaled Mount Washington in New Hampshire, which at 6,288 feet (1,917 meters) is the tallest peak in the northeastern United States. He later recalled how attracted he had become to "hiking on mountain trails and sharing the thrills of discovery with close friends." By age sixteen, Washburn had ascended the Matterhorn in Switzerland and Mont Blanc in the French Alps. The following year, he published his first book, *Among the Alps with Bradford* (1927).

Washburn received his undergraduate degree in 1933 from Harvard University, where he was a member of the mountaineering club. Its members climbed remote peaks in Alaska and Canada. He returned to Harvard years later, earning a master's degree in geology and geography in 1960.

Satisfying his appetite for adventure in another way—not unrelated to his interests in mountain climbing and photography—Washburn trained to become a pilot and flew solo for the first time at Boeing Field in Seattle in 1934. One year later, he earned his private flying license. By this time, to help plan expeditions, Washburn had taken to shooting aerial photographs of mountains that he was interested in climbing—and for their sheer beauty.

Washburn's most momentous and hair-raising early climb took place in 1937, when he attempted to climb Mount Lucania (17,146 feet, or 5,226 meters) in Canada's Yukon Territory. The third highest peak in Canada, Mount Lucania also was the highest unclimbed mountain in North America at the time. Two years earlier, members of a climbing party had quit their ascent to the summit and declared it unlikely that anyone would ever reach the peak because of the formidable terrain.

When the National Geographic Society sponsored Washburn, then twenty-six, for his attempt, the society's president at the time, Gilbert Grosvenor, said to him,

Bradford Washburn, one of America's leading mountaineers of the 1930s and 1940s, was also a pioneering figure in mountain photography and cartography. He later founded and directed the Boston Museum of Science. *(Robert Lackenbach/Time & Life Pictures/Getty Images)*

Yours is the first expedition we have entrusted to a man as young as yourself, and your remarkable record . . . might very naturally lead you to be a little over-confident and take risks . . . that an older man might not venture to take.

Washburn was accompanied on the climb by another young American mountaineer, Robert Bates, who also was twenty-six at the time, and he was flown to the site by Bob Reeve, a notable Alaskan bush pilot. Washburn instructed Reeve to land them on Walsh Glacier, just south of the mountain. Unknown to the team, however, an unusual warm spell had turned the top of the glacier to mush, and the plane was entrapped immediately upon landing. Several days passed before the ice hardened and Reeve could depart.

Washburn and Bates spent three weeks hauling supplies to their base camp. Finally, on July 9, they made their final assault from the base of the summit pyramid, wading through waist-high snow. "We fought on as I have never fought in my life," Washburn wrote.

The two climbers reached the summit later that afternoon. "Our yell of triumph could have been heard in Timbuctoo!" Washburn recorded in his journal.

WASHBURN'S CAMERA IN SPACE

As a mountain climber and photographer, Bradford Washburn took his cameras to astonishing heights to produce firsthand images for the armchair explorer. Yet he never imagined that one of his cameras would one day be used to take pictures in outer space. Such was the case in May 2009, two years after Washburn's death, when U.S. space shuttle astronaut John Grunsfeld used the camera during a *Columbia* mission to repair the Hubble Telescope.

Grunsfeld, himself a climber who later scaled Mount McKinley, had been a friend of Washburn's. The astronaut took with him on the *Columbia* a Zeiss Maximar B 4x5 camera, made in 1929, that Washburn had used as a "pocket" camera. In announcing his intention before the mission, Grunsfeld said:

Brad lived just a tremendous life. He is one of my heroes and during the 1920s did just a fantastic number of climbs all over. As part of that he started pioneering the use of cameras from airplanes. . . . I definitely plan to take some pictures of Hubble with the Zeiss camera but also of mountains, which I know Brad would appreciate.

Grunsfeld added that he would use the camera only inside the shuttle, because conditions in outer space might ruin the antique instrument. The camera, which belongs to the American Alpine Club, remains on display at the Bradford Washburn American Mountaineering Museum in Golden, Colorado.

On their return, Washburn and Bates trudged 150 miles (240 kilometers) from base camp through the surrounding wilderness to reach the small town of Burwash Landing. From there, a bush pilot took them to Valdez, Alaska.

Washburn's wife, Barbara, accompanied him on a number of expeditions, including on his fourth climb to the summit of Canada's Mount McKinley, in 1947. This made her the first woman to scale that mountain, which at 20,320 feet (6,194 meters) is the highest in North America.

In 1951, Washburn made the first-ever ascent of Mount McKinley by way of the mountain's West Buttress, thus opening a new route that is used by most climbers today. He later recalled,

> McKinley is the biggest and most beautiful peak of the really big mountains of the world that was really accessible to me. When we first went in there, it was unmapped and virtually unexplored.

In Alaska, Washburn took his photography to a new level, recording images of the wilderness from the ground and the air. As his prints revealed, he was interested in natural beauty as much or more than he was interested in scientific observation. His black-and-white photos later were shown at New York's Museum of Modern Art and in London's Victoria and Albert Museum.

As a cartographer, Washburn used aerial photography to survey the landscape and make measurements of its features. In 1960, for example, he used this technique to map Mount McKinley.

In 1974, with the help of staff members from *National Geographic* magazine, Washburn used helicopters to scale peaks in and around the Grand Canyon in Arizona and then measured contours and distances with lasers and reflecting prisms. The result was a detailed map of the Inner Canyon, followed four years later by a map of the central part of the canyon.

Perhaps his greatest cartographic achievement was a topographic map of the highest mountain in the world, Mount Everest, which is in the Himalayan Mountains on the border of Nepal and Tibet. The map was published in *National Geographic* in 1998 and distributed to more than 10 million readers.

In addition, Washburn was named director of the New England Museum of Natural History, in Boston, in 1939; he spent the next forty years working to improve it. Under his leadership, the museum was rebuilt and reestablished as the Boston Museum of Science on a site spanning the Charles River between Boston and Cambridge. Washburn retired as director of the museum in 1980, but he held the title of honorary director for the rest of his life. According to one observer, Washburn made the museum a "leading center for science" by bringing its exhibits more in line with recent research and theory.

Washburn wrote several more books, including *Mount McKinley: The Conquest of Denali* (1991). His writings and photographs also appeared in a number of magazines, including *Life* and *National Geographic*. He died from heart failure at his home in Lexington, Massachusetts, on January 10, 2007, at age 96.

Further Reading

Sfraga, Michael. *Bradford Washburn: A Life of Exploration.* Corvallis: Oregon State University Press, 2004.

Washburn, Bradford. *Mount McKinley's West Buttress: The First Ascent, Brad Washburn's Logbook, 1951.* Williston, VT: Top of the World, 2003.

Washburn, Bradford, and Lew Freedman. *Bradford Washburn: An Extraordinary Life.* Portland, OR: West Winds, 2005.

See also: National Geographic Society.

WATERTON, CHARLES (1782–1865)

1782: Born on June 3 in Wakefield, England

1804: Journeys to British Guiana to manage family estates

1812: Begins exploring the interior of British Guiana and collects the poisonous plant curare

1825: Publishes *Wanderings in South America,* about his four expeditions the continent

1865: Dies on May 27 in Wakefield

Eccentric English naturalist and explorer Charles Waterton traveled through British Guiana (now Guyana) in South America to collect the plant from which the poisonous substance curare—used by natives on arrowheads and later in Europe as a muscle relaxant—is derived.

Charles Waterton was born on June 3, 1782, at Walton Hall, his family's estate in Wakefield, West Yorkshire, England. His family was wealthy, aristocratic, and devoutly Roman Catholic. Charles embraced the faith as well and later would develop close ties with Catholic leaders at the Vatican in Italy. He was educated at a small Catholic school near the town of Durham in northern England and then Stonyhurst, a Jesuit school in Lancashire.

After a brief time in Spain, Waterton journeyed to British Guiana in 1804 to take care of an uncle's estates near Georgetown. In 1812, he began exploring the countryside. During his explorations, he collected a large vine found in the rainforest that Indians crushed and cooked to create a mixture called "curare." (The name comes from an Indian word meaning "poison.") The natives used it on the tips of arrows and darts to hunt wild game or, in some cases, in warfare to kill tribal enemies. Curare paralyzes the muscles and, in fatal doses, causes respiratory paralysis. Today, the plant is used in medicine to treat multiple sclerosis and cerebral palsy. Waterton, however, wanted to export curare to Europe to treat rabies. Because curare could relax the muscles, he thought it might be able to ease the convulsions attendant with rabies. Traveling on foot, Waterton explored along the Demerara and Essequibo rivers in British Guiana all the way to northern Brazil. On the way, he collected more flora as well as fauna, recorded details about the terrain, and observed indigenous peoples.

After returning briefly to England, he undertook a second expedition to British Guiana in 1816. He returned to England again and launched a third journey to British Guiana in 1820. And in 1824, after visiting the United States and several West Indian islands, he began a fourth exploration of British Guiana.

In his book *Wanderings in South America* (1825), Waterton wrote about the natives and their poisonous substance:

> Thus the savage of Guiana, independent of the common weapons of destruction, has it in his power to prepare a poison by which he can generally insure to himself a supply of animal food; and the food so destroyed imbibes no deleterious qualities. Nature has been bountiful to him. She has not only ordered poisonous herbs and roots to grow in the unbounded forests through which he strays, but has also furnished an excellent reed for his arrows, and another, still more singular, for his blow-pipe; and planted trees of an amazing hard, tough, and elastic texture, out of which he forms his bows. And in order that nothing might be wanting, she has superadded a tree which yields him a fine wax, and disseminated up and down a plant not unlike that of the pine-apple, which affords him capital bow-strings.

The book proved popular with young readers in Great Britain—among them Alfred Russel Wallace and Charles Darwin—who felt called to their own naturalist adventures. Especially enthralling to schoolchildren were Waterton's descriptions of experiences such as riding a crocodile:

> [I] jumped on his back. I immediately seized his fore-legs, and, by main force, twisted them on his back; thus they served me for a bridle. . . . He began to plunge furiously, and lashed the sand with his long and powerful tail. I was out of the reach of the strokes of it by being near his head. He continued to plunge and strike and made my seat very uncomfortable. It must have been a fine sight for an unoccupied spectator.

A best seller from the start, *Wanderings* has never been out of print since the original edition. Waterton's other notable work is *Essays on Natural*

History, Especially Concerning Ornithology, which first appeared in 1844 and includes an autobiography of the author.

As a taxidermist, Waterton preserved his specimens with a special solution of mercury chloride rather than by stuffing the carcasses. He amassed a large collection of preserved species, especially birds, which is now on display at the Wakefield Museum.

In the late 1820s, after completing his four journeys to British Guiana, Waterton retired to Walton Hall. He encircled the property with a 3-mile (5-kilometer) wall to contain wild birds and animals. For the next forty years, he managed the estate as a nature reserve, making him one of Europe's earliest conservationists. Waterton also was an early and outspoken critic of the pollution caused by England's industrial revolution.

Married briefly—his wife died in childbirth within a year of their 1829 wedding—Waterton was known to live a monkish existence, sleeping on bare boards with a block of wood as a pillow. He spent the rest of his life at Walton Hall, rising each day at three o'clock in the morning and reading a chapter of Miguel de Cervantes's *Don Quixote* (1605–1615).

Waterton died on May 27, 1865, from injuries sustained falling from a bridge on the grounds. He was buried near the spot where the accident occurred.

Further Reading

Aldington, Richard. *The Strange Life of Charles Waterton, 1782–1865*. London: Evans Brothers, 1949.

Edginton, Brian. *Charles Waterton: A Biography*. Cambridge, UK: Lutterworth, 1996.

Phelps, Gilbert. *Squire Waterton*. Wakefield, UK: EP, 1976.

WATKINS, GINO (1907–1932)

1907: Born on January 29 in London
1925: Enters Trinity College, Cambridge
1927: Explores and surveys Edgeoya (Edge Island) in the Arctic
1928–1929: Explores the upper Hamilton and Unknown rivers in northeastern Canada
1930–1931: Leads the British Arctic Air Route Expedition to Greenland and maps 280 miles (450 kilometers) of the coastline
1932: Returns to Greenland on an expedition sponsored by Pan American Airways to find a location for a refueling base
1932: Dies on August 20 while exploring Greenland

British Arctic explorer Gino Watkins led expeditions to investigate and map areas of Labrador, in far northeastern Canada, and Greenland. His last journey to Greenland resulted in his death at the age of only twenty-five.

He was born Henry George Watkins on January 29, 1907, in London. His father, who had the same name, worked for the government as a king's messenger, carrying important documents on diplomatic missions. At age twelve, "Gin" (the nickname he commonly used) sought entry into the Royal Navy training program to become an officer, but he failed the entrance exam. At sixteen, he entered Lancing College in Sussex, where he took up swimming, cross-country running, and rifle shooting. His interest in mountain climbing and exploration began during family trips to the French Alps and the Austrian Tirol, which he traversed with his father and guides.

In 1925, Gino Watkins entered Trinity College at the University of Cambridge, where his interest in Arctic exploration was piqued by a series of lectures on the polar regions by Scottish explorer James Wordie. During his Easter vacation in 1926, Watkins worked as a deckhand on a North Sea trawler and then was offered a place on an expedition to Greenland planned for the summer of 1927.

When the Greenland trip was canceled, Watkins approached the Royal Geographical Society proposing an expedition to survey and traverse uninhabited Edgeoya (Edge Island), located in the Arctic Ocean near Spitsbergen, between Greenland and the northwestern coast of Norway. The island was largely unexplored and had never been crossed, and the society agreed to fund the expedition.

Accompanying twenty-year-old Watkins on the expedition were eight scientists, including a biologist, a physicist, and a botanist, as well as a surveyor. The team sailed for the island on a Norwegian sealing ship, the *Heimen*, and arrived at Deevie Bay at Edgeoya on July 30, 1927. Over the next month, despite the challenge of gale-force winds and thick fog, the explorers were able to map much of the island and gather botanical specimens.

Watkins knew little about surveying, but as the leader of the mission, he kept the effort organized and disciplined. He recounted the journey in an article published by the Royal Geographical Society in August 1928. He also presented scientific data to a meeting of the fellows of the society and was elected to that body despite his young age.

Watkins's efforts on Edge Island led the Royal Geographical Society to provide him with funds for another expedition, this time to the interior of Labrador. The goal was to spend nine months mapping the headwaters of the Unknown River, the land adjacent to the Hamilton River (now called the Churchill River), and the southern boundary of Labrador. The exploration would require extensive travel along the region's waterways both in the summer, when currents flowed rapidly, and in the winter, when ice covered the frozen terrain. Watkins recruited two men, Lionel Leslie and James Maurice Scott, to accompany him, and he also had the help of a guide and experienced trapper, Robert Michelin.

The expedition began in late July 1928, when the men set out north up the Kenamu River in eastern Labrador. Heavy rains were followed by swarms of mosquitoes, from which they tried to protect themselves by smearing a mixture of butter and tar on their skin. The measure was largely unsuccessful. The men eventually made their way to the lower reaches of the Hamilton River and continued north to the town of North West River.

Watkins, Michelin, and Scott set out with dogsleds to Grand Lake and the Naskaupi River. (Leslie had left the expedition, as planned.) A 23-mile (37-kilometer) trek to Lake Nipishish took a week to complete. With rations running low, the team arrived back at North West River and the safety of shelter in late January 1929.

Watkins then pursued another objective, to survey the Falls District of the Unknown River. The expedition proceeded without major problems, at least until March 1829, when the team members reached the junction of the Hamilton and Unknown rivers, where the wooded gorge proved difficult to traverse. Despite the challenging terrain, Watkins and his colleagues pushed onward to the source of the Unknown River at Lake Ossokmanuan.

Because Lake Ossokmanuan also fed the Hamilton River, at least in part, the explorers had discovered a previously unknown geographic fact: the Hamilton and Unknown rivers make up an interconnected system. Time prevented Watkins and his colleagues from mapping the entire southern border of Labrador, but they did complete a valuable survey of previously uncharted regions.

After returning to England in spring 1929, Watkins determined to return to Greenland as part of the effort to survey an Arctic air route. For commercial air travel between Great Britain and North America to be viable, refueling stations would be needed in Iceland, in Greenland, on Baffin Island, and at Hudson Bay. (Airplanes at the time had far more limited flying ranges than they do today.) Such places would have to be more thoroughly surveyed before air bases could be built.

Raising money proved difficult because the Great Depression had begun, and Watkins spent a year organizing and funding the expedition. At the same time, he trained for his pilot's license on small aircraft, which he hoped to employ on the mission.

In July 1930, Watkins and his team of fourteen men set out on the British Arctic Air Route Expedition to Greenland. Again, his party consisted of several surveyors and scientists of different kinds, including a meteorologist, an ornithologist, and a geologist. Crisscrossing Greenland in seven separate forays, Watkins and his team employed motorboats and a seaplane to map 280 miles (450 kilometers) of coastline and monitor weather conditions.

Taking meteorological readings at Greenland's ice cap was an especially harrowing adventure, which nearly cost the life of a team member who became stranded at the station there under an avalanche of snow. The expedition also engaged in a 600-mile (960-kilometer) journey around the southern coast of Greenland by Watkins and two other men in an open boat. Upon returning to London, Watkins accepted a Founder's Medal from the Royal Geographical Society in recognition of his expedition.

In July 1932, Watkins set out on another journey to Greenland, this time to Tugtilik on the southeastern coast, to make weather observations. Pan American Airways sponsored the journey as part of the effort to identify viable locations for refueling stations. On August 20, Watkins, who was in charge of procuring food for the group, went seal hunting by kayak—a method he had perfected on the previous expedition. Colleagues warned him not to go hunting alone and to stay clear of a glacier at Lake Fjord from which ice had been falling. Watkins dismissed their concerns.

Days later, Watkin's empty kayak and a pair of his pants were found at Lake Fjord. His body was never located. The details of what happened at the fjord will never be known, but it is believed that Watkins may have left the kayak to make repairs and, while perched on an ice floe, was swept into the frigid water by ice crashing down from the glacier. The kayak in which he took his last journey is today on display at the Royal Geographical Society in London. It serves as a reminder of his accomplishment in mapping Arctic regions, his commitment to adventure, and, in the end, the recklessness that led to his death.

Further Reading

Lindsay, Martin. *Those Greenland Days: The British Arctic Air Route Expedition, 1930–1931*. London: W. Blackwood, 1932.

Ridgway, John. *Gino Watkins*. London: Oxford University Press, 1974.

Scott, James M. *The Land That God Gave Cain: An Account of H.G. Watkins's Expedition to Labrador 1928–1929*. London: Chatto and Windus, 1933.

WILKES EXPEDITION

1798: Charles Wilkes is born in New York City on April 3
1836: Congress approves the United States Exploring Expedition, an around-the-world scientific and surveying mission conducted by the U.S. Navy

1838: The government appoints Wilkes, a navy lieutenant, to head the expedition; ships set sail from Hampton Roads ,Virginia, on August 18

1842: The expedition ends in New York City on June 10

1877: Wilkes dies on February 8 in Washington, D.C.

The United States Exploring Expedition of 1838–1842, known as the Wilkes Expedition for its leader, Charles Wilkes, was an 87,000-mile (140,000-kilometer) journey undertaken by nine scientists and nearly 350 crew members aboard six ships to collect scientific knowledge, physical specimens, and mapping information, especially of the South Pacific Ocean. The expedition gathered the greatest quantity of scientific data of any ocean voyage of the mid-nineteenth century.

Among those who lobbied for funding of the expedition was John Cleves Symmes, Jr., of Ohio, an army captain during the War of 1812. Symmes was a proponent of the so-called holes in the poles theory, according to which the Earth was hollow and could be entered through openings at the two poles.

Thus, when Congress approved the expedition in 1836, it did so, in part, to find the polar entrances; however, the major objectives ultimately were a combination of commercial, diplomatic, and scientific goals. Congress declared that the expedition was to explore and survey "the Southern Ocean":

> to determine the existence of all doubtful islands and shoals, [so] as to discover, and accurately fix, the position of those which [were] in or near the track of our vessels in that quarter and [might] have escaped the observation of scientific navigators.

Finding someone to lead the expedition proved nearly as elusive as finding the polar entrances. In March 1838, the government finally turned to U.S. Navy officer Charles Wilkes, who headed the Department of Charts and Instruments. Born April 3, 1798, in New York City, Wilkes had attended boarding school and later Columbia College (now part of Columbia University). He entered the navy in 1818 and achieved the rank of lieutenant in 1826. He earned his reputation as an explorer on a surveying trip to Rhode Island's Narragansett Bay in 1832 and 1833.

The United States Exploring Expedition got under way on August 18, 1838, when Wilkes set sail from the Port of Hampton Roads, Virginia, in the expedition's flagship, the *Vincennes*. His fleet included five other navy vessels: the sloop *Peacock*, the brig *Porpoise*, the storeship *Relief*, and two schooners, the *Sea Gull* and the *Flying Fish*.

The nine scientists on the expedition, all young and talented, included naturalists, botanists, taxidermists, and a mineralogist. The chief botanist, William Brackenridge, a Scot, had been in charge of the Edinburgh Gardens. Geologist James Dwight Dana already had published his *System of Mineralogy* (1837), the leading text on the subject at that time. Horatio Hale of Harvard University served as philologist and ethnologist, and Charles Pickering of the Academy of Natural Sciences in Philadelphia served as the head naturalist.

After stopping at Rio de Janeiro, Brazil, then rounding the tip of South America, the ships proceeded west from Chile and Peru across the South Pacific to Samoa and to New South Wales in Australia. In December 1838, Wilkes sailed south from Sydney, Australia, into the Antarctic Ocean. But the expedition ships were poorly prepared for the harsh conditions, and the *Peacock* was nearly crushed by an iceberg. One of the vessels, the *Flying Fish*, crossed the 70th parallel in March 1839, taking it near the farthest southern point reached to that time by British explorer James Cook in 1774.

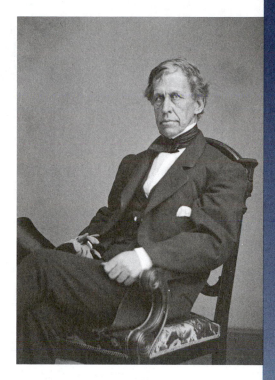

U.S. naval officer Charles Wilkes commanded the United States Exploring Expedition of 1838–1842, a global scientific survey of unprecedented scope He also wrote the official narrative of the expedition and edited the twenty-volume scientific reports. (*Library of Congress*)

The Wilkes Expedition arrived at Fiji and the Hawaiian Islands in 1840. In July, two sailors were killed by the locals while bartering for food on Malolo, an island in the Fiji archipelago. Wilkes retaliated by killing dozens of Fijians and destroying their villages. One of the explorers wrote,

> We continued as we had commenced, to destroy every house and plantation that we came across, and as we marched in three lines, I do not think that one escaped us.

The expedition continued on to explore the West Coast of the United States, including the Strait of Juan de Fuca, Puget Sound, and the Columbia River. Wilkes sent several men on an overland expedition to San Francisco and then sailed south and joined them there. He next headed the fleet west across the Pacific to the Philippines, Borneo, Singapore, and Polynesia. The expedition then crossed the Indian Ocean and rounded the Cape of Good Hope in South Africa, finally reaching New York on June 10, 1842.

Lieutenant Wilkes had completed his circumnavigation of the globe, covering a total distance that exceeded three times the Earth's circumference. In the process, however, he had lost two ships and twenty-eight men and had killed natives on Fiji. He was widely criticized for his dictatorial style and disliked by many expedition members.

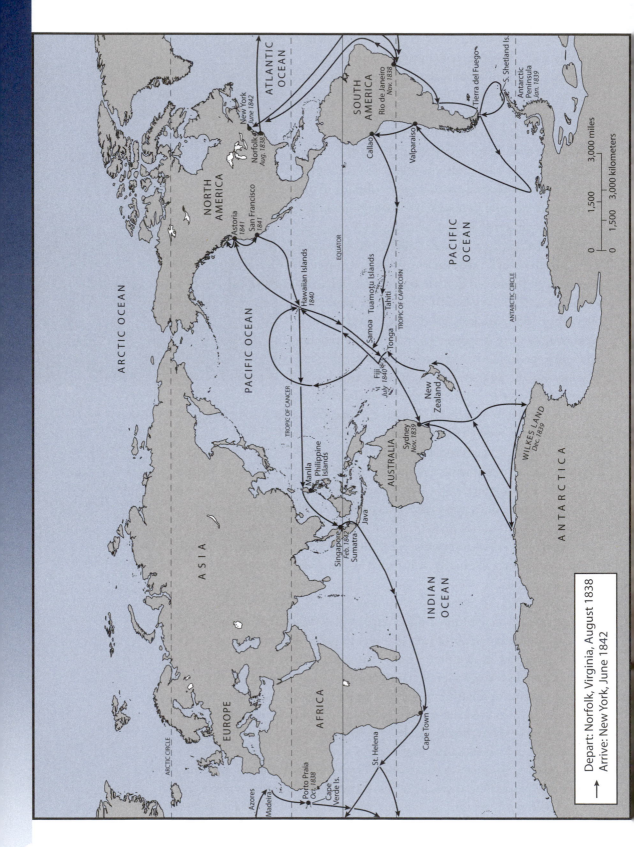

ATLANTIC OCEAN

ARCTIC OCEAN

NORTH AMERICA

New York
June 1842

Norfolk
Aug. 1838

Astoria
1841

San Francisco
1841

Hawaiian Islands
1840

EUROPE

PACIFIC OCEAN

TROPIC OF CANCER

EQUATOR

Manila

Philippine
Islands

Singapore
Feb. 1842

Sumatra

Java

ASIA

AFRICA

ARCTIC CIRCLE

Azores

Madeira

Porto Praia
Oct. 1838

Cape
Verde Is.

St. Helena

Cape Town

INDIAN OCEAN

Fiji
July 1840

Samoa

Tuamotu Islands

Tahiti

Tonga

TROPIC OF CAPRICORN

New
Zealand

AUSTRALIA

Sydney
Nov. 1839

SOUTH AMERICA

Rio de Janeiro
Nov. 1838

Callao

Valparaiso

Tierra del Fuego

S. Shetland Is.

Antarctic
Peninsula
Jan. 1839

PACIFIC OCEAN

ANTARCTIC CIRCLE

WILKES LAND
Dec. 1839

ANTARCTICA

0   1,500   3,000 miles

0   1,500   3,000 kilometers

Depart: Norfolk, Virginia, August 1838
Arrive: New York, June 1842

348

Upon returning home, Wilkes faced a navy court-martial for the loss of a ship on the Columbia River, for the mistreatment received by subordinate officers, and for the harsh discipline he had meted out to sailors. He was acquitted of all charges except the illegal flogging of sailors, for which the punishment was a public reprimand. One observer wrote,

> Wilkes's extreme arrogance & conviction that he would not only be acquitted, but it would [be] accomplished with a flourish of trumpets & a swipe at his accusers, has thus rendered his sentence doubly severe to himself.

Wilkes spent much of the rest of his life writing the *Narrative of the United States Exploring Expedition*, which was published in 1845 and consisted of five volumes and an atlas. He also edited the reports of the expedition, comprising twenty volumes of papers and eleven atlases over the course of publication from 1844 to 1874. Wilkes personally authored two of the volumes, one on meteorology and the other on hydrography. His *Western America, Including California and Oregon* (1849) and *Theory of Winds* (1856) were scientific works based on his observations and surveys.

The Wilkes Expedition yielded the largest collection of ethnographic objects and natural history specimens in America to that time. Among the thousands of anthropological artifacts were clubs from Fiji, feathered baskets from California, fishhooks from Samoa, and flax baskets from New Zealand. The collection was believed to be the largest ever gathered by one sailing expedition.

The botanists and naturalists returned home with an enormous variety of pressed plants—some 50,000 specimens of 10,000 species—as well as more than 1,000 living plants and the seeds for an additional 648 species. The zoologists brought back 2,150 birds, 134 mammals, and 588 species of fish (ready to be mounted), more than 200 jars of insects, and hundreds of envelopes containing other specimens. The geologists collected 300 fossil species, 400 species of coral, and 1,000 species of crustacean. The various collections formed the foundations of the U.S. National Herbarium and the U.S. Botanic Garden, today part of the Smithsonian Institution.

The scientific data compiled by the expedition was just as impressive. It included several notebooks of observations of native languages; a journal rich in ethnographic studies; 241 navigational charts, encompassing 280 Pacific islands (among them the first complete chart of the Fiji Islands), 800 miles (1,300 kilometers) of the Oregon coast, a 100-mile (160-kilometer) stretch of the Columbia River, the overland route from Oregon to San Francisco, and 1,500 miles (2,400 kilometers) of the Antarctic coast; and extensive meteorological, astronomical, magnetic, and oceanographic observations.

In all, the expedition amassed information on a scale and of a complexity that challenged the ability of contemporary scientific institutions to digest and analyze it. Wilkes died in Washington, D.C., on February 8, 1877, with the rank of rear admiral. In August 1909, his remains were moved to Arlington National Cemetery in tribute to his service and accomplishments.

Further Reading

Henderson, Daniel. *The Hidden Coasts: A Biography of Admiral Charles Wilkes.* Westport, CT: Greenwood, 1971.

Morgan, William James, et al., eds. *Autobiography of Rear Admiral Charles Wilkes.* Washington, DC: Naval History Division, Department of the Navy, 1978.

Philbrick, Nathaniel. *Sea of Glory: America's Voyage of Discovery, The U.S. Exploring Expedition, 1838–1842.* New York: Viking, 2003.

Stanton, William. *Great United States Exploring Expedition of 1838–1842.* Berkeley: University of California Press, 1975.

See also:
Antarctica.

GLOSSARY

aneroid barometer: A barometer without mercury, it consists of a partial vacuum chamber covered by a thin elastic disk. High atmospheric pressure pushes against the disk and causes it to bulge inward, while low pressure causes the disk to bulge outward. An aneroid barometer is smaller and more portable than a mercury barometer.

archaeology. The study of past human life and culture by the recovery and examination of remaining material evidence, such as buildings, tools, and pottery.

artificial satellite. An object that has been placed into orbit around the Earth or another celestial body. The first artificial satellite, *Sputnik 1*, was launched into orbit around the Earth by the Soviet Union in 1957. By 2010, thousands of satellites had been launched into orbit around the Earth through the efforts of more than fifty countries, while other satellites have circled the Moon and various planets.

astrolabe. The mariner's astrolabe consists of a disk or ring made of brass and marked off in degrees, with a movable arm at the center. By orienting the zero point on the disk with the horizon, a sailor can measure the altitude of any celestial object by sighting it along the arm. There is no precise date for the invention of the astrolabe, but it was likely in existence by the seventh century C.E. Although mariners used astrolabes into the 1800s, they have since become antiquated and are manufactured today mainly as conversation pieces.

Batesian mimicry. A form of biological resemblance whereby two or more species are similar in appearance, or in some other way, but only one actually carries the feature or features that make it repulsive to a predator, such as having a repugnant taste. This form of mimicry carries the name of its discoverer, nineteenth-century English naturalist Henry Walter Bates.

bathyscaphe. The name is taken from the Greek term meaning "deep ships." This deep-sea submergence vessel can be used without attachment to a ship's cable. Thus, it has more freedom of movement than some other deep-sea submersibles.

botanist. A scientist who specializes in the study of plants.

cartographer. A person who makes maps and charts.

cetaceans. Aquatic mammals, such as dolphins, porpoises, and whales.

chlorofluorocarbons: A family of chemical compounds, consisting of carbon, hydrogen, chlorine, and fluorine, which were developed for use in aerosol propellants and refrigerants. Chlorofluorocarbons are believed to react with the atmospheric ozone layer and cause its depletion.

chronometer: A timepiece used in scientific research that can accurately and precisely measure the duration of an event. In Switzerland, the Contrôle Officiel Suisse des Chronomètres (COSC) conducts tests and issues certificates that meet its standards. The official COSC definition of a chronometer states that it "is a high-precision watch capable of displaying the seconds and housing a movement that has been tested over several days, in different positions and at different temperatures, by an official neutral body."

continuous plankton recorder. A device used to collect plankton—tiny organisms in the water that form the basic food source of many larger marine animals—for study. Silk fabric is placed on a roller and towed by a ship. The forward motion of the ship supplies the energy to unroll the silk in stages, and plankton is collected on the fabric at a rate that closely corresponds to its concentration in the ocean.

deep-sea vents. Openings in the ocean floor from which mineralized water are emitted. These vents are formed where the sea floor is torn apart by the spreading of the Earth's tectonic plates.

egg clutch: Refers to a group of eggs produced by a bird or reptile, usually during a single time period, and laid in a nest.

Egyptology. A field of archaeology that focuses on the study of ancient Egyptian art, history, language, literature, and religion from the fifth millennium B.C.E. to the fourth century C.E.

entomology: The scientific study of insects, including their taxonomy, morphology, physiology, and ecology. Entomology also includes the study of the harmful and beneficial impacts of insects on human beings and their environment.

ethnographer. A person who studies a particular human culture firsthand and reports on the people's way of life based on direct observation.

folding: The term fold is used in geology when originally flat and planar surfaces become bent or curved. Folds form as a result of various types of stress and pressure.

fossils. The remains and other evidence of plants and animals found in sedimentary rock or other features of the Earth's crust from a past geologic age. These include organic remains and their impressions, as well as impressions of tracks, trails, and habitats.

functionalism: In anthropology, a theory that stresses how the patterns and institutions of a society are interdependent and interact to maintain cultural and social unity. Thus, for example, to anthropologist Bronsilaw Malinowski every custom, material object, idea, and belief that he studied fulfilled a vital cultural and societal function.

geodetic: Also called geodesy, it is the study of the size and shape of the Earth and its gravitational field, tides, and the movement of its crust and poles.

geology. The scientific study of the origin, history, and structure of the Earth.

herbarium: A collection of dried plant specimens properly mounted, identified by experts, and labeled by their proper scientific names, together with other information, such as where they were collected and how they grew. These specimens are filed in cases according to families and genera, and thus are made available for quick reference.

hot spring. A natural spring that discharges water over 980 degrees Fahrenheit (530 degrees Celsius). Hot springs are created when water enters a crack in the Earth's surface and forces out water that has collected beneath a fault and has been heated by hot rocks deeper in the Earth's interior.

Human-Occupied Vehicle (HOV). A deep-sea submersible capable of carrying passengers that is used in oceanic exploration.

hydrography: The measurement and description of the physical features and conditions of navigable waters, such as oceans, rivers, lakes, and the coastal areas that adjoin them. Information from hydrographic research provides accurate nautical charts and guides the study of shoreline erosion and the movement of sediment. Furthermore, hydrographic studies are instrumental in determining the use of marine resources, establishing maritime boundaries, building coastal facilities, and implementing environmental policies, including pollution control.

hygrometer: One of several devices that measures the relative humidity of the air. There are several types of hygrometers, ranging from psychrometers (see below) to electronic devices. For example, a hair tension hygrometer uses a strand of hair held under a known tension; the degree to which the hair curls in response to humidity reveals the amount of relative humidity. A cooled mirror dewpoint hygrometer measures relative humidity by detecting condensation on the surface of a mirror with an electronic device.

ice stations. First established by the Soviet Union and the United States, these scientific stations are located on ice floes in the Arctic. Ice stations have been used to conduct hydrological, meteorological, and magnetic observations of the Arctic region.

indigenous people: People who originate in a particular region or country (sometimes referred to as "native people"). The United Nations defines indigenous people as those having historical continuity with pre-invasion and pre-colonial societies.

indigo: A plant that is the natural source of a blue dye. Extraction of the dye was important to the economy of colonial America and other parts of the world, especially India. Since the early twentieth century, synthetic indigo has replaced the natural dye in most uses.

isothermal line: A line on a map that connects points of constant or equal temperatures.

JIM suit. An atmospheric deep-sea diving suit developed in 1971, it is designed to protect divers from the dangers associated with deep-sea compression.

lichen: Parasitic fungi which feed on algae or different types of bacteria.

mineralogy. The study of the distribution, identification, and properties of minerals (naturally occurring, inorganic substances that are characterized by crystalline structure, color, and hardness.)

natural selection. A theory most prominently associated with the natural scientist Charles Darwin, according to which the young in a species compete for survival. In this process, they pass on to the next generations (through heredity) variations, or adaptations to the environment, that are important to survival. According to Darwin, even the slightest variations may determine whether a specific species endures or dies out.

North Magnetic Pole. Arctic location where the magnetic field lines are oriented vertically before entering the Earth's surface. The magnetic pole is caused by the Earth's core emitting electrical currents; the pole drifts because the currents change.

oceanography. The exploration and scientific study of the ocean and its phenomena.

paleontology. The study of life-forms that existed in prehistoric or geologic times, usually as found in the fossils of plants, animals, and other organisms.

philology: This branch of linguistics is the study of human speech, mainly as it appears in literature and thus reveals cultural history.

psychrometer: Used for measuring atmospheric humidity, this instrument consists of two thermometers. The bulb of one thermometer is kept moist, and the effect of evaporative cooling is determined by comparing it to the other thermometer, which is kept dry.

rhumb line: A line that crosses all meridians of longitude at the same angle, it can be used for plotting a vehicle, an aircraft, or a ship's course over short distances and at low latitiudes.

samplers. Also known as corers, these hollow steel tubes are used to gather a core sample of layers from the Earth's crust on land, at the bottom of the ocean, and sometimes in other bodies of water. Samplers come in a various thicknesses and lengths, depending upon the type of material to be collected, and they provide a layered profile of the sediment in any given location.

scurvy: A breakdown of human collagen caused by a deficiency of vitamin C and characterized by spongy and bleeding gums, bleeding under the skin, and extreme weakness. It was a major threat to crews aboard sailing vessels during the Age of Discovery and later, due to inadequate diets at sea.

taxonomy. The science of classifying organisms.

tectonic plates. The large plates that make up the Earth's surface. Tectonic plates are in constant movement, shifting position by up to 2 inches (3 centimeters) per year. Consequently, the ocean floors are continually moving, spreading from the center, and sinking at the edges.

theodolite. An instrument used in surveying. It consists of two graduated circles placed at right angles and a telescope that turns on an axis and is situated at the center of the circles, all mounted on a pedestal. With this device, an explorer can measure horizontal and vertical angles and thus accurately survey land.

underwater sonar system: A system using sound waves to detect and locate submerged objects or to measure distances.

Van Allen radiation belt: Two belts (sometimes considered a single belt of varying intensity) of radiation outside the Earth's atmosphere, extending from about 400 to 40,000 miles (650 to 65,000 kilometers) above the Earth. The belts were named for James A. Van Allen, the American astrophysicist who first predicted their existence.

voyageur: A woodsman, boatman, or guide employed by a fur company to transport goods and supplies between remote stations in the North American wilderness, generally in the seventeenth through eighteenth centuries.

BIBLIOGRAPHY

The following is a selective list of books and Web sites pertaining to scientific expeditions and exploration since the fifteenth century. Please see the "Further Reading" lists accompanying individual articles for additional sources on specific subjects and people.

Books

Alexander, Caroline. *The Endurance: Shackleton's Legendary Antarctic Expedition.* New York: Alfred A. Knopf, 1998.

Ambrose, Stephen E. *Undaunted Courage: Meriwether Lewis, Thomas Jefferson, and the Opening of the American West.* New York: Simon and Schuster, 1996.

Ballard, Robert D., ed. *Archeological Oceanography.* Princeton, NJ: Princeton University Press, 2008.

———. *The Discovery of the Titanic.* New York: Warner, 1987.

Barden, Renardo. *The Discovery of America: Opposing Viewpoints.* San Diego, CA: Greenhaven, 1989.

Bascom, Willard. *The Crest of the Wave: Adventures in Oceanography.* New York: Harper and Row, 1988.

Bates, Henry Walter. *The Naturalist on the River Amazon.* 1863. New York: Routledge, 2004.

Baughman, T.H. *Pilgrims on the Ice: Robert Falcon Scott's First Antarctic Expedition.* Lincoln: University of Nebraska Press, 2008.

Beaglehole, J.C., ed. *The Journals of Captain James Cook on His Voyages of Discovery.* Rochester, NY: Boydell, 1999.

Beattie, Donald A. *Taking Science to the Moon: Lunar Experiments and the Apollo Program.* Baltimore: Johns Hopkins University Press, 2001.

Bernbaum, Edwin. *Sacred Mountains of the World.* Berkeley: University of California Press, 1997.

Berne, Jennifer. *Manfish: The Story of Jacques Cousteau.* San Francisco: Chronicle, 2008.

Berton, Pierre. *The Artic Grail: The Quest for the North West Passage and the North Pole, 1818–1909.* New York: Lyons, 2000.

Bond, Peter. *The Continuing Story of the International Space Station.* New York: Springer, 2002.

Bonta, Marcia M. *Women in the Field: America's Pioneering Woman Naturalists.* College Station: Texas A&M University Press, 1991.

Botting, Douglas. *Humboldt and the Cosmos.* New York: Harper and Row, 1973.

Bowleb, Peter. *Charles Darwin: The Man and His Influence.* New York: Cambridge University Press, 1996.

Bowman-Kruhm, Mary. *The Leakeys: A Biography*. Westport, CT: Greenwood, 2005.

Brown, Janet. *Charles Darwin: Voyaging*. New York: Alfred A. Knopf, 1995.

Bruce, James. *Travels to Discover the Source of the Nile in the Years 1768–1773*. 1790. New York: Horizon, 1964.

Brunier, Serge. *Space Odyssey: The First Forty Years of Space Exploration*. Cambridge, UK: Cambridge University Press, 2002.

Bryce, Robert. *Cook and Peary: The Polar Controversy Resolved*. Mechanicsville, PA: Stackpole, 1997.

Cadbury, Deborah. *Space Race: The Epic Battle Between America and the Soviet Union for Dominion in Space*. New York: HarperCollins, 2006.

Cameron, Ian. *To the Farthest Ends of the Earth: 150 Years of World Exploration by the Royal Geographical Society*. New York: E.P. Dutton, 1980.

Chaikin, Andrew. *A Man on the Moon: The Voyages of the Apollo Astronauts*. New York: Penguin, 2007.

Collins, David N., ed. *Siberian Discovery*. 12 vols. Surrey, UK: Curzon, 2000.

Counter, Allen S. *North Pole Legacy: Black, White and Eskimo*. Amherst: University of Massachusetts Press, 1991.

Cousteau, Jacques, with Frédéric Dumas. *The Silent World*. New York: Harper, 1953.

Crane, David. *Scott of the Antarctic: A Life of Courage and Tragedy*. New York: Vintage Books, 2007.

Davis, Wade. *One River: Explorations and Discoveries in the Amazon Rain Forest*. New York: Simon and Schuster, 1996.

DeGroot, Gerard. *Dark Side of the Moon: The Magnificent Madness of the American Lunar Quest*. New York: New York University Press, 2006.

Doubilet, David. *Pacific: An Undersea Journey*. Boston: Little, Brown, 1992.

Dugard, Martin. *Into Africa: The Epic Adventures of Stanley and Livingstone*. New York: Doubleday, 2003.

Earle, Sylvia. *Sea Change: A Message of the Ocean*. New York: Putnam, 1995.

Earle, Sylvia, and Al Giddings. *Exploring the Deep Frontier*. Washington, DC: National Geographic Society, 1980.

Fleming, Fergus. *Ninety Degrees North: The Quest for the North Pole*. New York: Grove, 2001.

Frost, Orcutt. *Bering: The Russian Discovery of America*. New Haven, CT: Yale University Press, 2003.

Gascoigne, John. *Science in the Service of Empire: Joseph Banks, the British State and the Uses of Science in the Age of Revolution*. New York: Cambridge University Press, 1998.

Godwin, Robert. *The Lunar Exploration Scrapbook: A Pictorial History of Lunar Vehicles*. Burlington, Canada: Apogee, 2007.

Hallett, Robin, ed. *Records of the African Association, 1788–1831*. London: Thomas Nelson and Sons, 1964.

Hanbury-Tenison, Robin , ed. *The Seventy Great Journeys in History*. New York: Thames and Hudson, 2006.

Hayes, Derek. *First Crossing: Alexander Mackenzie, His Expedition Across North America, and the Opening of the Continent*. Seattle: Sasquatch, 2001.

Henderson, Bruce. *True North: Peary, Cook and the Race to the Pole*. New York: W.W. Norton, 2005.

Herbert, Wally. *The Noose of Laurels: The Discovery of the North Pole*. London: Hodder and Stoughton, 1989.

Heyerdahl, Thor. *Green Was the Earth on the Seventh Day*. New York: Random House, 1996.

Horner, John, and Edwin Dobb. *Dinosaur Lives: Unearthing an Evolutionary Saga*. San Diego, CA: Harcourt Brace, 1998.

Hudson, Peter. *Two Rivers: Travels in West Africa on the Trail of Mungo Park*. London: Chapmans, 1991.

Huntford, Roland. *The Last Place on Earth: Scott and Amundsen's Race to the South Pole*. New York: Modern Library, 1999.

———. *Shackleton*. New York: Carroll and Graf, 1998.

Isaac, Glynn, and Elizabeth R. McCown, eds. *Human Origins: Louis Leakey and the East African Evidence*. Menlo Park, CA: W.A. Benjamin, 1976.

Jaffe, Mark. *The Gilded Dinosaur: The Fossil War Between E.D. Cope and O.C. Marsh and the Rise of American Science*. New York: Crown, 2000.

Jeal, Tim. *Stanley: The Impossible Life of Africa's Greatest Explorer*. New Haven, CT: Yale University Press, 2007.

Johnston, Alexa. *Reaching the Summit: Sir Edmund Hillary's Life of Adventure*. New York: DK, 2005.

Jones, Max. *The Last Great Quest: Captain Scott's Antarctic Sacrifice*. New York: Oxford University Press, 2003.

Lambert, David. *The Pacific Ocean*. Austin, TX: Raintree Steck-Vaughn, 1997.

Langley, Andrew, and Kevin Barnes. *The Great Polar Adventure: The Journeys of Roald Amundsen*. New York: Chelsea House, 1994.

Lavender, David Sievert. *The Way to the Sea: Lewis and Clark Across the Continent*. New York: Harper and Row, 1988.

Mackay, David. *In the Wake of Cook: Exploration, Science, and Empire, 1780–1781*. New York: St. Martin's, 1985.

Man, John. *Gobi: Tracking the Desert*. New Haven, CT: Yale University Press, 1999.

Marshack, Alexander. *The World in Space: The Story of the International Geophysical Year*. New York: Thomas Nelson, 1958.

Martin, Stephen. *A History of Antarctica*. Sydney, Australia: State Library of New South Wales Press, 1996.

Medina, Toribia José, ed. *The Discovery of the Amazon*. New York: Dover, 1988.

Mills, Eric L. *Biological Oceanography: An Early History*. Ithaca, NY: Cornell University Press, 1989.

Moorehead, Caroline. *Lost and Found: The 9,000 Treasures of Troy*. New York: Viking, 1996.

Morell, Virginia. *Ancestral Passions: The Leakey Family and the Quest for Humankind's Beginnings*. New York: Simon and Schuster, 1995.

Morison, Samuel Eliot. *Admiral of the Ocean Sea*. New York: MJF, 1997.

———. *The Great Explorers: The European Discovery of America*. New York: Oxford University Press, 1978.

Mouhot, Henri. *Travels in Siam, Cambodia, Laos, and Annam*. Bangkok, Thailand: White Lotus, 2000.

Moulton, Gary E., ed. *The Lewis and Clark Journals: An American Epic of Discovery*. Lincoln: University of Nebraska Press, 2003.

Munson, Richard. *Cousteau: The Captain and His World*. New York: William Morrow, 1989.

Myer, Valerie Grosvenor. *A Victorian Lady in Africa: The Story of Mary Kingsley*. Southampton, UK: Ashford, 1989.

Nansen, Fridtjof. *Farthest North*. New York: Modern Library, 1999.

National Geographic Society. *National Geographic Expeditions Atlas*. Washington, DC: National Geographic Society, 2000.

Newman, James L. *Imperial Footprints: Henry Morton Stanley's African Journeys*. Washington, DC: Brassey's, 2004.

Olds, Elizabeth. *Women of the Four Winds*. Boston: Houghton Mifflin, 1985.

Palmatary, Helen Constance. *The River of the Amazons: Its Discovery and Early Exploration, 1500–1743*. New York: Carlton, 1965.

Park, Mungo, with Kate Ferguson Marsters, ed. *Travels Into the Interior of Africa*. Durham, NC: Duke University Press, 2000.

Parry, J.H. *The Age of Reconnaissance, 1450–1650*. London: Phoenix, 1963.

Philbrick, Nathaniel. *Sea of Glory: America's Voyage of Discovery, The U.S. Exploring Expedition, 1838–1842*. New York: Viking, 2003.

Pond, Alonzo W. *Andrews: Gobi Explorer*. New York: Grosset and Dunlap, 1972.

Poole, Robert M. *Explorers House: National Geographic and the World It Made*. New York: Penguin, 2004.

Prager, Ellen J., and Sylvia A. Earle. *The Oceans*. New York: McGraw-Hill, 2000.

Reader's Digest. *Antarctica: The Extraordinary History of Man's Conquest of the Frozen Continent*. New York: Reader's Digest, 1990.

Reef, Catherine. *Black Explorers*. New York: Facts On File, 1996.

Sachs, Aaron. *Humboldt Current: A European Explorer and His American Disciples*. Oxford, UK: Oxford University Press, 2007.

Sattin, Anthony. *The Gates of Africa: Death, Discovery, and the Search for Timbuktu*. New York: St. Martin's, 2003.

Schultes, Richard, and Siri von Reis. *Ethnobotany: Evolution of a Discipline*. Portland, OR: Dioscorides, 1995.

Schwartz, Seymour I. *Putting "America" on the Map: The Story of the Most Important Graphic Document in the History of the United States.* Amherst, NY: Prometheus, 2007.

Schweinfurth, Georg. *The Heart of Africa: Three Years' Travels and Adventures in the Unexplored Regions of Central Africa from 1868 to 1871.* Trans. Ellen E. Frewer. 2 vols. Chicago: Afro-Am Books, 1969.

Scoresby, William, Jr. *An Account of the Arctic Regions.* 1820. New York: Augustus M. Kelley, 1969.

Smith, Charles H., and George Beccaloni, eds. *Natural Selection and Beyond: The Intellectual Legacy of Alfred Russel Wallace.* New York: Oxford University Press, 2008.

Speke, John Hanning. *Journal of the Discovery of the Source of the Nile.* 1863. Mineola, NY: Dover, 1996.

Stanton, William. *Great United States Exploring Expedition of 1838–1842.* Berkeley: University of California Press, 1975.

Tinting, Marion. *Women Into the Unknown: A Sourcebook on Women Explorers and Travelers.* Westport, CT: Greenwood, 1989.

Vaeth, J. Gordon. *To the Ends of the Earth: The Explorations of Roald Amundsen.* New York: Harper and Row, 1962.

Van der Post, Laurens. *Venture to the Interior.* New York: William Morrow, 1951.

Wallace, David Rains. *The Bonehunters' Revenge: Dinosaurs, Greed, and the Greatest Scientific Feud of the Gilded Age.* Boston: Houghton Mifflin, 1999.

Wallach, Janet. *Desert Queen: The Extraordinary Life of Gertrude Bell, Adventurer, Adviser to Kings, Ally of Lawrence of Arabia.* New York: Anchor, 2005.

Washburn, Bradford. *Mount McKinley's West Buttress: The First Ascent, Brad Washburn's Logbook, 1951.* Williston, VT: Top of the World, 2003.

Whitfield, Peter. *The Charting of the Oceans: Ten Centuries of Maritime Maps.* Rohnert Park, CA.: Pomegranate Artbooks, 1996.

Wilford, John Noble. *The Mapmakers.* New York: Alfred A. Knopf, 1981.

Williams, Glyndwr, ed. *Captain Cook: Explorations and Reassessments.* Rochester, NY: Boydell, 2004.

———. *Voyages of Delusion: The Quest for the Northwest Passage.* New Haven, CT: Yale University Press, 2003.

Winchester, Jim, ed. *Space Missions: From Sputnik to SpaceShipOne, The History of Space Flight.* San Diego, CA: Thunder Bay, 2006.

Winstone, H.V.F. *Howard Carter and the Discovery of the Tomb of Tutankhamun.* Manchester, UK: Barzun, 2006.

Woodcock, George. *Henry Walter Bates, Naturalist of the Amazon.* London: Faber, 1969.

Worster, Donald. *A River Running West: The Life of John Wesley Powell.* New York: Oxford University Press, 2001.

Web Sites

The Explorers Club. http://www.explorers.org.

The Hakluyt Society. http://www.hakluyt.com.

International Polar Year. http://www.ipy.org.

Kon-Tiki Museum. http://www.kon-tiki.no.

The National Academies, International Geophysical Year. http://www.nas.edu/history/igy.

National Association of Black Scuba Divers. http://www.nabsdivers.org.

National Geographic Society. http://www.nationalgeographic.com.

Roy Chapman Andrews Society. http://www.roychapmanandrewssociety.org.

Royal Geographical Society: http://www.rgs.org.

Russian Federal Space Agency: http://www.roscosmos.ru/main.php?lang=en.

Society of Woman Geographers. http://www.iswg.org.

U.S. National Aeronautics and Space Administration: http://www.nasa.gov.

U.S. National Aeronautics and Space Administration Landsat Program: http://landsat.gsfc.nasa.gov.

INDEX

Page numbers in italics refer to illustrations.

Abyssinia (Ethiopia), **1:**62–63; **2:**267

Academy of Natural Sciences, Philadelphia, **1:**183

Acadians, **1:**60

Account of the Arctic Regions, An (Scoresby), **2:**270

Acosta, Bertrand B., **1:**70

Acuña, Cristóbal de, **1:**6

Adams, Cyrus C., **1:**8

Adams, Harriet Chalmers, **2:**285–86

Adams, Jameson, **2:**280

Adare, Cape, Antarctica, **1:**22; **2:**276

Addington, Cape, Alaska, **2:**255

Adelaide, Cape, Canada, **1:**14

Aden, Yemen, **1:**65

Admiral of the Ocean Sea: A Life of Christopher Columbus (Morison), **1:**108–9

Advance Base, Antarctica, **1:**69, 72, 74

Adventure, HMS, **1:**87; **2:**234

Aegean Sea, **2:**199

Aerial photography, **2:**204, 339

Aetos, Mount, **2:**260

Africa, **2:**198, 251
    British exploration, **1:**3–5
    Bruce, **1:**61–64
    Burton and Speke, **1:**64–69; **2:**251, *251*, 317
    French exploration, **1:**3
    Kingsley, **1:**165–69, *167*
    Livingstone, **1:**184–87, *188*; **2:**251
    new colonies in, **1:**4
    Park, **1:**4; **2:**238–41
    Portuguese explorations, **1:**xi–xii, 3, 106–7

Africa *(continued)*
    Schweinfurth, **2:**267–69
    Stanley, **1:**184, 187–90, *188*, *189*; **2:**251
    Van der Post, **2:**326–30
    See also specific location

African Association, **1:**xiii, 3–5, 39; **2:**239

African plate, **1:**33

Agamemnon, death mask of, **2:**262–64, *263*

Agassiz, Alexander, **2:**226

Agassiz, Louis, **2:**225–26

Age of Discovery, **1:**xii, xiii, 105–12; **2:**200, 201, 216, 223, 232, 253

Age of Reconnaissance, 1450–1650, The (Parry), **1:**xii

Akka pygmies, **2:**267, 268

Aku-Aku (Heyerdahl), **1:**147

Al-Idrisi, Mohammed, **2:**199, 200

Alaska, **1:**12, 15, 27, 29, 30, 89; **2:**207, 208, 216, 218, 252, 254, 255, 256, 258, 337, 339

Albert, Lake, Africa, **1:**187, 189

Albert I, Prince of Monaco, **2:**222, 226

Albert Hall, London, **2:***251*

Albert P. Crary Science and Engineering Center, **1:**24

Alberta, Canada, **2:**194

Aldrin, Edwin "Buzz," **2:**292, *293*

Aleutian Islands, **1:**27, 149

Aleuts (native people), **2:**255

Alexander Mackenzie and Company, **2:**194–95

Alexandria Troas, Turkey, **2:**260

Alexandrian Museum, Egypt, **2:**199

Alfragan, **1:**108

Algeria, **1:**4

Algiers, **1:**61, 62

Allen, John, **1:**127

Allosaurus (dinosaur), **1:**80

Alone (Byrd), **1:**74

Alpine Club, **1:**121

Alps, **2:**337

ALSEP. *See* Apollo Lunar Surface Experiments Package

Alvin (submersible), **1:**31, 32–33, 35, 37, *37*

Amazon River and Basin, **1:**xiii, 5–8, *6*; **2:**207, 208, 265–66, 331, 332, 333
    Bates, **1:**7, 44–47
    Humboldt, **1:**5, 155
    Wallace, **1:**44; **2:**332

"America," **2:**199, 200

American Alpine Club, **2:**338

American Museum, New York, **1:**183

American Museum of Natural History (AMNH), New York City, **1:**16, 17, 18, 19, 20, 81, 130; **2:**229, 242

American Philosophical Society, **1:**91, 114, 180, 182

American Plate, **2:**231–32

American Revolution, **1:**61, 113, 115, 126

American Telephone and Telegraph Company (AT&T), **2:**305

Ames, Oakes, **2:**265

AMNH. *See* American Museum of Natural History

Among the Alps with Bradford (Bradford), **2:**337

Amundsen, Jens, **1:**9

Amundsen, Roald Engelbregt Grauning, **1:**xii, 8–16, *10,* 21, 22, 23, 28, 124; **2:**277

Northwest Passage, **1:**8, 10–13

South Pole, **1:***10,* 13–15; **2:**272, 275, 276, 277, 282

Amur River, **2:**252, 257, *257*

Anastasi, Adrian, **1:**53

Anatolia, Turkey, **2:**259, 260

Anaximander, **2:**199

Anchorage, Alaska, **1:**89

Anders, William, **2:**291

Anderson, Alexander, **2:**241

Anderson, William R., **1:**29

Andes Mountains, **1:**6, 56, 57, 98, 99, 157; **2:**218, 265

Andrea Doria (ship), **1:**36

Andrews, Charles Ezra, **1:**16

Andrews, Roy Chapman, **1:**xii, 16–21, *19,* 130

Aneityum Island, **1:**80

Angkor, Cambodia, **2:**209, 210

Angkor Wat, **2:**209, 210–11, *210*

Angola, **1:**166

ANGUS underwater camera, **1:**33, 35

Animal behavior, **2:**325

Animal Wife, The (Thomas), **2:**325

Antarctic Circle, **1:**21, 22, 87

Cook's crossing of, **2:**231, 234

Antarctic Ocean, **2:**347

See also specific voyage/ expedition

Antarctic Peninsula, **1:**21, 22

Antarctic Program, U.S., **1:**24

Antarctica, **1:**xiii, 11, 13, 21–25, *22,* 159, 160, 161, *161;* **2:**201, 225, 234

Amundsen, **1:**8, 9, 13–15, 21, 23

Byrd, **1:**21, 23, 69, 70, 71–74, *73;* **2:**218

Cook, **1:**21, 82, 87

glaciers, **1:**21, 25

Scott, **1:**13, 14, 22, 23; **2:**272–77, *273,* 278, 279

Shackleton, **1:**13–14, 22–23; **2:**278–84, *281, 282*

See also specific location

Anthropological Society of London, **1:**68

Anthropology

Heyerdahl, **1:**142–49, *143, 145, 146*

Leakey family, **1:**170–75; **2:**218

Anthropology, cultural. *See* Ethnography

Antioch, **1:**137

Anzhu, Pyotr, **1:**27

Apartheid, **2:**327–28

Apatosaurus (Brontosaurus; dinosaur), **1:**80

Aphrodite's Temple, Kíthira, **2:**264

Apollo Lunar Surface Experiments Package (ALSEP), **2:**292–93

Apollo Project (spacecraft), **2:**287, 290–94, 296

Apollo 7, **2:**291

Apollo 8, **2:**287, 291

Apollo 11, **1:**124; **2:**287, 292, 293, *293*

Apollo 12, **2:**292

Apollo 13, **2:**293–94

Apollo 15, **2:**294

Apollo 16, **2:**294

Apollo 17, **2:**294

Apollo 18, **2:**287, 295

Appalachian Mountains, **1:**32

Apurímac River, Peru, **1:**8

Aquarius (lunar lander), **2:**294

Arabia, **1:**65; **2:**267, 268, 322

Arabian Nights (*The Book of the Thousand Nights and a Night;* Burton, translator), **1:**69; **2:**322

Arabian Sea, **1:**148

Arabic, **2:**322, 323

Archaeology, **1:**51–54

Bell, **1:**51–54, *52*

Bingham, **1:**55–58, *57;* **2:**218

Carter, **1:**75–78, *77;* **2:**218

Schliemann, **2:**259–63, *262, 263*

See also Marine archaeology

Archaeopteryx (primitive bird), **2:**229, 230

Archimedes (bathyscaphe), **1:**33

Arctic, **1:**xiii, 11, 26–31, 160, *161;* **2:**202, 251, 342

Amundsen, **1:**8–9, 10–13, *10,* 15, 28

Bering, **1:**26, 27; **2:**253–55, *254*

Byrd, **1:**15, 28, 69, 70, *70*

Henson, **1:**23, 28, 140–42, *141;* **2:**243

Hudson, **1:**26, 27, 111–12

Nansen, **1:**9, 28; **2:**211–16, *212,* 222, 242

Nordenskjöld, **1:**9, 15, 28; **2:**219, 220–22, *220*

Peary, **1:**11, 13, 26, 28, 29, 140–42, *141;* **2:**218, 222, 242–45, *243*

Russian exploration, **2:**252–58

Scoresby, **1:**269–71

temperature, **1:**29, 31

twenty-first century, **1:**29, 31

Watkins, **2:**342–45

Arctic Circle, **1:**26

Arctic haze, **1:**160–61

Arctic Ocean, **1**:15, 28, 161; **2**:193, 194, 215, 219, 253, 255, 257, 343
See also specific voyage/expedition
Ares Valley, Mars, **2**:314
Argentina, **1**:98; **2**:208
Argo (submersible), **1**:34, 35
Argonauts of the Western Pacific (Malinowski), **2**:195, 197
Argun (ship), **2**:257
Aripuanã River, Brazil, **1**:7
Arizona, **2**:248, 339
Arkansas, **1**:115, 116
Arkansas River, United States, **1**:114
Arkhangelsk (Archangel), Russia, **1**:27; **2**:258
Arktika (ship), **1**:29
Armitage, Albert, **2**:274
Armstrong, Neil, **1**:124; **2**:287, 292, *293*
Arsenyev, Vladimir Klavdiyevich, **2**:253, 258
Artes Africanae; Illustrations and Descriptions of Productions of the Industrial Arts of Central African Tribes (Schweinfurth), **2**:269
Asia, **2**:200, 201, 286
See also specific location
Asie Centrale (Humboldt), **1**:156
Assam, **1**:165
Astoria, Oregon, **1**:181
Astrolabes, **1**:111, *111*
Atahuallpa (Inca emperor), **1**:110
AT&T. *See* American Telephone and Telegraph Company
Athabasca, Lake, Canada, **2**:193
Athabasca River, Canada, **2**:193
Atlantic Ocean, **2**:228, 231, 271
See also specific voyage/expedition

Atlantis (ship), **1**:37
Atlantis (space shuttle), **2**:298, 302, 309, 315
Atlas of America's Northwestern Coast from the Bering Strait to Corrientes Cape and the Aleutian Islands, **1**:27
Atlas of the Northern Part of the East Ocean, **1**:27
Aurora (ship), **2**:283
Australia, **1**:42, 50, 101; **2**:201, 231, 233, 234, 237, 269, 347
Cook's exploration, **1**:38, 41, 85, 87
Flinders's exploration, **1**:124–28
Unknown Coast, **1**:125, 126–27, 128
See also specific location
Australopithecus (primate species), **1**:173–74
A. afarensis, **1**:175
A. africanus, **1**:174
A. anamensis, **1**:175
A. boisei, **1**:170, 173, 174
Automobiles, **1**:18
Avasaksa, Lapland, **2**:202
Aylesbury, Countess of, **1**:5
Ayuthaya, Siam, **2**:209
Azov, Russia, **1**:148
Aztec Empire, Spanish conquest of, **1**:105, 110

Baalbek, Lebanon, **1**:62
Babylonia, **2**:199
Bacteria, **1**:34
Badoo, Africa, **2**:241
Baffin, William, **1**:27, 105, 112
Baffin Bay, **1**:105, 112
Baffin Island, **1**:27; **2**:325
Bagamoyo, Tanzania, **1**:187
Baghdad, Iraq, **1**:53
Baghdad Museum, **1**:52

Baghdad Sketches (Stark), **2**:321, 323
Bahamas, **1**:105, 108
Bahia, Brazil, **1**:49
Bahía Blanca, Argentina, **1**:49
Bahr-al-Ghazal, Sudan, **2**:268
Baikonur Cosmodrome, **2**:288, 304
Baja California, Mexico, **2**:201
Baku, Russia, **1**:135
Balchen, Bernt, **1**:70, 71–72
Ballard, Chester, **1**:32
Ballard, Robert Duane, **1**:xiii, 31–38, 34, 124; **2**:218
Bamako, Africa, **2**:240
Bangweulu, Lake, Zambia, **1**:186, *187*
Banks, Joseph, **1**:xiii, 3, 4, 38–43, 39, 83, 85, 87, 126, 127, 128; **2**:234, 238
Banks, William, **1**:39
Bantu tribes, **2**:198
Bar of Shadow, A (Van der Post), **2**:328
Barbados, **1**:142
Barbary states, **1**:4, 61
Barents Sea, **2**:256, 258
Barnum, P.T., **1**:183
Barometers, **2**:212, 214, 246, 247
Barrow, Alaska, **1**:30
Barrow, John, **2**:250
Bartram, William, **1**:114
Basra, Iraq, **1**:53
Bass, George, **1**:125–26
Bass Strait, **1**:126
Batavia, **1**:87
Bate, Sarah, **1**:39
Bates, Henry Walter, **1**:7, 44–47; **2**:331, 332
Bates, Robert, **2**:338–39
Batesian mimicry, **1**:44, 45–46
Bathyscaphes, **1**:33; **2**:222, 227, 236, *236*, 237
Baudin, Nicolas, **1**:126, 127
Bauer, Ferdinand Lukas, **1**:127

Bay of Whales, Antarctica, **1:**13, 71; **2:**280

Bayanzag Valley, Mongolia, **1:***130*

BBC. *See* British Broadcasting Company

Beagle, HMS, **1:**47–51, *48, 49,* 96, 97, *97,* 98–101, 102; **2:**225, 234

Bean, Alan, **2:**292

Beardmore Glacier, Antarctica, **2:**277

Beasts of the Sea, The (De Bestiis Marinis; Steller), **2:**255, 256

Beaufort, Francis, **2:**250

Beaufort Sea, **1:**89

Beaufoy, Hugh, **1:**4

Bechuanaland (Botswana), **1:**185; **2:**324, 327, 329

Bedouin, **1:**52

Beechy Island, **1:**11

Beetles, **1:**44

Belém (Para), Brazil, **1:**6, 44, 45

Belgian Antarctica Expedition, **1:**8, 9, 22

Belgica (ship), **1:**9, 22

Bell, Alexander Graham, **2:**216

Bell, Gertrude Margaret Lowthian, **1:**xii, 51–54, *52*

Bell Telephone Company, **2:**216

Bella Coola River, British Columbia, **2:**193, 194

Beloit, Wisconsin, **1:**16

Beloit College, **1:**16, 17

Bement, Arden, **1:**37

Bennett, Floyd, **1:**28, 70

Bennett, James Gordon, Jr., **1:**186, 187

Benowm, Africa, **2:**240

Berbera, Somalia, **1:**66

Berberis calliantha (evergreen shrub), **1:**165

Beregovoy, Georgi, **2:**291

Bering, Vitus Jonassen, **1:**26, 27; **2:**252, *253, 254, 255,* 256

Bering Island, **2:**255

Bering Sea, **1:**27; **2:**221, 255, 256

Bering Strait, **1:**27, 89; **2:**221, 252, 253

Berlin, Germany, **1:**156

Bernacchi, Louis, **2:**273, 274

Beyond Euphrates (Stark), **2:**321

Big bang theory, **2:**308

Big Nambas people, **1:**79

Bingham, Hiram, III, **1:**55–58, *57;* **2:**218

Binomial nomenclature, **1:**40

Bioko Island (Fernando Póo), **1:**68, 167

Bipedalism, **1:**174, 175

Birds

as evolved from dinosaurs, **2:**206, 229, 230

See also specific species

Bismarck (ship), **1:**36

Bjaaland, Olav, **1:**13

Black Sea, **1:**31, 36, 38; **2:**228

Blackburn, Reid, **2:**218

Blackwood's Magazine, **2:**318–19

Blanc, Cape, Mauritania, **1:**107

Blegen, Carl William, **2:**264

Bligh, William, **1:**125

Bloomsbury Group, **2:**328

Blue Nile River, **1:**61, 62–63

Blue poppy (*Meconopsis betonicifolia*), **1:**163, 164–65

Boer War, **2:**279

Bogotá, Colombia, **1:**156

Bojador, Cape, Africa, **1:**107

Bolívar, Simón, **1:**55–56

Bolivia, **2:**208

Bolshoy Baranov Cape, Russia, **1:**27

Bone Cabin Quarry, Wyoming, **1:**80, 81

Bongo people, **2:**268

Bonin Island, **2:**256

Bonpland, Aimé, **1:**5, 7, 152, 154, 155

Book de Magnete (Gilbert), **1:**14

Book of the Thousand Nights and a Night, The (Arabian Nights; Burton, translator), **1:**69; **2:**322

Boos, Franz, **1:**126

Boothia Peninsula, Canada, **1:**11, 12, 14, 28

Bor Guve, Mongolia, **1:**129, 130

Bora Bora Island, **1:**79

Borchgrevnik, Carsten, **1:**22

Borge, Norway, **1:**8, 9

Borman, Frank, **2:**290, 291

Borneo, **1:**17, 133, 134; **2:**347

Borup, Yvette, **1:**17

Boston Museum of Science, **2:**336, 337, 339–40

Botanic Garden, U.S., **2:**349

Botany

Banks, **1:**38–43; **2:**234

Humboldt, **1:**153–54

Kingdon-Ward, **1:**163–65

Mexia, **2:**207–9

Schultes, **2:**265–67

Schweinfurth, **2:**267–69

Wilkes Expedition, **2:**349

Botany Bay, Australia, **1:**38, 41, 85, 124, 125; **2:**234

Botswana (Bechuanaland), **1:**185; **2:**324, 327, 329

Boudeuse, La (ship), **1:**60

Bougainville, Louis-Antoine de, **1:**58–61, *59,* 154; **2:**231, 234

Bougainville Island, **1:**60; **2:**234

Bougainvillea (climbing plant), **1:**60

Bourke-White, Margaret, **2:**286

Bowdoin Bay, Greenland, **2:**242

Bowers, Henry Robertson, **2:**276–77

Bowman, Isaiah, **1:**56

Bowring, John, **2:**209

Brackenridge, William, **2:**347

Bradford Washburn American
Mountaineering
Museum, **2:**338

Brahmaputra River, **1:**138

Brand, Vance, **2:**295

Braun, Wernher von, **1:***159*

Brazil, **1:**5, 6, 44, 45, 49, 68, 98,
109, 133; **2:**207, 208,
347

Brazza, Pierre Savorgnan de,
1:166

Breed, William, **2:**248

Bright Angel shale, **2:**248

British Arctic Air Route
Expedition, **2:**342,
344–45

British Association for the
Advancement of
Science (British Science
Association), **1:**68;
2:269, 271, 321

British Broadcasting Company
(BBC), **2:**329

British Columbia, **1:**89, 142,
144, 176; **2:**193, 194

British East India Company,
1:64, 65

British Empire, **1:**43; **2:**250–51

British Guiana (Guyana), **2:**251,
340–42

British Military Intelligence,
1:53

British Museum, **1:**39, 43, 167

British Museum of Natural
History, **1:**79, 171

British National Antarctic
Expedition, **1:**22; **2:**272,
273–74, 275, 278, 279,
280

British Science Association
(British Association for
the Advancement of
Science), **1:**68

Brontosaurus (Apatosaurus;
dinosaur), **1:**80

Brothers of Freedom, **2:**323

Brown, Robert, **1:**127

Bruce, James, **1:**xii, 4, 61–64

Bruce, William Speirs, **2:**282

Bryce, Robert, **2:**244

Bube people, **1:**165, 167

Buddhism, **1:**129, 137

Budge, E.A. Wallis, **2:**264

Buffon, Georges Louis-Leclerc,
Comte de, **1:**63

Bull, Henryk John, **1:**21, 22

*Bulletin of the American
Geographical Society*, **1:**8

Bumpus, Hermon C., **1:**17

Bunarbashi, Turkey, **2:**260

Bureau of American Ethnology,
2:245, 249

Burma, **1:**17, 165

Burton, Richard Francis, **1:**xii,
64–69, 65, 166, 168,
186; **2:**251, 317–21

Bush, George W., **2:**298

Bushmen, **2:**324–25, 326, 327,
329

Bussa Rapids, **2:**241

Bute, Earl of, **1:**5

Butterflies, **1:**44, 45, 46

Bylot, Robert, **1:**27, 112

Byrd, Richard E., **1:**xii, 15, 21,
23, 28, 69–74, 70; **2:**218

Byron, John, **2:**233

Cabinda, Africa, **1:**166

Cabot, John, **1:**131

Cairo, Egypt, **2:**323

Cairo Museum, **1:**78

Calabar, Africa, **1:**166

Calder, William, III, **2:**263

Calicut, **1:**107

California, **1:**89; **2:**349
gold rush, **2:**260

California gray whales, **1:**17

Callao, Peru, **1:**146, 147

Calvert, Frank, **2:**260

Calypso (ship), **1:**92, 93–95, 93

Camarasaurus (dinosaur), **1:**80

Cambodia, **2:**209, *210*

Cameras, **2:**338
ANGUS underwater, **1:**33,
35
mapmaking and, **2:**204
See also Photography

Cameron, Verney Lovett, **2:**251

Cameroon, **1:**166

Cameroon, Mount, **1:**168

Camp Disappointment, **1:**183

Camposaurus (dinosaur), **1:**80

Camps and Trails in China
(Andrews), **1:**20

Canada, **1:**26, 27, 29, 59, 83,
105, 110, 112, 131–32;
2:193–95, 243, 256,
299, 308, 325, 336, 337,
339, 342, 343
See also specific location

Canary Islands, **1:**108

Canterbury Basin, New
Zealand, **2:**237

Cape Adare, Antarctica, **1:**22;
2:276

Cape Addington, Alaska, **2:**255

Cape Adelaide, Canada, **1:**14

Cape Blanc, Mauritania, **1:**107

Cape Bojador, Africa, **1:**107

Cape Chelyuskin, Russia, **1:**27

Cape Cod, Massachusetts,
2:226

Cape Crozier, Antarctica, **2:**276

Cape Evans, Antarctica, **2:**276

Cape Leeuwin, Australia, **1:**127

Cape Morris Jesup, Greenland,
1:28; **2:**242

Cape of Good Hope, Africa,
1:42, 87, 88, 107; **2:**347

Cape Prince of Wales, Alaska,
1:27

Cape Royds, Antarctica, **2:**280

Cape Shelagski, Russia, **2:**252,
257

Cape Times, **2:**328

Cape Verde Islands, **1:**49, 98,
107

Carchemish, **1**:52

Cárdenas, Garcia López de, **1**:110

Caribbean (West Indies), **1**:xiii, 113, 126, 163; **2**:226

Carmel, California, **1**:16, 20

Carnarvon, George Edward Stanhope Herbert, fifth Earl of, **1**:75, 76–78

Caroline Island, **2**:256

Carpentaria, Gulf of, **1**:127

Carr, Gerald, **2**:295

Carson, Rachel, **1**:95

Carter, Howard, **1**:xii, 75–78, 77; **2**:218

Carteret, Philip, **2**:234

Cartier, Jacques, **1**:105, 110

Cartography. *See* Maps and mapmaking

Cascade Mountains, **2**:194

Casiquiare Canal, **1**:155

Caspian Sea, **2**:321, 322

Cassini-Huygens (spacecraft), **2**:302, 315, 316

Castaneda, Carlos, **2**:266

Catastrophic theory, **1**:49, 102–3

Catholicism, **1**:xi; **2**:232, 340

Cave of a Thousand Buddhas, China, **1**:129

Celebes Island, **1**:17

Centaurus X-3, **2**:307

Central Africa, **1**:4, 166, *189*

Central America, **2**:200, 201, 242

See also specific location

Central Asia, **1**:135, 136–38, *136*, *138*

Central Asia and Tibet (Hedin), **1**:137

Central Asiatic Expeditions, **1**:16, 17–20

Central Kalahari Game Reserve, **2**:327, 329

Centrifugal force, **2**:202

Cernan, Eugene, **2**:294

Cetaceans, **1**:16, 17

CFCs (Chlorofluorocarbons), **1**:25

Chaffee, Roger, **2**:291

Challenger (space shuttle), **2**:285, 286, 297

Challenger Deep, **2**:227, 237

Challenger expedition, **2**:222, 225, 231, 232, 234, 235, 237

Chambers, Robert, **1**:102

Chandra (X-ray telescope), **2**:307

Chandrayaan-1 (lunar orbiter), **2**:311

Chang-Tang plateau, Tibet, **1**:123, 124

Chang'an (Xi'an), China, **1**:137

Chang'e 1 (lunar orbiters), **2**:302, 310–11

Chao Phraya River, Thailand, **2**:209

Chapman, Cora May, **1**:16

Charbonneau, Toussaint, **1**:178

Charles, Prince of Wales, **2**:326, 329

Charles Hansson (ship), **1**:12

Charles Island, **1**:50

Chatham Island, **1**:50, 99

Chechen Desert, **1**:138

Cheesman, Lucy Evelyn, **1**:78–80

Chelyuskin, Cape, Russia, **1**:27

Chelyuskin, Semyon, **1**:27; **2**:256

Chemosynthesis, **1**:34

Cherrie, George, **1**:7

Chesapeake Bay, United States, **2**:203

Chikyu (ship), **2**:237

Chile, **1**:98–99; **2**:208, 235, 347

Chimborazo, Mount, Ecuador, **1**:155, 157

Chimpanzees, **2**:218

China, **1**:17, 19, 121, 129, 135, 136, *136*, 137, 139, 163, 164; **2**:199, 252, 257, *257*, 258, 285, 287, 302, 308

manned space exploration by, **2**:287, 299–300

unmanned space exploration by, **2**:310–11

See also specific location

Chipewyan, Fort, Canada, **2**:193

Chirikov, Aleksi Illich, **1**:27; **2**:254, 255

Chitambo, Africa, **1**:187

Chlorofluorocarbons (CFCs), **1**:25

Choqquequirau, Peru, **1**:56

Christianity, **1**:xi, 107, 185

Christmas, Wilhelmina Anderson, **1**:20

Chronometers, **1**:67, 67, 83, 156; **2**:194, 203, 246

Chukchi Peninsula, Russia, **2**:254

Churchill River (Hamilton River), Canada, **2**:342, 343–44

Cíbola, **1**:105, 110

Circumnavigation of Earth, **1**:58, 59, 59, 105, 110; **2**:232, 233, 234, 256, 347

Civil Service Commission, **1**:58

Civil War, U.S., **1**:186; **2**:246

Clairaut, Alexis, **1**:59

Clarion Fracture Zone, **2**:235

Clark, Charles, **1**:89

Clark, James L., **1**:17

Clark, William, **1**:xiii, 114, 175–76, 177–83, *177*, *179*; **2**:194

Classes, classifying, **1**:40

Clatsop, Fort, Oregon, **1**:181–82

Clearwater River, United States, **1**:181

Climate change, **1:**31
  See also Global warming
Clipperton Fracture Zone, **2:**235
Cloverly Formation, Montana, **1:**81; **2:**230
Club of the Royal Philosophers, **1:**43
Coconino sandstone, **2:**248
Cod, Cape, Massachusetts, **2:**226
Coelurus, **1:**81
Colbert, Edwin H., **2:**229
cold war, **1:**23, 29, 58; **2:**287, 295, 302, 304, 310
Collins, Michael, **2:**290, 292
Colombia, **1:**154; **2:**265–66
Colonialism, **1:**169, 189
Colorado River, **2:**245–46, 247–49, 247
Columbia (*Apollo 11* command module), **2:**292
Columbia (space shuttle), **2:**287, 296, 298, 338
Columbia River, **1:**181, 183; **2:**347, 349
Columbia University, **2:**227
Columbus, Christopher, **1:**xi–xii, xiii, 105, 108–9, 131
Comet Grigg-Skjellerup, **2:**316
Commander Islands, **2:**254, 256
Commerçon, Philibert, **1:**60
Como Bluff, Wyoming, **1:**80–81, 91
Compasses, **2:**194, 212, 246, 269, 270, 271
Compton Gamma Ray Observatory, **2:**298
Concepción, Chile, **1:**99
Condemned to Devil's Island (Niles), **2:**285
Conformal maps, **2:**201–2
Congo, **1:**189–90
Congo, Democratic Republic of, **2:**268, 318

Congo and the Founding of Its Free State, The (Stanley), **1:**190
Congo River, **1:**3, 186, 189; **2:**241, 268
Connecticut, **1:**55, 58
Conrad, Charles "Pete," **2:**292, 295
Conservation, **2:**329, 342
Conshelf projects, **1:**92, 95–96
Constellation program, **2:**299
Continental Divide, **2:**193, 194
Continental drift, **1:**31, 32; **2:**228
Continentality principle (Humboldt), **1:**157
Continuous plankton recorder, **2:**227
Contributions to the Theory of Natural Selection (Wallace), **2:**334
Convicts, **1:**42
Cook, Frederick, **1:**13, 29; **2:**243, 244–45
Cook, James, **1:**xiii, 3, 4, 27, 41–42, 82–90, 83, 84, 86, 125, 152, 153, 154; **2:**203, 231, 233, 234, 347
  Antarctic Circle crossed by, **1:**21, 22, 87
  Antarctica circumnavigated by, **1:**82, 85, 87
  Australia, **1:**38, 41, 85, 87
  Northwest Passage, **1:**88–89
Cook and Peary: The Polar Controversy Resolved (Bryce), **2:**244
Cook Inlet, **2:**193
Cooley, William Desborough, **1:**131
Cope, Edward Drinker, **1:**xii, 81, 90–92; **2:**205, 207
"Cope's rule," **1:**91
Coral snakes, **1:**46
Corers, **2:**228

Corona (satellite), **2:**306
Coronado, Francisco, **1:**105, 110
Coropuna, Mount, Peru, **1:**57
Corps of Discovery, **1:**175–76, 178, 180, 182–83
Cortés, Hernán, **1:**105, 109–10
Coryndon Memorial Museum, **1:**172
Cosmic radiation, **1:**24, 159; **2:**302
Cosmos (Humboldt), **1:**153, 157
Cosmos Club, **2:**216
Cousteau, Jacques-Yves, **1:**xiii, 92–96, 93; **2:**218
Cousteau, Jean-Michel, **1:**96
Cousteau, Philippe, **1:**96
Cousteau Society, **1:**92, 95
Crary, Albert P., **1:**24
Crean, Tom, **2:**284
Crime and Custom in Savage Society (Malinowski), **2:**197
Crimean War, **2:**318
Crippen, Robert, **2:**296
Crocodiles, **2:**341
Crosley, John, **1:**127
Crozier, Cape, Antarctica, **2:**276
Cumberland, HMS, **1:**127
Cunningham, Walter, **2:**291
Curare, **2:**265–66, 340–41
Custis, Peter, **1:**116
Cutler, W.E., **1:**171
Cuzco, Peru, **1:**56, 110
Cyclops Mountains, New Guinea, **1:**80

Damascus, Syria, **1:**52, 68
Damāvand, Mount, Persia, **1:**136
Dana, James Dwight, **2:**347
Danielssen, Daniel Cornelius, **2:**212
Daphne Island, **1:**100
Dark Eye in Africa, The (Van der Post), **2:**329

Darwin, Charles, **1**:xiii, 45–46,
91, 96–105, *97*, 131,
157; **2**:206, *206*, 225,
331, 333, 334, *335*, 335,
341
Beagle voyage, **1**:47–51, *48*,
49, 97, *97*, 98–101, *102*;
2:225, 234
Darwin, Erasmus, **1**:97, 102
Darwin Medal, **2**:335
Darwinism. *See* Evolution,
Darwin's theory
Davis, John, **1**:21, 22, 27
Davis Strait, **1**:27
Davy, Humphry, **2**:270
Days Before History (Hall),
1:170
De Bestiis Marinis (*The Beasts of
the Sea*; Steller), **2**:255,
256
Death masks, **2**:259, 262–64,
263
Deep Ocean Engineering, **1**:117,
119
Deep Rover (submersible), **1**:119
Deep-sea drilling, **2**:222, 223,
227–28, 237–38
Deep Sea Drilling Project,
2:237
Deep Submergence Laboratory,
1:34
Deevie Bay, **2**:343
Defense Support Program
(DSP), **2**:306
Defoe, Daniel, **1**:125
Deinonychus (dinosaur), **2**:229,
230
Deir el Bahbri, Egypt, **1**:75
Dellenbaugh, Frederick, **1**:123
Demakopoulou, Katie, **2**:263
Demerara River, British Guiana,
2:341
Denali National Park (Mount
McKinley National
Park), Alaska, **2**:207,
208

Denmark, **1**:148
Denmark Strait, **1**:36
Depression, Great, **1**:20, 58;
2:344
Dersu Uzala (*Dersu the Hunter*;
Arsenyev), **2**:258
Des Moines River, United
States, **2**:246
Descent of Man, The (Darwin),
1:97, 103, 105
*Description from a Voyage
Around the World*
(Bougainville), **1**:60
Desert Storm, Operation, **2**:306
Devil's Island, **2**:285
DEW (Distant Early Warning)
Line, **1**:29
Dezhnyov, Semyon, **2**:253, 254
Dias, Bartholomeu, **1**:105, 107
Dias, Dinis, **1**:107
Dickson, James, **2**:238
Dinka people, **2**:268
Dinosaurs, **1**:19
birds as evolved from, **2**:206,
229, 230
eggs, **1**:16, 18–19, *19*, 130,
150–51; **2**:230
fossils, **1**:18, 21, 80–81,
90, 91, 129, 130, *130*,
150–51; **2**:206, 229–30
growth rates in, **1**:151
as warm blooded, **1**:151,
152; **2**:229, 230
See also specific species
Diomede Island, **1**:27
Diplodocus (dinosaur), **1**:80
Dipping needles, **1**:156
*Discoveries Made in Exploring
the Missouri, Red River,
and Washita by Captains
Lewis and Clark, Doctor
Sibley, and William
Dunbar*, **1**:116
Discovery (Byrd), **1**:74
Discovery (ship; Baffin
expedition), **1**:112

Discovery (space shuttle), **2**:298,
302, 309
Discovery, Age of. *See* Age of
Discovery
Discovery, HMS (ship; Cook
expedition), **1**:89
Discovery Expedition, **2**:273–74,
275, 278, 279, 280
Discovery of the Titanic, The
(Ballard), **1**:35
Dismorphia butterflies, **1**:45
Distant Early Warning (DEW)
Line, **1**:29
District of Columbia, University
of the (UDC), **1**:162–63
Diur people, **2**:268
*Divers Voyages Touching the
Discoverie of America*
(Hakluyt), **1**:131, 132
Dobrovolsky, Georgi, **2**:295
Dodoth people, **2**:324, 325
Dogs, **2**:325
Dogsleds, **1**:11; **2**:213, 243,
244–45, 275, 276, 277
Dolphin, HMS, **2**:233–34
Dörpfeld, Wilhelm, **2**:264
Drifting ice stations, **1**:26,
28–29, 30, *30*
Druze, **1**:51–52
DSP. *See* Defense Support
Program
Du Chaillu, Paul Belloni, **1**:166
Duke, Charles, **2**:294
Dunbar, William, **1**:xiii, 113–17
Dunbar-Hunter expedition,
1:xiii, 113–17
Dunhuang, **1**:129
Dunn, William, **2**:246
Dutch East India Company,
1:112
Dutch East Indies, **2**:233, 328
Dyhrenfurth, Norman, **1**:120,
122

Eagle (lunar lander), **2**:292, 293
Eagle City, Alaska, **1**:12

Eannes, Gil, **1**:107

Earhart, Amelia, **2**:285, 286

Earl of Pembroke (ship), **1**:86

Earle, Barbara, **1**:36

Earle, Sylvia Alice, **1**:117–20, *118*, 124; **2**:228–29

Early Apollo Scientific Experiments Package (EASEP), **2**:293

Early Man and the Ocean (Heyerdahl), **1**:148

Earth
circumference, **2**:199, 200–201
circumnavigation, **1**:58, 59, *59*, 105, 110; **2**:232, 233, 234, 256, 347
climate, **1**:21
equatorial bulge, **2**:202
magnetic field, **1**:24

Earthquakes, **2**:235

EASEP. *See* Early Apollo Scientific Experiments Package

East Africa, **2**:251

East India Company, **2**:317

East Indies (Spice Islands), **1**:xi, xiii, 110; **2**:232

East Pacific Rise, Siberian Sea, **1**:27; **2**:252, 257

Easter Island, **1**:87, 144, 147–48, 149; **2**:231

Ecuador, **1**:5, 6, 146, 154

Edge Island (Edgeoya), **2**:342, 343

Edsel Ford Range, Antarctica, **1**:72

Edward, Lake, Africa, **1**:189

Edward VII, King of England, **2**:281

Edwards, W.H., **1**:44

Egg Mountain, Montana, **1**:151

Eggs, dinosaur, **1**:16, 18–19, *19*, 130, 150–51; **2**:230

Egypt, **2**:267, 323

Egypt Exploration Fund, **1**:75

Egyptian Antiquities Service, **1**:75–76

Eisele, Donn, **2**:291

Eisenhower, Dwight D., **2**:304

El-Amarna, Egypt, **1**:75

Elasmosaurus (reptile), **2**:207

Elburz Mountains, Persia, **2**:322

Elephant Island, **2**:283, 284

Elephants, **2**:325

Elizabeth I, Queen of England, **1**:132

Elizabeth II, Queen of England, **2**:326, 330

Ellesmere Island, **1**:14, 27, 141; **2**:243

Ellicott, Andrew, **1**:114

Ellsworth, Lincoln, **1**:15, 23

Emma Dean (boat), **2**:246

Encounter Bay, Australia, **1**:126, 127

Endeavour (space shuttle), **2**:287, 297, 298, 309

Endeavour, HMS, **1**:38, 41–42, 82, 83, 85, 86, *86*; **2**:234

Endurance (ship), **2**:278, 281–84, *282*

England/English, voyages of discovery by, **1**:111–112, 131–132; **2**:232, 233

Enlightenment, **1**:3, 59, 60

Entomological Society of London (Royal Entomological Society), **1**:46

Entomology, **1**:44
Bates, **1**:44–47

Environment, evolution and, **1**:102, 104

Environmentalism, **1**:95–96, 119–20, 157; **2**:266, 326, 329–30

Epidemics, **1**:6–7

Equal-area maps, **2**:201–2

Equatoria, **1**:184, 189

Equatorial Guinea, **1**:167

Eratosthenes of Cyrene, **2**:199–200

Erebus, Mount, Antarctica, **2**:281

Erickson, Gregory, **1**:151

Erie, Lake, **1**:111

Eritrea, **2**:268

Erketu ellisoni (dinosaur), **1**:130

ESA. *See* European Space Agency

Eskimo Life (Nansen), **2**:213

Eskimos. *See* Inuit

Essays on Natural History, Especially Concerning Ornithology (Waterton), **2**:341–42

Essay on the Principle of Population, An (Malthus), **1**:101, 103

Essequibo River, British Guiana, **2**:341

Ethiopia (Abyssinia), **1**:62–63; **2**:267

Ethnobotany, **2**:265

Ethnography, **1**:12, 28; **2**:196–97, 285, 349
field-work, **2**:195, 196–97, *196*
functionalist approach, **2**:195, 197–98
Hanbury-Tenisons, **1**:133–35
Leakey family, **2**:218
Malinowski, **2**:195–99
participant observers in, **2**:197
Schweinfurth, **2**:267–69
Thomas, **2**:324–26

Etoile, L' (ship), **1**:60

Eudiometers, **1**:156

Euphrates River, **2**:199, 323

Eurasia, **1**:15

Europe. *See specific location*

European Space Agency (ESA), **2**:298, 299, 300, 302, 307, 308, 309, 312, 316

European Union, **2:**237

Evans, Cape, Antarctica, **2:**276

Evans, Edgar, **2:**276–77

Evans, Ronald, **2:**294

Everest, George, **1:**122

Everest, Mount, **2:**339
  expeditions to, **1:**xiii, 120–23, *121*

Evolution, **1:**50; **2:**331, *335*
  catastrophic theory, **1:**49, 102–3
  Darwin's theory, **1:**91, 96–97, *97*, 100–105, 143; **2:**205, 206, *206*, 331, 333
  geography and, **2:**332, 334
  Lamarck's theory, **1:**91, 102
  Wallace's theory, **1:**103–4; **2:**331, 332–34, *333*

Ewing, Maurice, **2:**228

Expeditions. *See specific expedition*

Explorer 1 (satellite), **1:**158, 159–60, *159*; **2:**301, 304

Explorer 6 (satellite), **2:**306

Explorer Comes Home, An (Andrews), **1:**20

Explorers. *See specific explorer*

Explorers Club, **1:**123–24, 142; **2:**285

Explorers Journal, **1:**123, 124

Exploring the Deep Frontier (Earle), **1:**119

Exploring with Byrd (Byrd), **1:**74

Expression of the Emotions in Man and Animals, The (Darwin), **1:**97, 105

Exxon Valdez oil spill, **1:**120

Faisal I, King of Iraq, **1:**51, 54

Falkland Islands, **1:**60, 98

Fallen Timbers, Battle of, **1:**177

Fang people, **1:**165, 166, 168

Farthest North (Nansen), **2:**214

Fatu Hiva Island, **1:**143

Ferdinand, King of Spain, **1:**xi, 108

Fernando Póo Island (Bioko), **1:**68, 167

Fernel, Jean, **2:**200–201

Ferrar, Hartley, **2:**273, 279

Fieldwork, **2:**195, 196–97, *196*

Fiji Islands, **2:**233, 235, 347, 349

Filchner, Wilhelm, **2:**282

Finches, **1:**50, 100

Finlay, Gregory and Company, **2:**193

Fiorelli, Giuseppe, **2:**260

First Crossing of Greenland, The (Nansen), **2:**213

First Pan American Scientific Congress, **1:**56

Fish
  fossils, **2:**206
  See also specific species

FitzRoy, Robert, **1:**47, 96

Fjord, Lake, Greenland, **2:**345

Flaming Cliffs, Gobi Desert, **1:**18, 19, 130

Flinders, Matthew, **1:**xiii, 42, 124–28

Florida, **1:**132

Florilegium (Banks), **1:**42

Floyd Bennett (airplane), **1:**71–72, 73, 73

Flying Fish, USS, **2:**346, 347

For Better, For Worse: To the Brazilian Jungle and Back Again (M. Hanbury-Tenison), **1:**133–34

Forbes, Edward, **2:**222, 223–24

Ford trimotor monoplane (Tin Goose), **1:**71–72, 73, 73

Forster, E.M., **2:**328

Forster, George, **1:**152, 153

Fort Chipewyan, Canada, **2:**193

Fort Clatsop, Oregon, **1:**181–82

Fort Mandan, North Dakota, **1:**178, 180, 181, 182

Fort Peck Reservoir, Montana, **1:**150, 152

Fort Pitt, Pennsylvania, **1:**113

Fossey, Dian, **1:**124; **2:**218

Fossils, **1:**16, 17–18; **2:**205–7, 248
  dinosaur, **1:**18, 21, 80–81, 90, 91, 129, 130, *130*, 150–51; **2:**206, 229–30
  extraction, **1:**20
  fish, **2:**206
  hominid, **1:**171–75, *171*
  mammal, **1:**173; **2:**206
  shells, **2:**247

Fracture zones, **2:**232, 235

Fram (ship), **1:**13, 14; **2:**211, *212*, 213–15

France/French, **2:**337
  voyages of discovery by, **1:**3, 110–11; **2:**232, 234

Franheim, **1:**13

Franklin, John, **1:**9, 11, 28; **2:**250, 251

Franz Josef Land, **2:**214, 215

Fraser River, Canada, **2:**194

Frazer, James, **2:**196

Freedom 7 (Mercury space capsule), **2:**287, 289

Freeman, Thomas, **1:**116

French Academy of Sciences, **1:**61

French and Indian War. *See* Seven Years' War

French Congo, **1:**165, 166, 167

French Guiana, **2:**285

French Polynesia, **1:**79

French Royal Academy of Sciences, **2:**202

Fridtjof, Mount, Antarctica, **1:**71

Friendship 7 (Mercury space capsule), **2:**287, 289

Frobisher, Martin, **1:**27

Frobisher Bay, Baffin Island, **1:**27

Fruneaux Group, **1:**126

Fuchs, Vivian E., **1**:24
Fuji Islands, **1**:149
Functionalism, **2**:195, 197–98
Fur trade, **2**:193
Furneaux, Tobias, **1**:87

Gagarin, Yuri, **2**:287, 288, 288, 305
Gagnan, Émile, **1**:93
Galápagos Islands, **1**:47, 50, 79, 96, 99–100, 147; **2**:231, 234
Galápagos Rift, **1**:33
Galileo (space probe), **2**:302
Gama, Vasco da, **1**:105, 107
Gambia River, Africa, **1**:3, 4, 107; **2**:239, 241
Garrett, Jim, **1**:119
Gelu, Lakpa, **1**:123
Gemini Project (spacecraft), **2**:287, 289–91, 296
    Gemini 3, **2**:290
    Gemini 4, **2**:290
    Gemini 6, **2**:290
    Gemini 7, **2**:290
    Gemini 10, **2**:290
Genera, **1**:40
Genus, classifying, **1**:40
Geodesy, **2**:200, 204
Géographe, Le (ship), **1**:126, 127
Geographical Distribution of Animals, The (Wallace), **2**:334
Geographical Journal, **2**:250, 251, 280
Geological Survey, U.S., **2**:199, 204, 207, 218, 245, 249
Geology, **1**:41; **2**:248, 349
George's River, Australia, **1**:124, 125–26
Germany, Nazi, **1**:139; **2**:198
Gibson, Edward, **2**:295
Giesecke, Albert, **1**:56
Gilbert, William, **1**:14
Giotto (spacecraft), **2**:302, 316
Gishe Abbay, **1**:63

Giza, Great Pyramid of, **1**:75
Gjoa (ship), **1**:10–11, 12, 28
Gjoa Haven, **1**:11, 12
Glacial melting, **1**:160
Glaciers, **1**:21, 25, 28
Glen Canyon, United States, **2**:247
Glenn, John, **2**:287, 289
Global Crop Diversity Trust, **1**:31
Global Positioning System (GPS), **1**:5, 6, 8, 14, 67
Global Seed Vault, **1**:31
Global warming, **1**:21, 29, 31
Glomar Challenger (ship), **2**:227–28
Goa, India, **1**:65
Goa and the Blue Mountains (Burton), **1**:65
Gobi Desert, **1**:xiii, 16, 17, 18, *19*, 21, 129–30, *130*, 135, 136, 139
Godthaab, Greenland, **2**:211, 213
Goethe, Johann Wolfgang von, **1**:158
Gold, **1**:4, 6, 110; **2**:232, 259, 261, *261*
Gold rush, California, **2**:260
Golden Bough, The: A Study in Magic and Religion (Frazer), **2**:196
Gondar, Abyssinia, **1**:62–63
Gondokoro, Sudan, **2**:319, 320
Good, Peter, **1**:127
Good Hope, Cape of, Africa, **1**:42, 87, 88, 107; **2**:347
Goodall, Jane, **2**:218
Gordon, Richard, **2**:292
Gore, John, **1**:89
Gorillas, **2**:218
Gould, Laurence, **1**:71
GPS. *See* Global Positioning System
Grafton, Duke of, **1**:5

Grand Canyon, Arizona, **2**:246, 247–48, 336, 339
Grand Lake, Labrador, **2**:344
Grand Wash, Arizona, **2**:248
Granger, Walter, **1**:18, 20, 80
Grant, James Augustus, **2**:251, 319
Grant, Peter, **1**:100
Gravity corer, **2**:228
Gray, Asa, **1**:96, 103
Great Barrier Inlet, Antarctica, **2**:280
Great Barrier Reef, Australia, **1**:85, 127; **2**:237
Great Bone Wars, **1**:91; **2**:207
Great Britain, **1**:3, 4; **2**:194, 211, 307
    imperialism, **1**:5, 53–54, 169
Great Depression, **1**:19–20, 58; **2**:344
Great Ice Barrier, Antarctica, **1**:23; **2**:279
Great Lakes, **1**:110–11
Great Northern Expedition, **1**:26, 27; **2**:252, 254–56
Great Plains, **1**:178
Great Slave Lake, Canada, **2**:193
Greece, **2**:215, 264
Greek Archaeological Society, **2**:263
Greely, Adolphus, **1**:123
Green River, United States, **2**:246–47, 247
Greenhouse gases, **1**:161
Greenland, **1**:9, 11, 26, 27, 28, 29, 69, 70, 112, 140–41, 160; **2**:211, 212–13, 219, 220, 222, 242, 244, 269, 270–71, 342, 343, 344–45
Greenland Sea, **2**:270
Greenwich Mean Time (prime meridian), **2**:203
Gregory, MacLeod and Company. *See* Finlay, Gregory and Company

Grenville (ship), **1:**83

Grigoryev, Alexander Mikhaylovich, **2:**258

Grissom, Virgil "Gus," **2:**289, 290, 291

Grosvenor, Gilbert Hovey, **1:**95; **2:**217, *218,* 337–38

Grosvenor, Gilbert Melville, **2:**218

Grunsfeld, John, **2:**338

Guadalcanal Island, **1:**36

Guam Island, **2:**236

Guerrero, Mexico, **2:**208

Guinea, Gulf of, Africa, **1:**165, 166

Guinness, Thomas Loel, **1:**93, 94

Gulf Stream, **2:**225, 226

Gulf War, **1:**120

Gunther, Albert Charles, **1:**167

Guyana (British Guiana), **2:**251, 340–42

Habeler, Peter, **1:**123

Haddon, Albert Cort, **1:**171

Hadley Rille, Moon, **2:**294

Hadrosaurs (dinosaur), **1:**151, 152

Hagoromo (satellite), **2:**310

Ha'il, Saudi Arabia, **1:**51, 52

Haise, Fred, **2:**293–94

Hajj, **1:**64, 65

Hakluyt, Richard, **1:**131–32, *132*

Hakluyt Society, **1:**xiii, 131–32

Hale, Horatio, **2:**347

Half Moon (ship), **1:**112

Hall, Henry Rushton, **1:**170

Halley, Edmund, **1:**88

Halley's Comet, **2:**302, 316

Hallucinogens, **2:**265–66

Ham (chimpanzee), **2:**305

Hamilton River (Churchill River), Canada, **2:**342, 343–44

Hanbury-Tenison, Marika, **1:**133–35

Hanbury-Tenison, Robin, **1:**133–35

Hanssen, Helmer, **1:**13

Harar, Somalia, **1:**64, 65

Hardy, Alister, **2:**227

Hargas, Marjorie, **1:**32, 36

Harmless People, The (Thomas), **2:**324, 325

Harrison, John, **1:**67, *67;* **2:**203

Harrison, Marguerite, **2:**285

Harvard University

    Botanical Museum, **2:**265, 266

    Oakes Ames Orchid Herbarium at, **2:**265, 266

Hassel, Sverre, **1:**13

Haverford College, **1:**91

Hawaii, **1:**89, 149

Hawaiian Islands, **2:**235, 347

Hawkes, Graham, **1:**117, 119

Hayden, Ferdinand, **1:**91

Heart of Africa, The: Three Years' Travels and Adventures in the Unexplored Regions of Central Africa from 1868 to 1871 (Schweinfurth), **2:**267, 268

Heart of the Antarctic, The (Shackleton), **2:**281

Heart of the Hunter, The (Van der Post), **2:**330

Hedin, Sven Anders, **1:**129, 135–39, *136*

Heezen, Bruce, **2:**228

Heimen (ship), **2:**343

Helen (ship), **2:**332

Heliconian butterflies, **1:**45; **2:**333

Hendrickson, Kai, **1:**56

Henrietta Marie (ship), **1:**163

Henry the Navigator, Prince of Portugal, **1:**xi, 105, 106–7, *106*

Henslow, John Stevens, **1:**97, 98

Henson, Matthew, **1:**xii, 26, 28, 140–42, *141;* **2:**243

Herbariums, **1:**39

Hermit shale, **2:**248

Hesperornis (early bird species), **2:**206

Heyerdahl, Thor, **1:**142–49, *143, 145, 146*

Hidatsa Indians, **1:**178

Hidden Life of Deer, The: Lessons from the Natural World (Thomas), **2:**326

Hidden Life of Dogs, The (Thomas), **2:**324, 325

Hillary, Edmund, **1:**120, *121,* 122, 124

"Hillary Step," **1:**122

Himalayan Mountains, **1:**121, 122, 138; **2:**339

Hindu culture, **1:**65

Hissarlik, Turkey, **2:**259, 260–62, *261*

Historic Naval Ship Association, **2:**236

History of British Starfishes and other Animals of the Class Echinodermata (Forbes), **2:**222, 223

History of the Expedition Under the Command of Captains Lewis and Clark, The, **1:**183

Hiten (spacecraft), **2:**310

Hitler, Adolf, **1:**139; **2:**198

HMS *Adventure. See Adventure,* HMS

HMS *Beagle. See Beagle,* HMS

HMS *Cumberland. See Cumberland,* HMS

HMS *Discovery. See Discovery,* HMS

HMS *Dolphin. See Dolphin,* HMS

HMS *Endeavour. See Endeavour,* HMS

HMS *Investigator. See Investigator*, HMS

HMS *Norfolk. See Norfolk*, HMS

HMS *Porpoise. See Porpoise*, HMS

HMS *Providence. See Providence*, HMS

HMS *Reliance. See Reliance*, HMS

HMS *Resolution. See Resolution*, HMS

HMS *Swallow. See Swallow* HMS

HMS *Terror. See Terror*, HMS

Hobart, Tasmania, 1:14

Hodgson, Thomas Vere, 2:273

Hofmann, Albert, 2:265

Hoghton Tower (ship), 2:278

Holistic view of nature, 1:153–54, 157

Homer, 2:259, 260, 261, 264

Hominids, 1:170, 171–75, *171, 172*
   Homo erectus, 1:173, 174
   Homo habilis, 1:173–74
   Homo sapiens, 1:173, 174, 175

Hoover, Herbert, 1:58, 72

Hopewell (ship), 1:112

Horn of Africa, 1:148

Hornemann, Friedrich, 1:4

Horner, John R. "Jack," 1:xii, 150–52; 2:230, 231

Horrocks, Jeremiah, 1:88

Hot springs, 1:115, 116

Hot Springs, Arkansas, 1:113, 115

Hot Springs National Park, 1:115

Houghton, Daniel, 2:239

Houssa, Africa, 2:239

HOVs. *See* Human Occupied Vehicles

How I Found Livingstone in Central Africa (Stanley), 1:190

Howland, O.G., 2:246

Hubbard, Gardiner Greene, 2:216

Hubbard Medal, 1:142

Hubble, Edwin, 2:308

Hubble Space Telescope, 2:298, 302, 308–9, *308*, 338

Hudson, Henry, 1:26, 27, 105, 111–12

Hudson Bay, Canada, 1:26, 27, 105, 112

Hudson River, United States, 1:112, 182

Hudson Strait, 1:112

Hudson's Bay Company, 2:193

Hughes Bay, Antarctica, 1:22

Human Occupied Vehicles (HOVs), 1:37
   See also specific HOV

Humboldt, Alexander von, 1:xiii, 5, 7, 152–58, *154*

Humboldt-Stiftung foundation, 2:268

Hunt, James, 1:68

Hunt, John, 1:122

Hunter, George, 1:xiii, 113–17

Huxley, Aldous, 2:266

Huxley, Thomas, 2:335

Huygens (space probe), 2:302, 316

Hydrographic Expedition of the Arctic Ocean, 1:28

Hydrographic Office, U.S., 2:204

Hydrographic survey, 1:47

Hydrothermal vents, 1:31, 33–34, 37, *37*

Hygrometers, 1:156

Hypsilophodontids, 1:151–52

Iberian Peninsula, 1:xi

IBG. *See* Institute of British Geographers

Ice mass, 1:23

Ice stations, drifting, 1:26, 28–29, 30, *30*

Icebergs, 1:26

Iceland, 1:26

Idaho, 1:181

Idrisi, Mohammed al-, 2:199, 200

Iguanas, 1:99

IGY. *See* International Geophysical Year

Ilios: The City and Country of the Trojans (Schliemann), 2:262

Illiad (Homer), 2:259, 261

Illinois Museum of Natural History, 2:246

Illinois River, Illinois, 2:246

Illustrations of British Entomology (Stephens), 1:98

Imperial Trans-Antarctica Expedition, 2:283

Imperialism, British, 1:53–54, 169; 2:250–51

In a Province (Van der Post), 2:328

Inca Land (Bingham), 1:58

Incas, 1:55, 56–57, 144, *146*; 2:200, 218
   Spanish conquest of, 1:56–57, 105, 110

Incas of Peru, The (Markham), 1:56

Independence Fjord, 2:242

India, 2:214, 285
   unmanned space exploration by, 2:311

Indian Ocean, 1:42, 107, 185; 2:221, 347
   See also specific voyage/ expedition

Indochina, 2:209

Indonesia, 1:87, 133, 134; 2:328–29

Indus River, 1:138, 148

Infrared Astronomical Satellite (IRAS), **2**:307

Infrared satellites, **2**:307

Infrared Space Observatory, **2**:307

Inman, Mason, **1**:100

Inner Africa Laid Open (Cooley), **1**:131

Inner Mongolia, **1**:16, 19

Insects. *See specific species*

Institute for Archaeological Oceanography, **1**:38

Institute for Exploration, **1**:36

Institute of British Geographers (IBG), **2**:250, 251

Institute of Marine Research (Berlin), **2**:227

Integrated Ocean Drilling Program (IODP), **2**:231, 237

Interior Department, U.S., **1**:118

International Council for Science, **1**:160

International Council for the Exploration of the Sea, **2**:215

International Council of Scientific Unions, **1**:23, 158

International Geographical Congress, **2**:204

International Geophysical Year (IGY), **1**:21, 23–24, 29, 30, 74, 158–60, *159*; **2**:303–4

International Polar Foundation, **1**:161

International Polar Year (1932–1933), **1**:159

International Polar Year (2007–2008), **1**:160–61, *161*

International Space Station (ISS), **2**:287, 296, 297, 298, 299–300, *300*

Internationalism, **1**:60

Inuit (Eskimos), **1**:11, 12, 26, 28, 140–41; **2**:211, 213, 243

Investigator, HMS, **1**:42, 126–27

IODP. *See* Integrated Ocean Drilling Program

Ionian Sea, **2**:260

Iran, **2**:322

Iraq, **1**:51, 53–54, 120, 142, 148; **2**:199, 322

Iraqi Archaeological Museum (National Museum of Iraq), **1**:51, 54

IRAS. *See* Infrared Astronomical Satellite

Irkutsk, Russia, **2**:257

Irvine, Andrew, **1**:122

Irwin, James, **2**:294

Isabella, Queen of Spain, **1**:xi, 108

Islam, **1**:xi, 107

Island Life (Wallace), **2**:334

Isle of Pines, **1**:88

Isothermal lines, **1**:156

ISS. *See* International Space Station

Issyk Kul, Lake, Russia, **1**:136

Italian city states, **1**:107

Ithaca, Greece, **2**:260, 264

Ituri forest, Africa, **1**:189

Ivanovna, Anna, Czarina of Russia, **2**:254

Iwo Jima, USS, **2**:294

Jackson, Frederick, **2**:215

Jacobsen, Christian, **2**:282

Jaketen pa Odin (*The Search for Odin*; Heyerdahl), **1**:148

James Caird (boat), **2**:283

James Island, **1**:50, 99

James Webb Space Telescope, **2**:309

Jameson, Robert, **2**:270

Japan, **1**:17, 149; **2**:237, 254, 285, 299, 307, 308

Japan (*continued*)
    unmanned space exploration by, **2**:310

Japan, Sea of, **2**:258

Japanese Experiment Module (JEM; Kibo), **2**:297

Japen Islands, **1**:80

Jason Junior (JJ; underwater vehicle), **1**:35

JASON Projects, **1**:35–36

Jebel Mountain, **1**:51

Jefferson, Thomas, **1**:114–15, 116, 155, 175–77, 180, 182, 183; **2**:194

JEM (Japanese Experiment Module; Kibo), **2**:297

Jet Propulsion Laboratory, **2**:313

Jewett, Ezekiel, **2**:205

"JIM Dive," **1**:117, 118–19

JIM suit, **1**:118–19

JJ. See Jason Junior

Johanssen, Hjalmar, **2**:213–15

JOIDES Resolution (ship), **2**:228, 237

Joint Oceanographic Institutions for Deep Earth Sampling (JOIDES), **2**:222, 227–28

Jolliet, Louis, **1**:110–11

Jones, Albert José, **1**:162–63

Joseph, Benjamin, **1**:112

Journal of a Voyage to Australia and Round the World, for Magnetical Research (Scoresby), **2**:272

Journal of a Voyage to the Northern Whale-Fishery, Including Researches and Discoveries on the Eastern Coast of West Greenland (Scoresby), **2**:269, 271

Journal of an Expedition Across Venezuela and Colombia, 1906–1907, The (Bingham), **1**:56

Journal of the Discovery of the Source of the Nile (Speke), **2:**317, 320
June, Harold, **1:**72
Jung, Carl, **2:**327, 329
Jupiter, **2:**302
    unmanned exploration, **2:**315
Jurassic Park (film), **1:**152
Jurassic Park III (film), **1:**152
Jussieu, Antoine de, **1:**126

K-19: The Widowmaker (film), **2:**217
Kaguya (lunar probe), **2:**310
Kaibab limestone, **2:**248
Kalahari Desert, Africa, **1:**184, 185; **2:**324, 326, 327, 329
Kalgan, **1:**18
Kama Sutra (Burton, translator), **1:**69
Kamalia, Africa, **2:**239, 240
Kamchatka (ship), **2:**256
Kamchatka Peninsula, **2:**253, 254, 254, 255
Kangaroo Island, **1:**127
Kansas River, United States, **1:**178
Kant, Immanuel, **1:**154
Kara Sea, **2:**221, 258
Karlskrona, Sweden, **2:**221
Kashgar, China, **1:**136
Katie Hines (ship), **1:**140
Kattwinkel, Wilhelm, **1:**173
Kayak Island, **2:**254
Kazakhstan, **2:**288, 304
Kealakekua Bay, Hawaii, **1:**82, 89
Kebrabasa Rapids, Africa, **1:**185
Kennedy, John F., **1:**38; **2:**289, 290, 292
Kenya, **2:**318, 326, 329
Kenya Wildlife Service, **1:**174
Kenyanthropus platyops (human ancestor), **1:**170, 175

Kepler Space Telescope, **2:**316–17
Kerguelen Islands, **1:**21
Kerwin, Joseph, **2:**295
Kew Gardens, **1:**42
Keynes, John Maynard, **2:**328
Khartoum, Sudan, **1:**63; **2:**267–68, 319
Khmer Empire, **2:**209–10, *210*
Kibo (Japanese Experiment Module; JEM), **2:**297
Kikuyu people, **1:**170
Kimeu, Kamoya, **1:**174
King Edward VII Land, Antarctica, **2:**280
King Haakon VII's Plateau, Antarctica, **1:**14
King Point, Canada, **1:**12
King snakes, **1:**46
King William Island, **1:**11, 28
Kingdom and the People of Siam, The (Bowring), **2:**209
Kingdoms, classifying, **1:**40
Kingdon-Ward, Frank, **1:**163–65
Kings. *See specific king*
Kingsley, Mary Henrietta, **1:**xii, 165–70, *167*
Kirishima (ship), **1:**36
Kíthira island, **2:**264
Kittis, Finland, **2:**202
Knorr (ship), **1:**34, 35, 160, *161*
Koettlitz Glacier, Antarctica, **2:**276
Kolobeng, Bechuanaland, **1:**185
Kolyma River, Russia, **2:**252, 257
Komandorski Islands, **1:**27
Komarov, Vladimir, **2:**291
Kon-Tiki (Heyerdahl), **1:**142, 147
Kon-Tiki (raft), **1:**142, *145*, 146, *146*, 147
Kon-Tiki (sun god), **1:**144
Koobi Fora, **1:**174, 175
Korea, **1:**17

Korean devilfish, **1:**17
Korean War, **1:**162
Korolyov, Sergey Pavlovich, **2:**288, 303
Kroepelin, Bjarne, **1:**143
Kubasov, Valeri, **2:**295
Kuiper Belt, **2:**316
Kurds, **1:**54
Kuro Shiro (Japan) Current, **1:**149
Kuruk Daria, China, **1:**136–37
Kuwait, **1:**120

La Boudeuse (ship), **1:**60
La Salle, René-Robert Cavelier, Sieur de, **1:**105, 111
Labrador, **1:**38, 39, 83, 131; **2:**343–44
Labrador Sea, **1:**27
Laetoli, **1:**174
Laika (dog), **2:**301, 303, *304*
Lake Regions of Central Africa (Burton), **1:**68
Lalor, William G., Jr., **1:**29
Lamarck, Jean-Baptiste, **1:**91, 102
Lamont-Doherty Earth Observatory, Columbia University, **2:**227, 228
Lancaster Sound, **1:**112
Land Nationalisation Society, **2:**331, 335
Land of Eagles, The (R. Hanbury-Tenison), **1:**134
Land of the Blue Poppy (Kingdon-Ward), **1:**164
Land reform, **2:**335
Landsat satellites, **2:**199, *203*, 204, 308
    Landsat 1, **2:**308
    Landsat 7, **2:**308
Laos, **2:**211
Lapatin, Kenneth D.S., **2:**263
Lapland, **2:**202
Larsen, Ole Aanderud, **2:**282

Latitude, **2**:200–201, *201*, 202
Lava flows, **1**:31, 33, 36
Lawrence, Charles L., **1**:73
Lawrence, T.E. (Lawrence of Arabia), **1**:52, 53, 54
Lawson, Nicholas, **1**:50, 100
Le Géographe (ship), **1**:126, 127
Le Naturaliste (ship), **1**:126
Le Roy, Pierre, **1**:67
Le Suroit (ship), **1**:34
League of Nations, **2**:211, 215
Leakey, Louis Seymour Bazett, **1**:170–74, *171*, *172*; **2**:218
Leakey, Louise, **1**:170, *172*, 175
Leakey, Mary Douglas Nicol, **1**:170, 171–74, *172*; **2**:218
Leakey, Meave Epps, **1**:170, 175
Leakey, Richard, **1**:170, *172*, 174–75
Leakey family, **1**:xii, 170–75; **2**:218
Lebanon, **1**:62; **2**:321, 322
Leeuwin, Cape, Australia, **1**:127
Leidy, Joseph, **1**:90
Lena River, Russia, **2**:252, 254, 255
Leonov, Alexei, **2**:287, 289, 295
Leopold II, King of Belgium, **1**:189–90
Leslie, Lionel, **2**:344
L'Etoile (ship), **1**:60
Lewin, Roger, **1**:174
Lewis, Meriwether, **1**:xiii, 114, 175–83, *177*, *179*; **2**:194
Lewis and Clark expedition, **1**:xiii, 113, 114, 175–84, *177*, *179*; **2**:194
Liberty Bell 7 (Mercury space capsule), **2**:289
Libya, **1**:4
Libyan Desert, **2**:267, 268
Life (magazine), **2**:340
Life, origin of, **1**:31, 33
Lindbergh, Charles, **1**:124

Linnaeus, Carl, **1**:39, 40, 154
Linnean Society, **1**:46, 104; **2**:333, 335
Lion Gate Project, Mycenae, **2**:259, 262
Litke, Fyodor Petrovich, **2**:252, 256–57
Little America (Byrd), **1**:74
Little America, Antarctica, **1**:71, 72
Little Sam (rhesus monkey), **2**:305
Liv Glacier, Antarctica, **1**:72
Livingstone, David, **1**:xii, 166, 184–87, *187*, *188*, *189*, 190; **2**:251, *251*, 252
Liwei, Yang, **2**:300
Lizarraga, Agustin, **1**:57
Logan, Mount, Canada, **2**:218
Logan Museum of Anthropology, **1**:16
Lohit gorge, **1**:165
Lolo Trail, United States, **1**:181
London Missionary Society, **1**:184
London *Sunday Telegraph*, **1**:133
London *Times*, **1**:80, 134, 138
Long, Thomas, **2**:257
Longitude, **2**:200, 201, *201*, 203
Longstaff, Cedric, **2**:279
Lonicera hildebrandiana (honeysuckle), **1**:165
Lop Desert, China, **1**:138
Lop Nur, China, **1**:136–37
Lord, Walter, **1**:32
Lord Sandwich (ship), **1**:86
Lorestan Province, Persia, **2**:322
Lost City of the Incas (Bingham), **1**:58
Lost World, The (film), **1**:152
Lost World of the Kalahari, The (Van der Post), **2**:329, 330
Louis XV, King of France, **1**:60
Louisiana (West Florida), **1**:113–14

Louisiana Purchase, **1**:175–76
Louisiana Territory, **1**:111, 113, 114, 116, 176, 183
Loulan, China, **1**:129, 135, 136, *136*
Lovell, James, **2**:290, 291, 293–94
Loyalty Review Board, **1**:58
LRO. *See Lunar Reconnaissance Orbiter*
Lualaba River, Africa, **1**:186, 189
Luanda, Africa, **1**:184, 185
Lucania, Mount, Canada, **2**:336, 337
Lumholtz, Carl, **1**:123
Luna program, **2**:301, 309–10
Lunar orbiters, **2**:301, 302, 309, 310–11
Lunar Prospector (spacecraft), **2**:310
Lunar Reconnaissance Orbiter (LRO; spacecraft), **2**:302, 310
Lunar rovers, **2**:294
Lusitania, RMS, **1**:36
Lyell, Charles, **1**:49, 102, 104

Machu Picchu, Citadel of the Incas (Bingham), **1**:58
Machu Picchu, Peru, **1**:55, 56–57, *57*; **2**:218
Mackay, Alexander, **2**:194
Mackenzie, Alexander, **1**:176; **2**:193–95
Mackenzie Pass, Canada, **2**:193, 194
Mackenzie River, Canada, **2**:193
MacMillan, Donald Baxter, **1**:70, 73
Madeira Islands, **1**:85, 107
Magellan (Venus orbiter), **2**:312
Magellan, Ferdinand, **1**:105, 110; **2**:232
Magnetism, **2**:271–72
Mahdi, **1**:189

Maiasaura (dinosaur), **1**:150
   M. peeblesorum, **1**:151
Mailu people, **2**:195, 196
Makela, Bob, **1**:150
Makololo tribe, **1**:185
Malakhov, Mikhail, **1**:29
Malaria, **1**:7, 66
Malawi (Nyasaland), **2**:326, 329
Malawi, Lake, Africa, **1**:186
Malay Archipelago, **2**:332, 333
Malay Archipelago, The: The Land of the Orang-Utan and the Bird of Paradise (Wallace), **2**:334
Malaysia, **2**:266
Maldive Islands, **1**:148
Malekula Island, **1**:79
Malinowski, Bronislaw, **2**:195–99, *196*
Mallory, George Leigh, **1**:120, 122
Malolo Island, **2**:347
Malthus, Thomas, **1**:101–2, 103; **2**:333
Maly Taymyr Island, **2**:258
Mammals
   fossils, **1**:173; **2**:206
   See also specific species
Manchuria, **2**:258
Mandan, Fort, North Dakota, **1**:178, 180, 181, 182
Mandan Indians, **1**:178
Mangbetu (Mombuttoo) people, **2**:268
Maori people, **1**:50, 85
Maps and mapmaking, **1**:xiii; **2**:199–204, 214
   aerial photography and, **2**:339
   Beagle, Voyage of, **1**:*48*
   conformal, **2**:201–2
   Cook, **1**:*84*
   distortion in, **2**:200, 201
   equal-area, **2**:201–2
   Heyerdahl, **1**:*146*

Maps and mapmaking
   (continued)
   Lewis and Clark Expedition, **1**:*179*
   Livingstone and Stanley, **1**:*188*
   National Geographic and, **2**:217
   oceanographic, **2**:224, *224*, *226*
   satellite imagery, **2**:199, *203*, *204*
   topographic, **2**:199, 203–4
   Washburn, **2**:336, 339
   Wilkes, **2**:348, 349
March of the Penguins (film), **2**:216, 217
Mare Serenitatis, Moon, **2**:309
Mariana Islands, **2**:233
Mariana Trench, **2**:222, 227, 231, 235, 236, *236*, 237
Marias River, United States, **1**:183
Marie Byrd Land, Antarctica, **1**:72
Marine archaeology, **1**:53, 93
   Ballard, **1**:31–38
   See also Oceanography
Marine Biological Laboratory, **2**:226
Marine biology, **2**:225–26
Marine chronometers, **2**:203
Marine ecosystems, **1**:162, 163
Mariner planetary probes, **2**:301, 311, 312–13
Mariners' compass, **2**:269, 270, 271
Markham, Clements, **1**:56; **2**:273, 279
Marquesas Fracture Zone, **2**:235
Marquesas Islands, **1**:79, 142, 143, 144, 149; **2**:232
Marquette, Jacques, **1**:110–11

Mars, **2**:301, 302
   unmanned exploration, **2**:312–15
Mars Exploration Rovers (MERs), **2**:302, *313*, 314–15
Mars Global Surveyor (orbiter), **2**:314
Mars Pathfinder (planetary probe), **2**:302
Marsh, Othniel Charles, **1**:xii, 80–81, 90, 91; **2**:205–7, *206*
Marshall, Eric, **2**:280
Marshall Islands, **2**:235
Marsili Seamount, **1**:35
Martin, Charles, **2**:217
Martinique, **2**:218
Martius, Carl Friedrich Philipp von, **1**:5, *7*
Maspero, Gaston, **1**:76
Mastodons, **1**:182
Matterhorn, **2**:337
Mattingly, Thomas, **2**:294
Maud (ship), **1**:15
Maupertuis, Pierre Louis Moreau de, **2**:202
Mauritania, **1**:107
Mauritius, **1**:127–28
Maury, Matthew Fontaine, **2**:222, 223, 224–25, *224*
Mauv limestone, **2**:248
May, Harriet, **1**:32
Mayas, **2**:200
Mazandaran Province, Persia, **2**:322
Mazatlán, Mexico, **2**:207, 208
McAuliffe, Christa, **2**:297
McClure, Robert, **1**:28
McIntyre, Loren, **1**:5, 8
McKinley, Ashley C., **1**:72
McKinley, Mount, Alaska, **2**:244, 336, 338, 339
McMurdo, Archibald, **1**:24

McMurdo Sound, Antarctica, **1:**13, 22, 24, *24;* **2:**273, 275, 276, 279, 280, 283

McMurdo Station, Antarctica, **1:**24, *24,* 25

McNairn, Stuart, **1:**57

McNish, Henry, **2:**283

Mead, Margaret, **2:**286

Meaning of Evolution, The (Simpson), **2:**229

Mecca, Saudi Arabia, **1:**64, 65

Meconopsis betonicifolia (blue poppy), **1:**163, 164–65

Medicine Bow Mountains, Wyoming, **1:**80

Medina, Saudi Arabia, **1:**64, 65

Mediterranean, **2:**199

Mediterranean Sea, **1:**93, 95, 107; **2:**199, 200, 223, 228

Meet Your Ancestors (Andrews), **1:**20

Melanesia, **2:**196, 232

Melbourne, Australia, **1:**86

Mendaña de Neira, Álvaro de, **2:**231, 232

Mendocino Escarpment, **2:**235

Mendoza, Argentina, **1:**98

Mercator, Gerardus, **2:**199, 201, *201*

Mercury, **2:**302

    unmanned exploration, **2:**311

Mercury Project, **2:**288–89, 296, 305

Merin, **1:**18

MERs. *See* Mars Exploration Rovers

Mesopotamia, **1:**148

Mesozoic era, **1:**81

MESSENGER probe, **2:**311

Messner, Reinhold, **1:**123

Meteor expedition, **2:**222, 227

Meteorology, **1:**15

Mexia, Ynes Enriquetta Julietta, **2:**207–9

Mexico, **1:**109, 110, 155; **2:**198, 207, 208, 265, 285

Mexico, Gulf of, **1:**105, 111, 118; **2:**225

Mexico City, **1:**156

Meyer, Grant, **2:**230

Miami, University of, **2:**227

Michel, Jean-Louis, **1:**31, 34–35

Michelin, Robert, **2:**344

Michigan, Lake, **1:**110

Mid-Atlantic Ridge, **1:**32; **2:**227

Middle Ages, **1:**xii

Middle East, **1:**137; **2:**321, 322

    Bell, **1:**51–54, *52*

    Stark, **2:**321–23, *322*

Midway, Battle of, **1:**36

Military Intelligence, British, **1:**53

Milky Way Galaxy, **2:**307, 308, 316

Mimicry, **1:**44, 45–46

Miocene period, **1:**172

Mir space stations, **2:**295–96, 300

Misha (dog), **2:**325

Missile Warning Center, **2:**306

Missionary Travels and Researches in South Africa (Livingstone), **1:**186

Mississippi River, United States, **1:**105, 111, 113, 115, 176, *177,* 178, 181; **2:**246

Missouri, **1:**176

Missouri Democrat, **1:**186

Missouri River, United States, **1:**177, 178, 182, 183

Mockingbirds, **1:**50

Mogao Caves, China, **1:**129

Molucca Islands, **2:**234, 333

Mombuttoo (Mangbetu) people, **2:**268

Mongolia, **1:**18, 129–30, *130*

Mongolian Academy of Sciences, **1:**130

Monroe, Louisiana, **1:**113

Mont Blanc, **2:**337

Montana, **1:**181, 183; **2:**230

    Great Falls of, **1:**181

Montcalm-Grozon, Louis-Joseph de, **1:**59

Montevideo, Uruguay, **1:**49

Montezuma II, Aztec emperor, **1:**110

Montreal Protocol, **1:**25

Moon

    Apollo project, **2:**287, 289, 290–94

    scientific experiments on, **2:**292–93, 294

    unmanned exploration, **2:**301–2, 309–11

Moors, **1:**xi; **2:**240

Morgan, J.P., **1:**18

Morison, Samuel Eliot, **1:**108–9

Morocco, **1:**4, 142, 162, 163

Morris Jesup, Cape, Greenland, **1:**28; **2:**242

Morrison formation, **1:**81

Mosul, Iraq, **1:**53

Motorized sleds, **2:**275, 276

Mouhot, Henri, **2:**209–11

Mount McKinley: The Conquest of Denali (Washburn), **2:**340

Mount McKinley National Park (Denali National Park), **2:**207, 208

Mountaineering

    Everest expeditions, **1:**xiii, 120–23, *121*

    Washburn, **2:**336–39, *337*

Mountains of the Moon, Africa, **1:**62

Mozambique, **1:**107

Mubarak, Sidi, **1:**66

Muir, John, **2:**248

Muller, Fritz, **1:**46

Mulu, Borneo, **1:**133, 134

Mulu: The Rain Forest (R. Hanbury-Tenison), **1:**134

Mundurucú Indians, **1**:45

Muravyov-Amursky, Nikolay Nikolayevich, **2**:252, 257, *257*

Murray, James, **2**:280

Murray, John, **2**:225, 234

Murray Fracture Zone, **2**:235

Museum of Natural History at Princeton University, **1**:150, 151

Muséum National d'Histoire Naturelle, **1**:126

Museums. *See specific museum*

Mushrooms, psychedelic, **2**:265

Muslims. *See Islam*

Mutesa, King, **2**:319

Muztagata Mountain, China, **1**:136

Mweru, Lake, Africa, **1**:186

My Life as an Explorer (Amundsen), **1**:9

Mycenae, Greece, **2**:259, 262–64, *263*

Myth in Primitive Psychology (Malinowski), **2**:197

Namibia, **2**:325

Nanai tribe, **2**:258

Nansen, Fridtjof, **1**:xii, 9, 28; **2**:211–16, *212*, 222, 242
    diplomatic career, **2**:211, 215

Nansen Cordillera, **2**:214

Napo River, South America, **1**:5, 6

Napoleon I, Emperor of France, **1**:126

Nares, George Strong, **2**:251

"Nariokotome Boy," **1**:174

Narragansett Bay, Rhode Island, **2**:346

Narrative of the United States Exploring Expedition (Wilkes), **2**:349

Narrative of Travels on the Amazon and Rio Negro, A (Bates and Wallace), **2**:331, 332

NASA. *See* National Aeronautics and Space Administration

Naskaupi River, Labrador, **2**:344

Natal Advertiser, **2**:327

Natchez, Mississippi, **1**:113–14, 115, 116

National Academy of Sciences, **2**:207

National Advisory Committee on Oceans and Atmosphere, **1**:119

National Aeronautics and Space Administration (NASA), **1**:118; **2**:288–92, 294–98, 304, 309, 311–17, *313*

National Archaeological Museum, Athens, **2**:263

National Association of Black Scuba Divers (NABS), **1**:163

National Geographic, **1**:23, 33, 57; **2**:216, 217, 218, *218*, 286, 339, 340

National Geographic Adventure, **2**:217

National Geographic Expeditions Atlas, **2**:218–19

National Geographic Explorer, **1**:36

National Geographic Kids, **2**:217

National Geographic News, **1**:100

National Geographic Society, **1**:xiii, 7, 8, 36, 38, 72, 94, 95, 142, 173; **2**:216–19, *218*, 244, 245, 337
    scientific exploration sponsored by, **2**:218–19
    television and film, **2**:216, 217

National Geographic Traveler, **2**:217

National Herbarium, U.S., **2**:349

National Marine Sanctuaries, U.S., **1**:117, 120

National Maritime Museum, **1**:86

National Museum of Iraq, **1**:51, 54

National Museums of Kenya, **1**:174, 175

National Oceanic and Atmospheric Administration (NOAA), **1**:117, *118*, 120, 160

National Science Foundation (NSF), **1**:37, 118, 151

National Wildlife Federation, **1**:120

Nationalism, **1**:60

Native Americans, **1**:116, 177, 178, 180, 182, 183; **2**:194, 248, 249
    European contact with, **1**:108–9
    languages, **2**:246, 249
    See also specific native people

Natural selection, **1**:44, 45–46, 47, 50, 96–97, *97*, 101–5; **2**:206, 331, 335

Naturalist on the River Amazon, The (Bates), **1**:46

Naturaliste, Le (ship), **1**:126

Nature, holistic view of, **1**:153–54, 157

Nautilus (submarine), **1**:26, 29

Navy, U.S., **1**:23–24, 32, 34, 36, 118; **2**:227, 346

Nazi Germany, **1**:139; **2**:198

Near-Infrared Camera and Multi-Object Spectrometer (NICMOS), **2**:309

Nebraska, **2**:206

Negro Explorer at the North Pole, A (Henson), **1:**140, 142

Negroland of the Arabs Examined and Explained, The (Cooley), **1:**131

Nelson, David, **1:**42

Nepal, **1:**121; **2:**339

Nephila spiders, **1:**79

Neptune, **2:**315
    unmanned exploration, **2:**316

Netherlands, the/Dutch, **2:**307
    voyages of, **2:**232, 233

Netsilik people, **1:**12

Nevado Mismi, Peru, **1:**8

New Caledonia, **1:**80, 88

New England Museum of Natural History, **2:**336, 339

New Guinea, **1:**79–80, 87; **2:**195, 196, 233, 235

New Hampshire, **2:**336

New Hebrides (Vanuatu), **1:**60, 78, 79; **2:**231, 234

New Holland. *See* Australia

New Horizons (space probe), **2:**302, 315, 316

New Mexico, **2:**229

New Orleans, Louisiana, **1:**113, 116

New Siberian Islands, **1:**27

New South Wales, Australia, **1:**42; **2:**347

New Theoretical and Practical Treatise on Navigation, A (Maury), **2:**224

New York Bay, United States, **1:**112

New York Herald, **1:**186, 187, 189; **2:**207

New York Times, The, **1:**29, 56, 104, 130; **2:**244, 245, 325

New Yorker, The, **1:**95

New Zealand, **1:**41, 50, 82, 83, 85, 89, 101, 125, 149; **2:**231, 233, 234, 235, 237, 275, 280, 349

Newfoundland, **1:**38, 39, 82, 83, 131; **2:**244

Newton, Isaac, **2:**202

Nez Perce Indians, **1:**180, 181

Ngami, Lake, Africa, **1:**184, 185

Niam-Niam people, **2:**268

Nicaragua, **1:**140; **2:**242

NICMOS, **2:**309

Niger (ship), **1:**38, 39

Niger River, **1:**3, 4; **2:**238, 239–41, 268

Nigeria, **2:**241

Night of the New Moon, The (Van der Post), **2:**328

Night to Remember, A (Lord), **1:**32

Nile River, **1:**5, 184; **2:**264, 267–68
    Bruce, **1:**61, 62–63
    Burton and Speke, **1:**65–68, 69; **2:**317, 318–21, *318*

Nile River Valley, **1:**75

Niles, Blair (Mary Blair Rice), **2:**285

Nilsen, Thorvald, **1:**13

Nimrod expedition, **2:**278, 279–81

Niña (ship), **1:**108, 109

Nipishish, Lake, Labrador, **2:**344

Nippur, **2:**199

NOAA. *See* National Oceanic and Atmospheric Administration

Nobel Peace Prize, **2:**211, 215

Nobile, Umberto, **1:**8, 15, 28

Nome, Alaska, **1:**12, 15

Nootka Indians, **1:**90

Nootka Sound, British Columbia, **1:**89

Nordenskjöld, Nils Adolf Erik, **1:**15, 28; **2:**219–22, *220*, 258

Nordic Genetic Research Center, **1:**31

Norell, Mark A., **1:**130

Norfolk, HMS, **1:**126

Norfolk Island, **1:**88

Norge (dirigible), **1:**15

Norsemen, **1:**26

North America, **2:**200, 201
    British colonization, **1:**132
    Dunbar-Hunter Expedition, **1:**xiii, 113–17
    Lewis and Clark Expedition, **1:**xiii, 114, 175–84, *177,* *179*
    Mackenzie, **2:**193–95
    Pacific Coast, **1:**175–78, *177;* **2:**193, 194, 253–54, 256, 258, 347
    Powell, **1:**xiii; **2:**245–49, *247*
    Russian exploration, **1:**27; **2:**253–54, 256, 258
    See also specific location

North American plate, **2:**235

North Dakota, **1:**178

North East Land, **2:**220–21

North Equatorial Current, **1:**149

North Magnetic Pole, **1:**8, 9, 11–12, 14, 28

North Pole, **1:**11, 13, 15, 26, 28–29, *29,* 30, 69
    Byrd, **1:**70, *70*
    Henson, **1:**40, 41–42, *41;* **2:**243
    Nansen, **2:**211, *212,* 213–15
    Nordenskjöld, **2:**220–21
    Peary, **1:**140, 141–42, *141;* **2:**218, 242–45

North Pole-1, **1:**28, 30

North Pole-2, **1:**30

North Pole-32, **1:**30, *30*

North Sea, **1:**119

North Warning System, **1**:29

North West Company, **2**:193, 195

North West River, Labrador, **2**:344

North Western Shipping Company, **2**:278

Northeast Passage (Northern Route), **1**:15, 28, 135; **2**:219, 220, 221–22, 253, 258

Northwest Passage, **1**:9, 26–28, 42, 82, 89, 132, 176; **2**:193, 194, 253

  Amundsen, **1**:8, 10–13

  Baffin, **1**:112

  Cook, **1**:88–89

  Hudson, **1**:111–12

Norway, **1**:8, 9, 15, 161; **2**:213, 215

Norwegian Archaeological Expedition, **1**:147

Notebooks on the Transmutation of Species (Darwin), **1**:101

Notes of a Botanist (Spruce), **2**:265

Nova Scotia, **2**:256

Novaya Zemlya, Russia, **2**:252, 256

Noville, George O., **1**:70

NR-1 (submarine), **1**:36

NSF. *See* National Science Foundation

Nunavut, Canada, **1**:11

Nyasaland (Malawi), **2**:326, 329

Oakes Ames Orchid Herbarium (Harvard University), **2**:265, 266

Oates, Lawrence, **2**:276–77

Oaxaca, Mexico, **2**:198, 208, 265

Ob River, **2**:254

Observations on the Coast of Van Diemen's Land (Flinders), **1**:126

Ocean currents, **1**:15, 149

Ocean Drilling Program, **2**:237

Ocean floor, **2**:224, 226, 227–28, 231, 235–36

Oceanic Institute, **1**:32

Oceanographic Museum, Monaco, **2**:222, 226–27

Oceanography, **1**:xiii; **2**:204, 222–29, *224*, *226*, 231

  Ballard, **1**:31–38; **2**:218

  Cousteau, **1**:92–96, *93*; **2**:218

  Earle, **1**:117–20, *118*, 124; **2**:228–29

  Jones, **1**:162–63

  nineteenth century, **2**:223–26

  twentieth century to present, **2**:226–29

Oceans, The (Prager and Earle), **2**:228–29

Odysseus, **2**:260

Odyssey (*Apollo 13* command module), **2**:293–94

Odyssey (Homer), **2**:259

Office of Coast Survey, **2**:242

Office of Naval Research, **1**:32

Ogowe River, French Congo, **1**:167–68

Ohio River, United States, **1**:111, 115; **2**:246

Old Southwest, United States, **1**:113, 115

Old Way, The: A Story of the First People (Thomas), **2**:324, 326

Olduvai Gorge, Tanganyika, **1**:171, 173–74

Olsen, George, **1**:16, 19

Olympus Mons, Mars, **2**:301, 313

"On the Anomaly in the Variation of the Magnetic Needle" (Scoresby), **2**:270

"On the Habits of Butterflies of the Amazon Valley" (Wallace), **2**:333

On the Hunt for Paradise (Heyerdahl), **1**:143

On the Origin of Species (Darwin), **1**:45–46, 97, 103, 104; **2**:334

"On the Tendency of Species to Form Varieties; and on the Perpetuation of Varieties and Species by Natural Means of Selection" (Darwin and Wallace), **1**:104; **2**:335

"On the Tendency of Varieties to Depart Indefinitely from the Original Type: Instability of Varieties Supposed to Prove the Permanent Distinctness of Species" (Wallace), **2**:333

On the Trail of Ancient Man (Andrews), **1**:20

Ontario, Lake, **1**:111

Oodaaq Qeqertaag, Greenland, **2**:242

Operation Deep Freeze, **1**:69, 74

Opportunity (Mars rover), **2**:302, 315

Orbis Terrarum (Ortelius), **2**:200

Orchomenus, Greece, **2**:264

Orders, classifying, **1**:40

Oregon, **1**:89, 175, 181

Orellana, Francisco de, **1**:5, 6

Origin of the Fittest, The: Essays on Evolution (Cope), **1**:92

Origins (Leakey and Lewin), **1**:174

Orinoco River, South America, **1**:7, 133, 152, *154*, 155

Orion (space capsule), **2**:299

Orkney Islands, **1**:160

Orodromeus makelai (dinosaur), **1**:152

Ortelius, Abraham, **2**:200

Osborn, Henry Fairfield, **1**:18, 21

Oslo, Norway, **1**:9

Ossokmanuan, Lake, Labrador, **2**:344

Ostrom, John H., **1**:xii, 152; **2**:229–31

Ottoman Empire, **1**:51, 54, 62

Ouachita River, United States, **1**:113, 116

Outer Mongolia, **1**:19

Oviraptor (dinosaur), **1**:19

Oxford University, **1**:64

Ozone hole, **1**:24, 25

Pacific exploration, **2**:231–38
    Beagle (ship), **1**:47–51, *48*, *49*, 96, 97, *97*, 98–101, 102; **2**:225, 234
    Bougainville, **1**:58–61, *59*
    Challenger Expedition, **2**:231, *232*, 234, 235, 237
    Cheesman, **1**:78–80
    early period, **2**:232–34, *235*, 237
    Flinders, **1**:124–28
    modern period, **2**:237–38
    ocean floor, **2**:227, 228, 231, 235–36
    Trieste (bathyscaphe), **2**:222, 227, 231, 236, *236*, 237
    Wilkes Expedition, **2**:347, *348*, 349
    See also Cook, James
Pacific Northwest, **1**:149, 176
    British claims in, **2**:194

Pacific Northwest (*continued*)
    Native Americans, **1**:144

Pacific Ocean, **1**:181; **2**:193, 194, 226, *226*, 228
    currents in, **1**:149
    See also specific voyage/ expedition

Pacific Plate, **2**:231–32, 235

Paez, Pedro, **1**:63

Pageos satellite, **2**:204

Paine, Thomas, **1**:57

Pakistan, **1**:142, 148

Paleontology, **2**:205–7, *206*
    Andrews, **1**:16–21, 30
    Como Bluff, **1**:80–81, 91
    Cope, **1**:81, 90–92; **2**:205, 207
    Gobi Desert, **1**:29–30, *30*
    Horner, **1**:150–52; **2**:230, 231
    Marsh, **1**:80–81, 90, 91; **2**:*206*
    Ostrom, **1**:152; **2**:229–31

Palestine, **1**:51

Palmyra, Syria, **1**:62

Pamir Mountains, **1**:136

Pampas Indians, **1**:49

Pan American Airways, **2**:342, 345

Papanin, Ivan, **1**:26, 28, 30

Papilio memnon butterfly, **1**:46

Papua New Guinea, **1**:78, 79

Para (Belém), Brazil, **1**:44, 45

Paris, France, **1**:156

Paris Institute, **1**:155

Paris Peace Conference, **1**:53

Park, Mungo, **1**:xii, 3, 4; **2**:238–41, 239

Parkinson, Sydney, **1**:41

Parry, J.H., **1**:xii

Parry, William, **1**:11

Parsnip River, Canada, **2**:194

Participant observers, **2**:197

Pasha, Emin (Eduard Schnitzer), **1**:184, 189

Passive Seismic Experiment Package (PSEP), **2**:293

Patagonia, **1**:47

Pathfinder (Mars lander), **2**:313–14

Patsayev, Viktor, **2**:295

Pattern of Peoples, A: A Journey Among the Tribes of Indonesia's Outer Islands (R. Hanbury-Tenison), **1**:134

Paul Block Bay, Antarctica, **1**:72

Paulet Island, **2**:283

Payne, Katy, **2**:325

PBS. *See* Public Broadcasting System

Peabody, George, **2**:205

Peabody Museum of Natural History, Yale University, **2**:205–6, 230

Peace River, Canada, **2**:194

Peacock, USS, **2**:346, 347

Peale, Charles Willson, **1**:178, 182, *182*
    museum of, **1**:182, *182*, 183

Peary, Robert Edwin, **1**:xii, 11, 13, 26, 28, 29, 124, 140–42, *141*; **2**:218, 222, 242–45, *243*

Peary Land, Greenland, **2**:242

Pechora River, Russia, **2**:258

Peck, Annie, **2**:286

Peel Sound, Canada, **1**:11

Pelée, Mount, Martinique, **2**:218

Peloponnese, **2**:264

Pembroke (ship), **1**:82

Penikese Island, Massachusetts, **2**:226

People of the Lake (Leakey and Lewin), **1**:174

People's History of the United States, A (Zinn), **1**:109

Peress, Salim Joseph, **1**:119

Persia, **1**:51, 136, 138; **2**:321, 322

Persian Gulf, **1:**120, 148

Personal Narrative of a Pilgrimage to Al-Medinah and Meccah, A (Burton), **1:**65

Personal Narrative of Travels to the Equinoctial Regions of the New Continent (Humboldt), **1:**155

Peru, **1:**5, 6, 7, 8, 56, 142, 143–44, *146,* 147, 154; **2:**207, 208, 347

Petchaburi, Thailand, **2:**211

Peter I "the Great", Czar of Russia, **1:**27; **2:**253, 254

Petrie, Flinders, **1:**75

Petropavlovsk, Russia, **2:**256

Peyote, **2:**265

Pfennig, David, **1:**100

Philadelphia, University of, **1:**91

Philadelphia Academy of Natural Sciences, **1:**90–91

Philippines, **1:**17, 110; **2:**232, 347

Philosophia Botanica (Linnaeus), **1:**40

Philosophical Transactions, **1:**46

Phipps, Constantine John, **1:**39

Phoebe (Saturn moon), **2:**302, 316

Phoenix, Howard, **1:**53

Photography, **2:** 204, 336, 337, *337,* 338, 339–40
See also Cameras; Satellites, imagery

Photojournalism, **2:**216, 217

Photosynthesis, **1:**34

Physical Geography of the Sea, The (Maury), **2:**222, 225

Physical Society of London, **2:**274

Piccard, Auguste, **2:**236

Piccard, Jacques, **2:**227, 236, 237

Pickering, Charles, **2:**347

Pickering, William, **1:***159*

Pietowski, Andrew, **1:**5, 8

Pikes Peak, Colorado, **2:**245, 246

Pinta (ship), **1:**108, 109

Pioneer (solar probes), **2:**311, 312, 315

Pioneer (Venus probes), **2:**312

Pisania, Africa, **2:**239, 240, 241

Pitcairn, Robert, **2:**234

Pitcairn Island, **2:**234

Pitt, Fort, Pennsylvania, **1:**113

Pizarro, Francisco, **1:**105, 110

Planetary orbiters, **2:**301, 302, 314

Planetary probes, **2:**301–2, 311–15

Plankton, **2:**227

Plant geography, **1:**154

Plants
medicinal uses, **2:**265–66
taxonomy, **1:**40

Plants of the Gods: Origins of Hallucinogenic Use (Schultes and Hofmann), **2:**265

Plate tectonics, **1:**32, 33, *37;* **2:**231

Platte River, United States, **1:**178

Player, Ian, **2:**329

Pleistocene period, **1:**173

Plesiosaur (dinosaur), **1:**91

Pluto, **2:**302
unmanned exploration, **2:**316

Pogue, William, **2:**295

Polar Plateau, Antarctica, **2:**274, 276

Polish Institute of Arts and Sciences, **2:**198

Pollution, **1:**92, 95–96, 148, 160–61, 163; **2:**342

Polo, Marco, **1:**108, 129

Polynesia/Polynesians, **1:**142–44, *146,* 147–48, 149; **2:**232, 233, 347

Pompeii, Italy, **2:**260

Pond, Peter, **2:**193

Porpoise, HMS, **1:**127

Porpoise, USS, **2:**346

Portugal/Portuguese, voyages of discovery by, **1:**xi–xii, 3, 6, 105, 106–7, 110; **2:**232

Portuguese Angola, **1:**185

Potsherds, **1:**53

Powell, Emma, **2:**246

Powell, John Wesley, **1:**xiii, 123; **2:**245–49, *247*

Powell, Ric, **1:**163

Powell, Walter, **2:**246

Powell expeditions, **2:**245–49

Prager, Ellen J., **2:**228–29

Preobraschenie Island, **2:**221

Priam, **2:**261

"Priam's Treasure," **2:**259, *261*

Pribilof Islands, **2:**256

Primates, **1:**53, 103
See also specific species

Prime meridian (Greenwich Mean Time), **2:**203

Prince of Wales, Cape, Alaska, **1:**27

Prince of Wales Island, **2:**255

Prince William Sound, Alaska, **1:**27, 89, 120

Princeton University, Museum of Natural History at, **1:**150, 151

Principall Navigations, Voiages, and Discoveries of the English Nation, The (Hakluyt), **1:**131, 132, *132*

"Principle of continentality" (Humboldt), **1:**157

Principles of Geology (Lyell), **1:**102

Proceedings (Royal Geographical Society), **2:**251

Proconsul africanus (hominid species), **1:**170, 172

Project FAMOUS, **1:**33

Project Mercury, **2:**288–89

Pronchishchev, Maria, **2:**256

Pronchishchev, Vasili, **2:**252, 255–56

Protoceratops (dinosaur), **1:**19, 129, 130

Providence, HMS, **1:**125

Providential Cove, Australia, **1:**126

Prussia, King of, **1:**152

Przhevalsky, Nikolai, **1:**136

PSEP (Passive Seismic Experiment Package), **2:**293

Psychedelic mushrooms, **2:**265

PT-109 (boat), **1:**38

Pterodactyl, **2:**206

Ptolemy, **1:**62; **2:**200

Public Broadcasting System (PBS), **2:**305

Puerto Rico, **1:**126

Puget Sound, **2:**347

Pursh, Frederick, **1:**183

Quebec, **1:**82

Queen Elizabeth Islands, **1:**30

Queen Hatshepsut, temple of, Egypt, **1:**75

Queen Maud Mountains, Antarctica, **1:**22, 71, 72

Queens. *See specific queen*

Quest (whaling ship), **2:**284

Quest of the Snow Leopard (Andrews), **1:**20

Question of Survival for the Indians of Brazil, A (R. Hanbury-Tenison), **1:**134

Quinn, Patricia, **1:**161

Quito, Ecuador, **1:**5, 6, 155

Quivedo, Ecuador, **1:**146

Quivira, Kansas, **1:**110

Ra (boat), **1:**148

Ra II (boat), **1:**142, 147–48

Ra Expeditions (Heyerdahl), **1:**148

Rainbow Falls, Tibet, **1:**164

Rain forests, **1:**134; **2:**266
    See also specific location

Rait, Alexander, **1:**113

Raleigh, Sir Walter, **1:**132

Ramses VI, tomb of, Egypt, **1:**76

Ramsey, William, **1:**52

Ranger lunar probes, **2:**310

Raroia Island, **1:**147

Ras Michael, King of Abyssinia, **1:**63

Raven, Peter H., **2:**218–19

"Reciprocity," **2:**198

Reck, Hans, **1:**173

Red Canyon, Utah, **2:**246

Red River, United States, **1:**114, 116

Red Sea, **1:**62, 94, 95, 148, 162, 163; **2:**267

Redwall limestone, **2:**248

Reeve, Bob, **2:**338

Reinach, Saloman, **1:**52

Reindeer Moon (Thomas), **2:**325

Reliance, HMS, **1:**125, 126

Relief, USS, **2:**346

Reptiles. *See specific species*

Resolution, HMS, **1:**22, 42, 82, 87, 89; **2:**222, 234, 269–70

Resolution Cove, British Columbia, **1:**89

RGS. *See* Royal Geographical Society

Rhode Island, **2:**346

Rhode Island, University of, **1:**38

Rhododendrons, **1:**165

Rice, Mary Blair (Blair Niles), **2:**285

Ride, Sally, **2:**297

Rift valley, Africa, **1:**32

Right whales, **1:**16, 17

Riiser-Larsen, Hjalmar, **1:**15

Ringapat, King, **1:**79

Rio da Duvida (River of Doubt), Brazil, **1:**7–8

Rio de Janeiro, Brazil, **2:**347

Río de la Plata (River Plate), South America, **1:**49

Rio Grande, **1:**110

Ripon Falls, Africa, **2:**317, 319

River of Disappointment (Mackenzie River), Canada, **2:**193

River of Doubt (*Rio da Duvida*), Brazil, **1:**7–8

River Plate (Río de la Plata), South America, **1:**49

Robb, George, **1:**53

Robinson, George, **2:**233

Robinson Crusoe (Defoe), **1:**125

Rockefeller, John D., Jr., **1:**18

Rockefeller Mountains, Antarctica, **1:**71

Rocky Mountains, North America, **1:**176; **2:**206, 246

Roggeveen, Jakob, **1:**144, 148

Rohlfs, Gerhard, **2:**268

Rome, ancient, **1:**35, 36, 62

Rondon, Cândido Mariano da Silva, **1:**7

Roosevelt, Anna, **1:**124

Roosevelt, Eleanor, **2:**286

Roosevelt, Theodore, **1:**5, 7–8

Roosevelt, USS, **2:**243, 243

Rosenstiel School of Marine and Atmospheric Science, University of Miami, **2:**227

Ross, Alexander, **1:**113

Ross, James Clark, **1:**11, 12, 14, 24

Ross, John, **1:**11, 28, 113

Ross Ice Shelf, Antarctica, **1:**13, 21, 23, 71; **2:**277, 280

Ross Island, Antarctica, **1:**24

Ross Sea, Antarctica, **1:**22, 24, 72; **2:**228

Rowett, John Quiller, **2:**284

Royal African Society, **1:**169

Royal Charter (ship), **2:**271

Royal Entomological Society. *See* Entomological Society of London

Royal Geographical Society (RGS), **1:**xiii, 3, 5, 65, 66, 121, 134, 138, 169, 186, *187;* **2:**209, 250–52, *251,* 273, 279, 280, 281, 285, 317, 318–19, 320, 321, 335, 343, 345

Royal Horticultural Society, **1:**43, 165

Royal Magazine, **2:**279

Royal Navy, **1:**82

Royal Scottish Geographical Society, **1:**165; **2:**279, 323

Royal Society of London for the Improvement of Natural Knowledge, **1:**38, 39, *39,* 40, 41, 42, 43, 44, 46, 58, 59, 83, 88; **2:**238, 270, 271, 273, 331, 335

Royal Swedish Academy of Sciences, **2:**220

Royds, Cape, Antarctica, **2:**280

RPM Nautical Foundation, **1:**53

Rubber trees, **2:**266

Rush, Benjamin, **1:**178

Rusinga Island, **1:**172

Rusizé River, Africa, **1:**187

Russell, Israel C., **2:**218

Russia, **1:**xiii, 22, 26, 27, 148, 161; **2:**211, 215, 285, 299, 307, 308
    exploration by, **1:**27; **2:**252–58

Russia *(continued)*
    manned space exploration by, **2:**287
    See also Soviet Union

Russian Geographical Society, **2:**256

Ruvuma River, Africa, **1:**186

Ruwenzori Mountains, Africa, **1:**189

Sacagawea, **1:**178

Sage grouse, **1:**177

Sahara Desert, **1:**133

Sahlquist, Gustava, **1:**9

St. Helens, Mount, Washington, **2:**218

St. Lawrence Bay, Nova Scotia, **2:**256

St. Lawrence Island, **1:**27

St. Lawrence River, **1:**82, 105, 110

St. Louis, Missouri, **1:**115, 175, 181, 183

St. Matthew Island, **2:**256

St. Paul (ship), **2:**254, 255

St. Peter (ship), **2:**254–55

Salyut 1 space station, **2:**287, 295

Samoa, **1:**60; **2:**231, 234, 235, 347, 349

Samplers, **2:**228

San Andreas Fault, California, **2:**235

San Francisco, California, **2:**347

San Juan Basin, New Mexico, **2:**229

San Salvador, **1:**50

Sanders, Robert, **1:**151

Sandwell, David, **2:**228

Sansanding, Africa, **2:**241

Santa María (ship), **1:**108, 109; **2:**236

Santarém, Brazil, **1:**45

Santiago, Chile, **1:**56, 98

Santiago Island, **1:**50

São Francisco River, Brazil, **1:**68

Sarawak, **1:**134

Satellites, **2:**296, 298, 302–9
    defense-related, **2:**306
    Hubble Telescope, **2:**298, 302, 308–9, *308*
    imagery, **2:**199, *203,* 204, 226, 228, 237
    infrared, X-ray, and remote-sensing, **2:**307–8
    lunar orbiters, **2:**301, 302, 309, 310–11
    planetary orbiters, **2:**301, 302
    Sputnik program, **2:**301, 303–5
    spy, **2:**304, 306
    television, **2:**301, 305, *306*
    weather, **2:**301, 306–7

Saturday Club, **1:**3

Saturn, **2:**302
    unmanned exploration, **2:**315–16

Saudi Arabia, **1:**51, 52, 54

Sauropods, **1:**130

Saville, Marshall, **1:**123

Schirra, Walter "Wally," **2:**290, 291

Schliemann, Heinrich, **1:**xii; **2:**259–64, *261, 263*

Schmitt, Harrison, **2:**294

Schnitzer, Eduard (Emin Pasha), **1:**184, 189

Schomburgk, Robert, **2:**251

Schools. *See specific school*

Schroder, B.H., **2:**260

Schultes, Richard Evans, **1:**xiii; **2:**265–67

Schweinfurth, Georg August, **2:**267–69

Scientific Results of a Journey in Central Asia, 1899–1902 (Hedin), **1:**135, 138

Scientific revolution, **1:**xii, xiii; **2:**200

Scoresby, William, **2:**269–72

Scorpion, USS (submarine), **1:**34

Scott, David, **2:**294

Scott, James Maurice, **2:**344

Scott, Robert Falcon, **1:**xii, 13, 14, 22, *22*, 23; **2:**272–77, *273*, 278, 279

Scottish Renaissance, **1:**113

Scripps Institution of Oceanography, **2:**227, 228

Scuba, **1:**92, 93, 94, 117, 162

Scurvy, **1:**85; **2:**255–56, 279

SDI (Strategic Defense Initiative), **2:**306

Sea bears, **2:**256

Sea Gull, USS, **2:**346

Sea of Japan, **2:**258

Sealers, **1:**22

Search for Odin, The (*Jaketen pa Odin*; Heyerdahl), **1:**148

SEASAT satellite, **2:**226

Second Boer War, **1:**169

Sedgwick, Adam, **1:**97

Seed and the Sower, The (Van der Post), **2:**328

Semliki River, Africa, **1:**189

Sen, Gertrude Emerson, **2:**285

Senate, U.S., **1:**55, 58

Senegal River, Africa, **1:**3

Serengeti Plains, Africa, **1:**173

Seven Years' War, **1:**59, 62, 82

Severnaya Zemlya archipelago, **1:**28; **2:**258

Sextants, **2:**194, 212, 214, 246

Sexual Life of Savages in North-Western Melanesia, The (Malinowski), **2:**197

Shackleton, Ernest, **1:**xii, 13–14, 22–23, 124; **2:**273, 278–84, *281*, *282*

Shackleton-Rowett Expedition, **2:**278, 284

Shelagski, Cape, Russia, **2:**252, 257

Shelby, Gertrude Mathews, **2:**285

Shells, fossilized, **2:**247

Shenzhou 5 (spacecraft), **2:**287, 300

Shepard, Alan, **2:**287, 288–89, 305

St. *See entries under* Saint

Sherpas, **1:**122–23

Shih Chan-chun, **1:**122

Shiites, **1:**53

Shilluk people, **2:**268

Shiloh, Battle of, **1:**186; **2:**246

Shire River, Africa, **1:**186

Shoshone Indians, **1:**178

Siam (Thailand), **2:**209

Siberia, **1:**26, 27, 89, 153, 156; **2:**252–53, 254, 255, 256, 257–58

Sibiryakov, Aleksandr Mikhaylovich, **2:**252, 257–58

Sierra Leone, **1:**166

Sierra Madre Mountains, Mexico, **2:**208

Sikhote-Alin mountain range, **2:**258

Silent World, The (Cousteau), **1:**92, 94

Silent World, The (film), **1:**93, 95

Silk Road, **1:**129, 136, 137

Simpson, George Gaylord, **2:**229

Singapore, **2:**347

Sino-Swedish Expedition (1926–1935), **1:**139

Sitka, Alaska, **2:**256

Sixth International Geographical Conference (1895), **1:**22

Skate, USS (submarine), **1:**29

Skylab 1; **2:**295, 296

Skyward (Byrd), **1:**74

Slava Rossii (ship), **1:**26, 27

Slave trade, **1:**3, 66, 163, 185

Slaves/slavery, **1:**4, 113, 114

Slayton, Donald "Deke," **2:**295

Sleds

dogsleds, **1:**11; **2:**213, 243, 244–45, 275, 276, 277

motorized, **2:**275, 276

Slice of Spice (M. Hanbury-Tenison), **1:**134

Small-pox, **1:**6

Smith, Donaldson, **1:**123

Smith, Walter, **2:**228

Smithsonian Institution, **2:**349

Snake River, United States, **1:**181

Snakes

coral, **1:**46

king, **1:**46

Snowflakes, **2:**270

Social Lives of Dogs, The: The Grace of Canine Company (Thomas), **2:**326

Society Islands, **1:**149

Society of Woman Geographers (SWG), **2:**285–86

Sojourner (Mars rover), **2:**302, 314

Sokoto River, Nigeria, **2:**241

Solander, Daniel Carl, **1:**38, 39, 41

Solar system, unmanned exploration, **2:**311–16

Solar wind, **2:**293

Solomon Islands, **1:**60; **2:**231, 232, 234

Somalia, **1:**65–66

Somaliland, **2:**317, 318

Sonar, **2:**227

South Africa, **2:**326–27, 347

South America, **1:**55–56, 98, 133, 149; **2:**200, 201, 207, 265–66, 285, 286, 331, 332, 333, 340–42, 347

Humboldt, **1:**57, 152, 154–55, *154*, 156

See also Amazon River and Basin; *specific location*

South American plate, **2**:235

South Asia, **1**:133

South Equatorial Current, **1**:149

South Georgia Island, **1**:21; **2**:278, 283–84

South Magnetic Pole, **2**:281

South Pole, **1**:8, *12*, 21, *22–23*, *22*

    Amundsen, **1**:*10*, 13–15; **2**:272, 275, 276, 277, 282

    Byrd's flights over, **1**:*69*, 70, 71–72, *73*, 74

    Scott, **2**:272, 273, 274–77, 279

    Shackleton, **2**:278, 279, 280–81

South Sandwich Islands, **1**:21

"South-Wales Farmer, The" (Wallace), **2**:331

Southampton Island, **1**:112

Southeast Asia, **2**:209, 238–39

Southern Gates of Arabia, The (Stark), **2**:321

Southern magnetic hemisphere, **2**:269, 271–72

Southern Tibet (Hedin), **1**:138

Soviet Union, **1**:23, 29, 158, 159

    manned space exploration by, **2**:287, 288, *288*, 289, 291, 294–96

    unmanned space exploration by, **2**:301–5, 306, 307, 309–10, 311–12

    See also Russia

Soyuz Project (spacecraft), **2**:287, 291

    Soyuz 1, **2**:291

    Soyuz 3, **2**:291

    Soyuz 4, **2**:287, 291

    Soyuz 5, **2**:287, 291

    Soyuz 11, **2**:295

    Soyuz 19, **2**:287, 295

    Soyuz TM-21, **2**:296

Space exploration, manned, **1**:xiii; **2**:287–301

    Apollo Project, **2**:287, 290–94, 296

    Gemini Project, **2**:287, 289–91, 296

    International Space Station, **2**:287, 296, 297

    Mercury Project, **2**:288–89, 296

    scientific research, **2**:290, 292–93, 294, 295–97, *297*, 298, 299–300, *300*

    Soyuz Project, **2**:287, 291, 295

    space shuttles, **2**:285, 286, 287, 296–99, 338

    space stations, **2**:287, 294–96

Space exploration, unmanned, **1**:xiii; **2**:301–17

    Moon, **2**:301–2, 309–11

    planetary, **2**:311–16

    planetary probes, **2**:301–2, 311–13

    scientific research, **2**:302–4, 308–17

    Sun, **2**:311

    See also Satellites

Space shuttles, **2**:285, 286, 287, 296–99, 302, 309, 338

Space stations, **2**:287, 294–96

"Space transportation system" (STS). *See* Space shuttles

Spacelab, **2**:297, 298

Spacewalks, **2**:287, 289, 290, 309

Spain/Spanish, **1**:105

    voyages of discovery and conquest by, **1**:xi–xii, 6, 105, 107, 108–11; **2**:232–33

Species, classifying, **1**:40

Speke, John Hanning, **1**:xii, 65–68, 69, 186, 189; **2**:251, 317–21, *318*

Spencer Gulf, Australia, **1**:127

Sperm whales, **1**:117, 118

Sphacteria Island, **2**:264

Spice Islands (East Indies), **1**:xi, xiii, 110; **2**:232

Spirit (Mars rover), **2**:302, 314–15

Spiritualism, **2**:331, 335

Spitsbergen Island, **1**:15, 31; **2**:215, 219, 220–21, 343

Spix, Johann Baptist von, **1**:5, 7

Spöring, Herman, Jr., **1**:41

Spruce, Richard, **2**:265

Sputnik program (satellites/spacecraft), **2**:301, 303–5

    Sputnik 1, **1**:158, 159; **2**:301, 303

    Sputnik 2, **2**:288, 301, 303, *304*

    Sputnik 3, **2**:303, 304

    Sputnik 4, **2**:304

    Sputnik 5, **2**:304

    Sputnik 7, **2**:305

    Sputnik 8, **2**:305

    Sputnik 9, **2**:305

    Sputnik 10, **2**:305

Spy satellites, **2**:304, 306

Sri Lanka, **1**:148; **2**:266

Stafford, Thomas, **2**:290, 295

Stanley, Henry Morton, **1**:xii, 184, 186–90, *187*, *188*, *189*; **2**:251

Star Town (Zvezdny Gorodok), Russia, **2**:288

Star Wars program (SDI), **2**:306

Stark, Freya Madeleine, **2**:321–23, *322*

Starokadomsky Island, **2**:258

Stegosaurus (dinosaur), **1**:80

Steller, Georg Wilhelm, **2**:254–55, 256

Stephens, J.F., **1**:98

Strait of Georgia, **1**:176

Strait of Juan de Fuca, **2**:347

Strait of Magellan, **2:**234

Strategic Defense Initiative (SDI), **2:**306

Stromness, South Georgia Island, **2:**284

STS ("Space transportation system"). *See* Space shuttles

Submarines, **1:**29, 31, 32, 34, 35, 36

Submersibles, **1:**31, 32–33, 35, 37, *37*, 119, 134; **2:**222, 227, 236, *236*, 237

Sudan, **1:**63, 184, 189; **2:**267–68, 319

Suez Canal, **2:**221

Sullivan, Kathryn D., **1:**124; **2:**285, 286

Sulzberger Bay, Antarctica, **1:**72

Sumatra, **2:**238–39

Sumerians, **1:**148

Sun, **1:**24; **2:**302
    unmanned exploration, **2:**311

Sundance formation, Wyoming, **1:**81

Sunnis, **1:**54

Supai formation, Grand Canyon, **2:**248

Suroit, Le (ship), **1:**34

Surveying, **2:**202
    topographic, **2:**199, 203–4

Surveyor (lunar probes), **2:**301, 310

Survival International, **1:**133; **2:**327

Survival of the fittest, **1:**103

Sustainable Seas Expeditions, **1:**117, 120

Sutlej River, Tibet, **1:**138

Sverdrup, Harald, **1:**15

Swallow, HMS, **2:**234

Sweden, **1:**149; **2:**215

Swedish Academy, **2:**222

Swedish Museum of Natural History, **2:**220

SWG (Society of Woman Geographers), **2:**285–86

Swigert, John, **2:**293–94

Switzerland, **2:**337

Sydney, Australia, **1:**85, 125

Symmes, John Cleves, Jr., **2:**346

Syria, **1:**51, 62; **2:**322

Syria: The Desert and the Sown (Bell), **1:**51, 52

System Naturae (Linnaeus), **1:**40

System of Mineralogy (Dana), **2:**347

Tabei, Junko, **1:**120, 123

Tae Kwan Do, **1:**162

Tagging Along (M. Hanbury-Tenison), **1:**133–34

Tahiti, **1:**40, 41, 50, 79, 85, 87, 89, 101, 125, 143; **2:**231, 233, 234
    Bougainville, **1:**58, 59, 60–61
    Cook, **1:**83

Talcahuano, **1:**98–99

Tana, Lake, Africa, **1:**63

Tanganyika, Lake (Sea of Ujiji), Africa, **1:**64, 66–67, 69, 184, 187, 189, 190; **2:**317, 318–19

Tanzania (Tanganyika), **1:**66, 171, 173; **2:**318

Tapajós River, Brazil, **1:**45

Tapeats sandstone, **2:**248

Tarim River, China, **1:**136–37, 138

Tasman, Abel Janszoon, **2:**231, 233

Tasmania (Van Diemen's Land), **1:**14, 125, 126; **2:**231, 233

Tatum, Bill, **1:**34

Taxidermy, **1:**16; **2:**342

Taxonomy, **1:**40

Taymyr Peninsula, Russia, **1:**27; **2:**255, 258

Tectonic plates, **1:**32, 33, 37; **2:**231

Tehran, **1:**136

Teixeira, Pedro, **1:**5, 6

Tektite underwater project, **1:**118

Telescopes, **2:**194
    Hubble, **2:**298, 302, 308–9, *308*, 338
    infrared, **2:**307
    James Webb, **2:**309
    Kepler, **2:**316–17
    X-ray, **2:**307

Television and Infrared Observation Satellite (*TIROS 1*), **2:**301, 306–7

Television satellites, **2:**301, 305, 306–7, *306*

Teller, Alaska, **1:**15

Telstar 1 (satellite), **2:**301, 305, *306*

Telstar 2 (satellite), **2:**305

Temple Butte, Grand Canyon, **2:**248

Tenochtitlán, Mexico, **1:**105, 110

Tenzing Norgay, **1:**120, *121*, 122

Tereshkova, Valentina, **2:**287, 289

Terra Australis, **2:**201

Terra Nova (ship), **1:**22; **2:**272, 274–75

Terra Nova expedition, **2:**274–77

Terror, HMS, **1:**24

Testament to the Bushmen (Van der Post), **2:**330

Thagard, Norman, **2:**296

Thailand (Siam), **2:**209

Tharp, Marie, **2:**228

Thatcher, Margaret, **2:**330

Theodolites, **1:**156; **2:**212, 214

Theory of Winds (Wilkes), **2:**349

Thermometers, **2:**214, 246, 270

Thomas, Elizabeth Marshall, **2:**324–26

Thomas, Lowell, **1:**124

Thomson, Charles Wyville, **2:**225, 234

Thomson, Joseph, **2:**251

Thousand and One Churches, A (Bell and Ramsey), **1:**52

Thresher, USS (submarine), **1:**31, 34, 35

Through the Dark Continent (Stanley), **1:**190

Tibet, **1:**121, 122, 124, 138, 163, 164–65; **2:**339

Tidal dynamics, **1:**15

Tierra del Fuego, South America, **1:**47, 49–50, 88

Tiger (ship), **1:**112

Tigris (boat), **1:**142, 148

Tigris River, **2:**199

Timbuktu (Tombouctou), **1:**4; **2:**239, 240

Time (magazine), **2:**313

Tin Goose (airplane), **1:**71–72, 73, 73

Tinian Island, **2:**233

TIROS 1 (satellite), **2:**301, 306–7

Tiryns, Greece, **2:**264

Titan (Saturn moon), **2:**302, 316

Titanic, RMS, **1:**31, 32, 33, 34–35, 34; **2:**218

Titanic Historical Society, **1:**34

Titov, Gherman, **2:**288

Tobol River, **2:**258

Tobolsk, Kazakhstan, **2:**252, 258

Tokelau, **2:**233

Tom Thumb (boat), **1:**126

Tonga, **2:**235

Tonga-Kermadec Trench, **2:**235

Tonti, Henri de, **1:**111

Topographic surveys, **2:**199, 203–4

Torell, Otto, **2:**220

Torne River, Finland, **2:**202

Tornia, Finland, **2:**202

Toroweap limestone, **2:**248

Torres Strait, **2:**233

Tortoises, **1:**50, 99–100

Toscanelli, Paolo, **1:**108

Trade, **1:**169, 185

fur, **2:**193

slave, **1:**3, 66, 163, 185

Trade routes, **1:**36, 107, 129, 137; **2:**193, 239

Transactions (American Philosophical Society), **1:**114

Transhimalaya (Hedin), **1:**138

Transit of Venus, **1:**40–41, 82, 83, 85, 88

Travels in the Interior Districts of Africa (Park), **1:**4; **2:**239, 239, 240

Travels in West Africa (Kingsley), **1:**165, 168, 169

Travels to Discover the Source of the Nile in the Years 1768–1773 (Bruce), **1:**63

Trees, rubber, **2:**266

Tribe of the Tiger, The: Cats and Their Culture (Thomas), **2:**326

Trieste (bathyscaphe), **2:**222, 227, 231, 236, 236, 237

Trieste, Italy, **1:**64, 68

Trieste II (bathyscaphe), **2:**236

Tripolitania, **1:**4

Tristão, Nuno, **1:**107

Tritonia (diving suit), **1:**119

Trobriand Islanders, **2:**195, 196–98, 196

Trojan Antiquities (Schliemann), **2:**262

Trojan War, **2:**259, 262, 264

Troy, **2:**259, 260–62, 261, 264

Troy and Its Remains (Schliemann), **2:**262

Truth, Sojourner, **2:**314

Tuamotu Archipelago, **1:**79, 147, 149; **2:**233

Tucker, H.Z., **1:**56

Tugtilik, Greenland, **2:**345

Tunis, **1:**62

Tunisia, **1:**4

Turkana, Lake, Africa, **1:**174, 175

Turkey, **2:**215, 259, 260, 261

Tutankhamen, King

curse of, **1:**76

mummy of, **1:**77, 77, 78

tomb of, **1:**75, 76–78, 77; **2:**218

Twenty Thousand Leagues Under the Sea (Verne), **1:**32

Two Medicine Formation, Montana, **1:**150

Two Trips to Gorilla Land (Burton), **1:**166

Tyrannosaurs Rex (dinosaur), **1:**150, 152

U.S. Antarctic Program. *See* Antarctic Program, U.S.

U.S. Botanic Garden. *See* Botanic Garden, U.S.

U.S. Civil War. *See* Civil War, U.S.

U.S. Geological Survey. *See* Geological Survey, U.S.

U.S. Hydrographic Office. *See* Hydrographic Office, U.S.

U.S. Interior Department. *See* Interior Department, U.S.

U.S. National Herbarium. *See* National Herbarium, U.S.

U.S. National Marine Sanctuaries. *See* National Marine Sanctuaries, U.S.

U.S. Navy. *See* Navy, U.S.

U.S. Senate. *See* Senate, U.S.

Ubangi River, Africa, **2:**268

UDC (University of the District of Columbia), **1:**162–63

Uele (Welle) River, Africa, **2:**267, 268

Uganda, **2:**318, 319, 324, 325

Uhuru (satellite), **2:**307

Ujiji, Sea of (Lake Tanganyika), Africa, **1:**64, 66–67, 69, 184, 187, 189, 190; **2:**317, 318–19

Ujiji, Tanzania, **1:**67–68, 187

Ukhaa Tolgood fossil field, Mongolia, **1:**130

Ukhaidir, Mesopotamia, **1:**52

Ultraviolet rays (UVBs), **1:**25

Ulysses (planetary probe), **2:**315

Ulysses (solar probe), **2:**298

Under a Lucky Star (Andrews), **1:**20

Undersea World of Jacques Cousteau, The (television specials), **1:**95

Underwater Adventure Seekers (UAS), **1:**162

Union-Castle Line, **2:**279

United Nations Human Rights Council, **2:**327

United States, **1:**29
  manned space exploration by, **2:**287, 288–99, 297
  unmanned space exploration by, **2:**301–2, 304–9, 310–17
  See also entries under U.S.; *specific location*

United States Exploring Expedition. *See* Wilkes Expedition

University of Miami, **2:**227

University of Philadelphia, **1:**91

University of Rhode Island, **1:**38

University of the District of Columbia (UDC), **1:**162–63

Unknown Coast, Australia, **1:**125, 126–27, 128

Unknown River, Canada, **2:**342, 343–44

Upper atmosphere, **1:**24

Upper Atmosphere Research Satellite, **2:**298

Ural Mountains, **1:**153; **2:**219, 252, 258

Uranus, unmanned exploration, **2:**316

Urubamba River, Africa, **1:**57

USS *Flying Fish*. *See Flying Fish*, USS

USS *Iwo Jima*. *See Iwo Jima*, USS

USS *Peacock*. *See Peacock*, USS

USS *Porpoise*. *See Porpoise*, USS

USS *Relief*. *See Relief*, USS

USS *Roosevelt*. *See Roosevelt*, USS

USS *Scorpion*. *See Scorpion*, USS

USS *Sea Gull*. *See Sea Gull*, USS

USS *Skate*. *See Skate*, USS

USS *Thresher*. *See Thresher*, USS

USS *Vincennes*. *See Vincennes*, USS

USS *Washington*. *See Washington*, USS

USS *Yorktown*. *See Washington*, USS

Ussuri River and basin, **2:**253, 258

Utah, **2:**246

Utopian philosophers, **1:**58

UVBs (ultraviolet rays), **1:**25

V-2 rocket, **2:**301, 302

Váez de Torres, Luis, **2:**233

Vahsel Bay, Antarctica, **2:**283

Valdivia, Chile, **1:**98

Valles Marineris, Mars, **2:**313

Valley of the Kings, Egypt, **1:**76, 77

Valleys of the Assassins, The (Stark), **2:**321

Van Allen, James, **1:**159; **2:**304

Van Allen radiation belts, **1:**159; **2:**304

Van der Post, Laurens, **2:**326–30

Van Diemen, Anthony, **2:**233

Van Diemen's Land. *See* Tasmania

Van Putten, Mark, **1:**120

Van Veen sampler, **2:**228

Vanuatu (New Hebrides), **1:**60, 78, 79; **2:**231, 234

Variation of Animals and Plants Under Domestication, The (Darwin), **1:**105

Vega (ship), **2:**221

Velociraptor (dinosaur), **1:**130

Venera (planetary probes), **2:**301, 311–12

Venezuela, **1:**7, 154, 155

Venture to the Interior (Van der Post), **2:**326, 329

Venus, **2:**301, 302
  transit of, **1:**40–41, 82, 83, 85, 88; **2:**234
  unmanned exploration, **2:**311–12

Venus Express (planetary probe), **2:**312

Verne, Jules, **1:**32

Vertebrata of the Tertiary Formations of the West, The (Cope), **1:**92

Vesconte, Petrus, **2:**199, 200

Vespucci, Amerigo, **1:**109; **2:**200

Vestiges of the Natural History of Creation (Chambers), **1:**102

Victoria, Lake, Africa, **1:**67–68, 69, 172, 184, 187, 189; **2:**317, 318–19, *318*

Victoria, Queen of England, **2:**250

Victoria Falls, Africa, **1:**185

Victoria Land, Antarctica, **2:**274

Vietnam War, **1:**32

Viking (planetary probes), **2:**313

Viking (ship), **2:**212

Vilcabamba, Peru, **1:**56

Vilkitsky, Boris, **2:**253, 258

Vilkitsky Island, **2:**258

Vincennes, USS, **2:**346

Vine, Allyn, **1:**37

Virgin Islands, **1:**126

Virginia, **1:**132

Vishnu schists, **2:**248

Vision for Space Program, **2:**310

Vladivostok, Russia, **2:**258

Volcanoes, **1:**155

Volkov, Vladislav, **2:**295

Voskhod 2, **2:**289

Vostok 1, **2:**287, 288, *288*

Vostok 6, **2:**287, 289

Voyage of the Vega, The (Nordenskjöld), **2:**219, 222

Voyage to Terra Australis: Undertaken for the Purpose of Completing the Discovery of that Vast Country, and Prosecuted in the Years 1801, 1802, and 1803, in His Majesty's Ship the Investigator (Flinders), **1:**128

Voyage Up the River Amazon, Including a Residence at Para (Edwards), **1:**44

Voyager planetary probes, **2:**315, 316

Voyages from Montreal on the River St. Lawrence Through the Continent of North America to the Frozen and Pacific Oceans in the Years 1789 and 1793 (Mackenzie), **1:**176; **2:**194

Voyageurs, **2:**193

Waguha people, **1:**190

Waigeo Island, **1:**80

Waldseemüller, Martin, **2:**199, 200

Wallace, Alfred Russel, **1:**xiii, 44, 97, *97*, 103–4; **2:**252, 331–36, *333*, 335, 341

"Wallace's Line," **2:**332

Wallis, Samuel, **2:**231, 233–34

Walsh, Don, **2:**227, 236, 237

Walsh, Henry Collins, **1:**123

Walsh Glacier, **2:**338

Wanderings in South America (Waterton), **2:**340, 341

Wang Yuanlu, **1:**129

Ward Hunt Island, **1:**29

Warrior Herdsmen, The (Thomas), **2:**324, 325

Washburn, Barbara, **2:**339

Washburn, Bradford, **1:**xiii; **2:**336–40, *337*, 339

Washington (state), **1:**176

Washington, George, **1:**182

Washington, Mount, **2:**336

Washington, USS, **1:**36

Waterton, Charles, **2:**340–42

Watkins, Henry George "Gino," **2:**342–45

Watson, H.C., **1:**104

Wayne, Anthony, **1:**177

Weather satellites, **2:**301, 306–7

Weber, Richard, **1:**29

Weddell Sea, Antarctica, **2:**282, 283

Wedgwood, Josiah, **1:**97

Weitz, Paul, **2:**295

West Africa, **1:**3–5, 165, 166

West African Studies (Kingsley), **1:**165, 169

West Florida (Lousiana), **1:**113–14

West Indies (Caribbean), **1:**xiii, 113, 126, 163; **2:**226

West Road Valley, Canada, **2:**194

Westall, William, **1:**127

Western America, Including California and Oregon (Wilkes), **2:**349

Whale Hunting with Gun and Camera (Andrews), **1:**20

Whale Island, **2:**194

Whales

   California gray, **1:**17

   right, **1:**16, 17

   sperm, **1:**117, 118

Whales, Bay of, Antarctica, **1:**13, 71; **2:**280

What Led To the Discovery of the Source of the Nile (Speke), **2:**320

Wheeler, George, **1:**91

White, Edward, **2:**290

White Nile River, **1:**62, 63, 68, 186, 187, 189; **2:**268

White Sea, **1:**27

Wichita, Kansas, **1:**31, 32, 110

Wild, Frank, **2:**280

Wilkes, Charles, **2:**225, 345–50, *347*

Wilkes, James, **1:**22

Wilkes Expedition, **2:**345–50, *348*

   scientific discoveries by, **2:**349–50

Wilkes Land, Antarctica, **1:**24; **2:**237

Wilkins, George Hubert, **1:**23

Willow Creek, Montana, **1:**150–51

Wilson, Edward, **2:**273, 276–77, 279

Winter Quarters Bay, Antarctica, **2:**273

Wisherd, Edwin "Buddy," **2:**217

Wisting, Oscar, **1:**13, 15

Wolfe, James, **1:**82

Wolves, **2:**325

Women's rights, **1:**169

Woods Hole, Marine Biological Laboratory at, **2:**226

Woods Hole Oceanographic Institution, **1:**32, 34, 34, 36, 37, 161; **2:**227

Woolf, Leonard, **2:**328

Woolf, Virginia, **1:**54; **2:**328

Worcester (ship), **2:**238

Worden, Alfred, **2:**294

Wordie, James, **2:**343

World Data Centers, **1:**159

World Meteorological Organization, **1:**160

World War I, **1:**36, 53, 54, 70; **2:**322

World War II, **1:**36, 38, 144; **2:**266, 302, 323, 328

World Wilderness Congress, **2:**326, 330

World Without Sun (film), **1:**95

Worsley, Frank, **2:**284

Wrangel, Ferdinand Petrovich, **2:**252, 257

Wrangel Island, **2:**257

Wreck Reef, Australia, **1:**127

Wyoming Territory, **2:**246, 247

X-ray satellites, **2:**307

Xi'an (Chang'an), China, **1:**137

Xingu people, **1:**133

Xinjiang Autonomous Region, **1:**137

XMM-Newton (X-ray telescope), **2:**307

Yakutska (ship), **2:**255

Yale University, **1:**56, 57
Peabody Museum of Natural History, **2:**205–6, 230

Yangtze River, **1:**164

Yarlung Zangbo River, **1:**164, 165

Yeager, Chuck, **1:**124

Yelcho (tug), **2:**284

Yellowstone National Park, **1:**115

Yellowstone River, United States, **1:**183

Yemen, **2:**323

Yenisei River, **2:**221, 254, 255

Yeniseysk, Russia, **2:**257

Yorktown, USS, **1:**36

Yorktown, Virginia, **1:**61

Young, Brigham, **1:**68

Young, John, **2:**290, 294, 296

Yugor Strait, **2:**221

Yukon Territory, **2:**337

Yunnan Province, China, **1:**164

Zalambdalestes (early mammal species), **1:**19

Zambezi River, Africa, **1:**184, 185, 186

Zambia, **1:***187*

Zanzibar, **1:**66, 187; **2:**318, 319, 320

Zenit (satellite), **2:**306

Zinjanthropus boisei. See Australopithecus, A. boisei

Zinn, Howard, **1:**109

Zoological Society of London, **2:**209
Insect House, **1:**79

Zoology, Wilkes Expedition, **2:**349

Zvezdny Gorodok (Star Town), Russia, **2:**288